ST. JOHN OF THE CROSS

An Appreciation

Daniel A. Dombrowski

STATE UNIVERSITY OF NEW YORK PRESS

Published by
State University of New York Press, Albany

© 1992 State University of New York

For information, address State University of New York
Press, State University Plaza, Albany, N.Y. 12246

Production by Diane Ganeles
Marketing by Bernadette LaManna

Library of Congress Cataloging-in-Publication Data

Dombrowski, Daniel A.
    St. John of the Cross : an appreciation / Daniel A. Dombrowski.
        p.   cm. — (SUNY series in Latin American and Iberian thought
    and culture)
        ISBN 0-7914-0887-6 (hard : alk. paper). — ISBN 0-7914-0888-4
    (pbk. : alk. paper)
        1. John of the Cross, Saint, 1542–1591.   2. Mysticism—Catholic
    Church—History—16th century.   3. Catholic Church—Doctrines—
    History—16th century.   4. Mysticism—Spain—History—16th century.
    I. Title.   II. Title: Saint John of the Cross.   III. Series.
    BX4700.J7D56   1992
    271.7302—dc20
        [B]   90-28577
                                                                          CIP

10 9 8 7 6 5 4 3 2 1

Contents

Acknowledgments

I am grateful to the Institute for Carmelite Studies for permission to quote from the Kavanaugh-Rodriguez translation of John of the Cross's works, including the translations of his poetry found at the beginning of each chapter. Helpful insights regarding John of the Cross have been received either personally or through the audiocassette medium from (in alphabetical order): Don Buggert, Mary Cruise, Elda Maria Estrada, Constance Fitzgerald, Anthony Morello, and Eileen Stich. I am especially appreciative of the comments offered to me by Aloysius Deany.

Abbreviations

A = *Ascent of Mount Carmel*

D = *Dark Night of the Soul*

L = *Living Flame of Love*

S = *Spiritual Canticle*

M = minor works

P = poems

Introduction

Twentieth century philosophers and theologians may legitimately ask why they should be concerned about a sixteenth-century Spanish mystic. I do not intend to give an exhaustive response to this question in this introduction. Rather, I will respond to the question throughout the book in my attempts to relate John of the Cross's thought to six contemporary areas. Hence, those who wonder whether they have the time or interest to read this book should immediately jump to chapter one to see if the beginnings of my response to the above question are persuasive.

My method or hermeneutical stance can be stated quite plainly as an effort to mediate between two extremes: (1) An *author-centered* approach to John of the Cross would in effect concentrate on queries regarding what John of the Cross exactly said, why he said it, and so forth. Although there is a necessary and foundational role provided by this sort of "interpretation," in that without it no other sort of interpretation could exist, an overconcentration on this approach leads to a sort of intellectual paralysis. That is, this sort of approach can easily turn John of the Cross into a museum piece who would be of interest merely for the purposes of positivistic historiography. Such a historiography is fueled by the desire to have every aspect of every major historical figure accurately compiled and categorized.

(2) A *text-centered* approach would use the works of John of the Cross as springboards from which to jump into contemporary issues, or would use the texts of John of the Cross to trigger or amplify contemporary religious experience. The obvious danger in this ap-

1

proach is that by *using* John of the Cross's works for contemporary purposes one runs the risk of inventing a John of the Cross who never existed and of rewriting his texts for him, in ways perhaps that he would not approve. This approach in effect suggests that we should not so much be concerned with what John of the Cross said or why he said it, but rather we should be concerned with having John of the Cross's works act as spurs.

There are both strengths and weaknesses in each of these hermeneutical commitments, and obviously it is not the aim of this book to develop a full-blown theory of interpretation. Rather, my aim is to do justice to John of the Cross and his writings, an aim which does not necessarily play into the hands of the author-centered approach. I will assume that there is merit in both of these approaches and that they can be used to keep each other honest. If my interpretations are successful, I will both acknowledge the insistency of the sanjuanistic sources *and* deliver on their contemporary value.

I must admit that I intend to lean more in the direction of text-centered (2) than author-centered (1). There are three reasons for my choice to lean in this direction. First, excellent work has been done on the biographical details of John of the Cross's life, and on what he meant to say in his writings, but there is no book that I know of which argues for John of the Cross's significance in relation to contemporary philosophy, and not enough has been done regarding his significance for contemporary theology, and this despite the fact that those who know his thought well insist that there is such significance. Second, I do not find sufficient evidence to engage in a hermeneutics of suspicion whereby previous interpreters are accused of bias or distortion. Even with regard to gender issues in religion, liberation theology, and issues in theology of the environment, where the charge of systematic distortion of the text is most likely, previous interpreters have had some worthwhile things to say. I am adding to a tradition rather than tearing one down. Third, John of the Cross is dead but his works live on. The permanence of the written word as opposed to the transitoriness of life or of the spoken word forces one to take the text-centered approach seriously once the works of a historical figure are put in good scholarly shape by the Herculean efforts of various editors and translators.

Although I am "merely" adding to a tradition, my additions are at times so bold and so novel that I will no doubt offend some parties. In the book, I will indicate (with John of the Cross on my side, I think) why boldness in religion is a virtue.

The chapters of the book are arranged in a logical order: (1) I will use John of the Cross to supplement the thought of Thomas Merton in defense of the contemplative life in the twentieth century. I will show that John of the Cross's notion of *interiority* is not a piece of antiquarian lore; rather, it speaks directly to what can be called, for lack of a better designation, the "existential burdens" of contemporary individuals. In this chapter, I will also deliver an apologia for asceticism, an effort which will be an uphill climb when one considers the (to some extent legitimate) bad press asceticism has received in recent centuries. (2) Next I will show, contra the possible charge of quietism, that the contemplative life is not inconsistent with vigorous *praxis*. In fact, I argue that John of the Cross helps us to illuminate and deepen certain important themes in liberation theology, particularly its Latin American variety. In this argument I will rely on John of the Cross's own *praxis* as a spiritual director, on his tendance of the sick and poor, and on his political impact on the internecine Catholic reformation of sixteenth-century Spain. That is, chapters one and two together will provide an example of unity-in-difference which, I allege, says some profound things about what it means to be an individual in society.

Also, at the beginning of chapter two can be found a brief summary of John of the Cross's life and writings for those who are unfamiliar with them. Because chapter two deals with John of the Cross's *praxis,* in particular, and with the relationship between solitude and *praxis* in the life of the mystic, in general, I consider it essential in this chapter to discuss exactly what John of the Cross *did* with his life. My fear is that if I did not discuss his biography in this chapter that I would be open to the familiar charge from pragmatists, utilitarians, Marxists, and defenders of a strong institutional church that there is something pollyannish about mysticism. That is, it is fruitful in the effort to show the praxic implications of John of the Cross's thought that he personally could not only act in the world but act efficaciously.

(3) John of the Cross is also instructive regarding *gender issues* in religion. Although in one sense he follows the dominant patriarchal trend in favor of God the Father, in other senses he counterbalances patriarchy through his contact with Teresa of Avila, his emphasis on affectivity in the attempt to achieve unity with God, and his pervasive use of marriage metaphors in the illustration of this unity. I will allege that his dipolar theism allows him to do justice to what have been traditionally conceived of as "masculine" steadfastness and "feminine" receptivity in God. (4) John of the

Cross's incorporation in his writings of themes, which have traditionally been thought of as "feminine," is not unconnected with his deep *respect for nature,* a respect which is often diminished in traditional theism because, as Jurgen Moltmann has shown, the God of Judaism and Christianity is very often (unwittingly) the inheritor of the tendency in Greek religion to have father sky god subjugate mother earth goddess. In this regard, I will favorably treat John of the Cross as a proto-romantic. Specifically, I will rely on Thomas McFarland to understand and apply John of the Cross's romanticism as it surfaces in the tension between human reality as a shattered fragment and the desire for reticulative wholeness. That is, chapters three and four are attempts to engage John of the Cross with contemporary issues regarding male bias in religion and regarding the connection between male bias in philosophy of religion and ecology.

As my first name indicates, I am male, hence some feminists will at least initially be sceptical as to whether the version of feminism, which I defend in chapters three and four, is *totally* purged of male bias. In these chapters, I make a strong effort to bring about a polar equality between what have traditionally been considered male (divine) attributes and female (divine) attributes, and it is in this effort that my feminism can primarily be found. However, I am aware of the fact that *some* women philosophers of religion and theologians (but certainly not all) will still be bothered by my drive for logical rigor in the use of abstract concepts and by my attempt to synthesize only after initially drawing some sharp dichotomies. If this drive is at odds with feminism, which I doubt, then to a certain extent I am not a feminist. In any event, my feminism is exhibited not only in my attempt to defend polar equality with respect to the divine attributes but also in my attempt to show the intelligibility in chapter four of John of the Cross's God, who is characterized not only by (traditionally male) abstract properties but also by the concrete, embodied (traditionally female) properties associated with natural description.

(5) Because he is a great poet (indeed one of the greatest in the Spanish language), and because he is instructive regarding the distinctions between literal and symbolic *uses of language,* John of the Cross can be used to clarify certain current problems in religious discourse. These clarifications prepare the way for (6), a detailed consideration of John of the Cross's *mysticism* in its different forms, and of the contemporary uses or abuses of mysticism. Charles

Hartshorne is consulted in this chapter, both for the purpose of helping us to understand John of the Cross's mysticism and to provide a vehicle through which John of the Cross's thought can be appropriated in the present for the purpose of responding to certain canards or caricatures of mysticism. John of the Cross's similarities to, and differences from, Eastern mysticism will also be treated in chapter six.

The above groupings (chapters one and two together, three and four together, and five and six together) are not ironclad. For example, the study of interiority in chapter one prepares the way for chapter four's treatment of the sublime in John of the Cross, and chapter one's emphasis on meditation eases the transition to a consideration of a quite different phenomenon, contemplation, in chapter six. And chapter three's critique of mind-body dualism is continuous with chapter five's defense of the language of faith, and so forth.

Throughout the book I use the Kavanaugh-Rodriguez translations of John of the Cross's works and the Biblioteca de Autores Cristianos edition in Spanish, although at certain points other translations (especially Peers's translation, which is more literal than Kavanaugh-Rodriguez) will be consulted. I should note that when I cite John of the Cross's Spanish I will do so accurately according to the original Spanish rather than by making sure that the Spanish words I cite agree in gender and number with my own prose. This procedure may, at times, shock the reader who knows Spanish well, but it will allow my text to read more easily and it will more accurately render John of the Cross's own words. Further, except in the cases of John of the Cross's poetry cited at the beginning of each chapter, the criterion I have used in the choice of which passages to quote both in translation and in the original Spanish is philosophical or theological rather than aesthetic. That is, where the conceptual content of John of the Cross is at stake, or where conceptual content might be misconstrued, I have given the Spanish as well as English.

It should now be obvious, however, that the whole point to this book is to represent John of the Cross's views fairly so as to do intellectual work with them. In this regard I am working very much in the spirit of William James's *Varieties of Religious Experience*. My hope is that readers who are already familiar with John of the Cross's works will be engaged by my contemporary, philosophical appreciation of them. And readers who are unfamiliar with his writings will learn, in the course of what I trust is a clearly written book, a great deal about John of the Cross's four major works (*The Ascent of Mount Carmel, Dark Night of the Soul, The Spiritual Canticle,* and *The Living Flame of Love*) as well as about his minor works and his poetry.

Some final words should be said about my attempt to appropriate John of the Cross's works for the purposes of contemporary philosophy and theology. John of the Cross *himself* is impatient with any pedantic narrow-mindedness with respect to his poetry just as he is impatient with biblical literalism. He is quite clear in the Prologue to *The Spiritual Canticle* that he cannot adequately explain the stanzas of his poems, yet it is best to leave them (*mejor dejarlos*) alone or to explain them in the broadest sense so that each reader can profit from them. Narrow-minded (or pedantically literal) interpretation of religious classics, he thinks, makes them unadaptable to many palates. If there is no reason to be bound by John of the Cross's interpretations of his own poems there is little reason to feel ill at ease by transcending the interpretations of his works offered by his commentators.

It is only by reading John of the Cross with a synoptic vision that he becomes "relevant." And relevant he is. Consider that his scathing critique of visions and personal revelations and his excoriating remarks regarding biblical literalism are no less opportune and necessary today (thanks to fundamentalism in various religions!) than they were in the sixteenth century. And his hard-nosed approach to the spiritual life offers a convincing antidote, I think, to the attenuated, yet pervasive, conception held by contemporary believers and nonbelievers alike that religion is a type of sentimentality or little more than a life of good works.

No thinker in any discipline is to be regarded as a terminus, a full stop, after which nothing remains to be said. Science does not end with Isaac Newton, nor does religion end with *any* particular religious classic. Additions and explications are dynamic phenomena brimming all around us, phenomena that characterize life itself, including religious life.[1] Nonetheless there is good reason to at least pause, if not stop, at the classics in religion. And when one considers that part of religion usually called "mysticism" (a slippery term to be treated in chapter six) one must come to terms with the golden age of Spanish mysticism in the sixteenth century, which constitutes a peak in the field analogous to Renaissance painting or nineteenth-century symphonic orchestration. Writings become classics precisely because they must be reread in order to be understood. There are several reasons to reread John of the Cross now. It is perhaps trivial to notice that 1991 is the four-hundredth anniversary of his death, but these sorts of demarcations are often occasions for reconsideration of a past thinker. More importantly, John of the Cross's powerful vision of the interior life and the gregarious chatty nature of contemporary philosophy and theology are in desperate need of each other.

I would like to make it clear at the outset that readers who are primarily interested in John of the Cross as a poet or those who are primarily interested in inspirational reading can find more appropriate books to read on John of the Cross than this one. Even in chapter five on language I have treated aesthetic concerns as secondary. This is a book that will treat John of the Cross as a philosopher and theologian concerned with the issues mentioned above in my synopsis of the six chapters. Specifically, I will be treating John of the Cross as a critic of some traditional views of God, views which have been criticized in the twentieth century most forcefully by an intellectual movement called "process philosophy" or "process theology." My emphasis should not be interpreted as an implicit condemnation of the work of those who have had as their focus either John of the Cross as a poet or John of the Cross as an inspirational spiritual writer, but as a complement, at times a dialectical complement, to the work of these other writers.

CHAPTER 1

Solitude

1. One dark night,
   En una Noche oscura
Fired with love's urgent longings
   Con ansias en amores inflamada
Ah, the sheer grace!
   ¡Oh dichosa ventura!
I went out unseen,
   Salí sin ser notada,
My house being now all stilled;
   Estando ya mi casa sosegada.
2. In darkness, and secure,
   2. *A oscuras, y segura*
By the secret ladder, disguised,
   Por la secreta escala disfrazada
Ah, the sheer grace!
   ¡Oh dichosa ventura!
In darkness and concealment,
   A oscuras y en celada,
My house being now all stilled;
   Estando ya mi casa sosegada.
3. On that glad night,
   3. *En la noche dichosa*
In secret, for no one saw me,
   En secreto, que nadie me veía,
Nor did I look at anything,
   Ni yo miraba cosa,
With no other light or guide
   Sin otra luz y guía

Than the one that burned in my heart;
 Sino la que en el corazón ardía.
4. This guided me
  4. *Aqúesta me guiaba*
More surely than the light of noon
 Más cierto que la luz del mediodía,
To where He waited for me
 A donde me esperaba
Him I knew so well
 Quien yo bien me sabía
In a place where no one else appeared.
 En parte donde nadie parecía.
5. O guiding night!
  5. *¡Oh noche que guiaste!*
O night more lovely than the dawn!
 ¡Oh noche amable más que el alborada!
O night that has united
 Oh noche que juntaste
The Lover with His beloved,
 Amado con amada,
Transforming the beloved in her Lover.
 Amada en el Amado transformada.
6. Upon my flowering breast
 En mi pecho florido,
Which I kept wholly for Him alone,
 Que entero para él solo se guardaba,
There He lay sleeping,
 Allí quedó dormido,
And I caressing Him
 Y yo le regalaba,
There in a breeze from the fanning cedars.
 Y el ventalle de cedros aire daba.
7. When the breeze blew from the turret
  7. *El aire de la almena,*
Parting His hair,
 Cuando ya sus cabellos esparcía,
He wounded my neck
 Con su mano serena
With his gentle hand,
 En mi cuello hería,
Suspending all my senses.
 Y todos mis sentidos suspendía.
8. I abandoned and forgot myself,
  8. *Quedéme y olvidéme,*
Laying my face on my Beloved;
 El rostro recliné sobre el Amado,

All things ceased; I went out from myself,
   Cesó todo, y dejéme,
Leaving my cares
   Dejando me cuidado
Forgotten among the lilies.
   Entre las azucenas olvidado.

St. John of the Cross, "The Dark Night"/"Noche Oscura"

Introduction to Solitude

As Thomas Merton has noticed,[1] there is a certain tyranny exerted on human beings by diversion or distraction, by what Pascal called "divertissement." Yet John of the Cross writes a great deal about solitude (*soledad*), not so much to convince people to become solitary, but to become more aware of the condition of solitude in which they already exist. He thinks that all human beings are solitary, even if many of them work as hard as they can to forget this fact. Nor do they have to work hard to forget their solitude in that culture (especially contemporary culture, with its electronic media and fetish for commodities) that makes diversion systematic by graciously providing a person with opportunities all through the day and night to avoid his own company.

My procedure in this chapter will be to describe in a general way this solitude and its enemies in contemporary culture, and then carefully to consider the texts of John of the Cross in order to introduce his approach to the sort of contemplative life which he thinks best takes advantage of human solitude. In the process, we will have occasion to consider several features in John of the Cross's thought: asceticism, meditation, the dark night of the soul, and contemplation.

It should be noted at the outset, and this point will be developed in chapter two on *praxis* (action), that solitude does not mean a reversal of John Donne's claim that no man is an island. Even the worst society provides some goods essential for human life. That is, John of the Cross is well aware of the fact that there are individualistic illusions pursued under the pretense of solitude. (When Frank Sinatra sings that he did it *his* way we cannot help but notice that he is a *cultural* artifact. Those who protest too much about their individuality are precisely those who are abjectly dependent on society.)

The good that society provides an individual is, most importantly, the opportunity to transcend individual*ism* in the service of others. But one cannot provide such service by diversion, for its function is to "anesthetize the individual as individual, and to plunge him in the warm, apathetic stupor of a collectivity which, like himself, wishes to remain amused."[2] Such amusement may be blatant, as in watching football games on television while doing twelve-ounce curls with a can of beer, or hypocritical, as in the seriousness of political conventions or in the precise plans to invest money.

There are those for whom solitude is a problem, and reading John of the Cross will be of little use to them. His appeal is found in those who have less need of diversion than they are told, to those who can detach (*ajención*) themselves from the engineers of human personality and from the cult of publicity. Further, John of the Cross can only appeal to those who are not afraid of the abyss. In avoiding diversion one gives up the possibility of a neat, tidy, self-referential illusion about oneself.

But to be alone is not necessarily to be lonely; this is the whole point to John of the Cross's religious view of what he calls "holy solitude" (*soledad santa*). When one is called to be a solitary (the passive voice to be explained in chapter six), one need not be a monk (etymologically, one who is isolated). John of the Cross is concerned with an interior solitude that can exist even in an active life like Henry Thoreau's, or better, even in an extremely active life like his own. One achieves true solitude not by literally leaving society but by transcending it; not by eschewing fellowship but by realizing that human solidarity is not achieved through Rotarian optimism. For John of the Cross each person is a metaphysical one, a spiritual center, and if there is a higher unity it is found at a divine level (as we will see in chapter four in what John of the Cross believes to be a mystical body—of Christ). In between these two unities some chase the mirage of "union" found in the fictions and conventions of social groups. These fictions can take possession of an individual and divert him, that is, divide him against himself.

Political and economic systems have a tendency to treat persons as instruments. As we will see, John of the Cross's severe *nada* has led some to suppose that he, too, sees human beings as instruments in the service of God. Yet John of the Cross almost always uses *nada* in conjunction with *todo*. Without emptiness the solitary remains an individualist whose nonconformity terminates in a James Dean-like rebellion without a cause. Negation properly understood, however, awakens one to *all* that matters. John of the Cross's vocation is not a call to a narcissistic or solipsistic religion, but a call to be awake.

The hope of John of the Cross is to live hidden in the sense that his solitude is not easily seen. He was a trenchant opponent to anything flashy in religion, as he was to any ec-centric desire for recognition. It is true that there is something severe in John of the Cross's Weltanschauung, a severity which surfaces in many ways, for example, in the opposition to what many contemporary religious seekers assume to be the goal of their search: the heightening of *self*-consciousness. But the point to his severity is *decisively* to break with social and psychological fictions.

Despite the severity of John of the Cross's view of solitude, or perhaps because of it, the tendency of his thought is toward unity. The false or superficial solitary wants society to advert to his separateness, hence he needs society as a ventriloquist needs a dummy. The solitude John of the Cross has in mind does not call attention to itself, but it takes with a grain of salt the claims made in the modern world for collective achievement and happiness. The unity that is the *telos* of his thought has nothing to do with patriotism; in fact, he may very well despise the arrogance of his own nation as that of any other. The unity that he is concerned with is, as we will see in chapter four, stripped of the fiction which many people require in religion and politics and culture.

Homer was correct in implying that the solitary is likely to be either bestial or godlike. Polyphemus the Cyclops, who lived apart from human culture, is an example of the former. His anthropophagy is the fruit of his solitude. John of the Cross, however, defends in text after text a solitude that is really shared by everyone. What the true solitary renounces is not fellowship with others, but rather the fictive community of fans, say, at a frenzied rock concert. The solitary is united with others on a deeper, emotional, even metaphysical level. He is united with others in their common solitude, a commonality which, as we will see, is the ground of sym-pathy.

Many will no doubt find the solitary person a bit unsocial, despite his deep sympathy. In any event, the true solitary does not waste time searching for solitude—a sure sign of a lost soul—in that he is already found by it. The simplicity of the solitary's life would be lost if the search for solitude itself became a principal means of diversion. Further, there are many who try with idle chatter to "save" the solitary from his solitude, perhaps because the veneer of religion they are familiar with makes them ill-prepared to appreciate the bond they already have with the solitary.

If every Christian, and perhaps every artist, is supposed to be in the world but not of it, then there has never been a truer Christian or artist than John of the Cross. To be "in" the world means that there is no need to retreat to the desert in order to reach union with God, especially when it is realized that the contemporary desert is not necessarily a retreat, as in its oil rigs, its dirt bikes, and its nuclear test sites. It is an internal withdrawal that John of the Cross has in mind. To despair of the elaborate facades that human beings build is not to despair of humanity. The solitary has the humility to realize that to better the human condition *in* the world it is not necessarily the case that the only contribution is made in an overt, social way. I will try to deliver on this promissory note as the book advances.

I do not wish to deny that love for others must eventually take some visible, or at least symbolic, form. I am only claiming, along with John of the Cross: (1) that interior withdrawal from others (or a mute witness to a profound truth) can in fact be a type of love for them; and (2) that an unreflective attachment to action for its own sake plays into the hands of a corruptive, even demagogic, fiction. Merton calls this fiction "the virus of mendacity."[3] The solitary escapes mendacity in a Socratic fashion by being critical first and foremost of himself. And although the desert is not necessary for such criticism, it must be admitted that there is a healing silence in natural wilderness that facilitates self-knowledge. Further, and this point will be amplified in chapter five, silence is needed for language to have meaning because without intervals between utterances all of our words would run together into a Babel, as they often do.

In my discussion of action, it will be clear that John of the Cross is not necessarily concerned with those who are condemned to isolation by circumstance or, perhaps, by temperament. Familiar with activity himself, John of the Cross directs his attention at those who "leave" activity for the sake of an internal wilderness. Because these solitaries have not so much chosen their solitude as they have been chosen by it, they often experience torment *at first,* but, as we will see, eventually they become acclimated to the positive features of poverty, emptiness, and anonymity.

There are Wordsworthian spots of time in every person's life, when, like Puck, we notice what fools mortals can be. But to be *completely* honest with oneself requires a "wretched austerity,"[4] which is mitigated a bit if one lives in a religious community or if one is ensconced within a counter-culture. (From the perspective of mysticism, Christianity itself is a counter-culture, even in, perhaps especially in, nominally Christian cultures.) The smaller group is still a group, however, and the solitary must to some extent be a stranger (*extrañez*) or a wanderer even among friends. There is something ironic about solitude in community, perhaps even something oxymoronic about it, but there is nothing positively inconsistent in a solitude which no longer possesses an instinctive, knee jerk response to the otherwise automatic mechanisms of a group, but a solitude which nonetheless belongs to the group.

The solitary certainly has eccentricities and faults, but he is not a failure just because he lies outside the computations and plans of those in the dominant culture, including those within mainstream academia, who can commodify people or treat them as instruments as well as any technocrat. Only when one works from the assumption that these computations and plans are preeminent can one see the solitary as irrelevant. From the perspective of the technocrat the solitary is, at best, indistinguishable from the pragmatic individualist, but the latter is a construction of eighteenth- and nineteenth-century commercial culture rather than of mystical religion.

Although it is easier to have religion filtered to us through the slogans and assumptions of a particular organization or a particular culture, the solitary is nonetheless happy on his difficult road, even if he does not always "have a good time." It is easier for culture to recreate a god in its own image through catchwords and advertisements than it is to approach God on the divine's own terms. There is something "other" not only to God, but also to the individual human being. Even when viewing one's own past self one senses an alterity, say when one is startled by a photo of "oneself" when in high school. One of the jobs of the solitary is to come to terms with this otherness and with divine otherness.

It will eventually become apparent that the solitary self is not only not selfish, it is not even permanent. It vanishes unmysteriously in mystical contemplation, especially that false, superficial, social self which postures in everyday life. The shallow "I" of individualism can be commodified, prostituted, and pandered to. The inner "I" is elusive, yet when uncovered it is the fertile ground of divinity itself.

Unity-in-Variety

Thus far I have spoken in very general terms of John of the Cross's notion of solitude. Now I would like to consider several specific texts of his that amplify this theme of solitude. I would like to begin by noticing the pragmatic tendency in John of the Cross's thought. That is, all of his efforts aim at the solution of a problem or at the amelioration of some irritant. He notices those who feel interiorly alien from all things (*extrañez de todas las cosas*), an estrangement which causes a distasteful weariness (*tedio*) with the world (D, II, 9; L, 3, 39).[5] Once the spirit has a taste of the solution to these difficulties, its previous food seems bitter. In a holy idleness, the soul comes to realize that it is advantageous for the soul to be sick (*enfermar*), for then it searches for God as a cure. It is this hope for a cure which, in a way, makes the soul's suffering quite unwearisome (*sufrir sin fatigarse*). According to John of the Cross, the really sick person only desires health, and the really sick soul only desires God (D, 2, 19; S, 10, 1).

But the soul must not only suffer, it must realize that it suffers in order for progress to be made. Hence John of the Cross is quick to point out that self-knowledge (*conocimiento de sí*) is the first requirement for advancing to God (S, 4, 1). To know that one's life is in need of a cure is one thing, to know where to find a cure is another. John of the Cross's advice is straightforward and prompts the title to this chapter: God must be sought within the soul, which is the divine hiding place. John of the Cross relies on Luke 17:21 and on several simple metaphors to describe the knowledge of self he has in mind: the self is like a sick person desiring health, a hungry person craving food, or an empty vessel waiting to be filled (S, 1, 6–8; S, 9, 6).

No reflective person in our age would be convinced by Job's friends to the effect that a suffering soul is caused by hidden wickedness. What is more likely is that the contemporary suffering soul would first psychologize his condition and then procrastinate due to the assumption that the suffering would go away or could be bought out by a trip to a few stores (see A, prologue; M, prayer). But procrastination, by definition, only postpones the problem. For John of the Cross, the old person must die and the new person live *now* in order to achieve union with God (L, 2, 33). This effort is facilitated by the dynamism of life itself, a dynamism which presupposes what Alfred North Whitehead calls the "perpetual perishing" of the drops of experience that make up our lives.

It is not my aim to disparage psychology of religion as a discipline, but rather to suggest that the whole notion of a "spiritual crisis" is trivialized if it is reduced *simpliciter* to psychological components. Further, psychological reductionism is a knife that can cut both ways, as William James noticed; it can reduce a spiritual crisis to certain psychological excitations *and* it can reduce the atheist's beliefs to a malfunctioning liver.[6] The assumption many contemporaries make, an assumption which initially seems harmless, that spiritual suffering is due exclusively to psychological conditions, is one of the cataracts noticed by John of the Cross, a small speck clearly seen which clouds our vision of a big object. God, for John of the Cross, lies on the other side of the cataract (L, 3, 72–73). Never one to be bothered by the mixing of metaphors, John of the Cross sees the removal of the cataract as the cause of an awakening (*recuerdo*) of God in the soul, and those who are recently awake breathe the most deeply, they are most in-spired (L, 4, 2). Like Merton, John of the Cross himself was inspired by Isa. 8:6, where the life-giving waters of Siloe flow, unnoticed, in silence (L, 3, 64).

It might be asked, how could a soul suffer and not know it? John of the Cross's response would consist, like Thoreau's,[7] in pointing out that many, if not most, human beings live lives of *quiet* desperation, a desperation hidden by the cataract of their own sleepy assumptions regarding what life can be. John of the Cross does not write an ode to dejection, but brags as lustily as chanticleer if only to wake us up. Wakeful individuals wedge their feet downward through the mud and slush of prejudice and mere opinion, the alluvion which covers the globe, until they hit rock bottom, until they hit God.

In order to stay awake in life human beings need training. Hitting something solid is not as easy, as the cliché has it, as falling off a horse. That is, spiritual progress for John of the Cross requires asceticism. It was a commonplace in Greek culture that virtue consisted in a mean between two extremes. Moderation (*sophrosyne*) was a key virtue, perhaps *the* key virtue, consisting in a mean between self-indulgence (*pleonexia*), or thinking too much of oneself, on the one hand, and thinking too little of oneself (*mikropsychia*), on the other. In that Western culture has exhibited pleonexic tendencies at least from the time of Adam Smith, it is not too surprising that many recent interpreters of Christian thinkers like John of the Cross either see asceticism as an example of *mikropsychia* or as an embarassing feature for which one must give an *apologia*. My thesis in this section of the chapter is that defenders of John of the Cross need not be embarassed by his asceticism and that asceticism need not be a type of *mikropsychia*. Integral to this thesis will be an emphasis on the athletic nature of *askesis*.

Another sixteenth-century Spanish writer like Saint Ignatius of Loyola makes it clear in *The Spiritual Exercises* that there is a difference between moderation and penance. The former consists in denying ourselves what is excessive, luxurious, flashy; that is, eliminating what we might want as opposed to what we really need. But penance consists in temporarily denying ourselves what is essential for us to have; it does not eliminate that which is

excessive but that which is integral to our well being. Two preliminary examples would be avoiding frequent desserts after meals
(moderation) as opposed to fasting (penance).

   In which category is asceticism to be placed? In order to respond
to this question one must realize that the etymology of the word
askesis shows an athletic origin. The word does not so much refer
to self-denial as to the practice or training required to compete in
an athletic event. It must be emphasized that ascetic training is
also needed to avoid *pleonexia,* that is, to obtain moderation so as
to reach God. Or as Porphyry implies, asceticism enables us to
escape from barbarism so that we may "enter the stadium naked
and unclothed, striving for the most glorious of all prizes, the
Olympia of the soul."[8]

   E. R. Dodds is an example of a scholar who seems to think that
Christianity introduces a hatred for the body and contempt for the
human condition.[9] His negative attitude is understandable when
we realize that he relies on an anonymous early Christian thinker
who compares the human body to a filthy bag of excrement and
urine. The moderation of John of the Cross can be seen if we offer a
better model for ascetic discipline. If I am not mistaken, John of
the Cross's notion of solitude is connected with the concepts of
interior beauty or of being "centered." If I am correct about this
connection, then solitude can be seen as a mean between two sets
of extremes, as the following diagram indicates:

Diagram 1

B = too much order or asceticism
   lack of *discreción*

A = *centro*
   sobriedad y templanza
   to be centered in
      the spiritual life
   soledad
   mas profundo centro

D = hopeless
      profundity

E = superficiality
   golosina de
   espiritu
   ornato de
   muñecas

C = too much disorder
   distracción
   vana codicia
   excess "needs"

I will now work my way around this circle, starting with *distracción* (C). If one wanted to hear beautiful music, one would be disappointed if forced to hear a two-year-old bang piano notes at random. Too much disorder is as distasteful in one's spiritual life as it is in music or politics. John of the Cross is intent to show that an excessive reliance on sensation creates a sort of ugliness called "distraction" (*distracción*). This ugliness is intensified when inordinate attachment to appetites becomes habitual, for then it becomes less likely that one will create a beautiful life for oneself (A, I, 9, 11; A, III, 26). A vain covetousness (*vana codicia*) leads to a slavish clinging to things, like a wood boring insect who continually gnaws. The oddity is that this tawdry attachment to things is often rationalized as the search for beauty through ornamentation (a search which presupposes that the object ornamented cannot stand on its own aesthetic worth), style (*modo*), or craftsmanship (A, III, 35).

For John of the Cross, trying to journey to God without shaking off the appetites and the cares of the world is like dragging a cart uphill (M, sayings, 53). The heaviness of the burden is caused by the fact that the habit of meddling with exterior attachments multiplies one's needs. In addition to invariant biological needs (like food) and those variable needs connected with some particular historical epoch (for example, in our culture, a telephone), John of the Cross realizes that there are those "needs" created by our anxiety (*nuestra solicitud es la que nos necesita*). These latter "needs" are such impediments to beauty that John of the Cross hyperbolizes by saying that we should not attach ourselves to anything (M, sayings, 26; M, letters, 10, 20). It is this sort of talk on John of the Cross's part that plays into the hands of critics like Dodds who assume that Christian asceticism is life-negating.

A more favorable treatment of John of the Cross would have us notice that he is only advocating the view that the soul should divest (*desasida*) itself of distractions to solitude (S, 40, 2). He has no hope of eliminating biological desire altogether; there will always be some herd of appetites which escape even the ascetic's control; there will always remain inclinations under the sway of bad habits; and there will always be certain angry predispositions, which, like foxes, pretend to be asleep, but which have a certain degree of hegemony over us nonetheless (S, 14, 30; S, 16, 5; S, 26, 18; D, I, 5).

There is nothing wrong with eating, as long as we do so mindfully, that is, as long as we carefully notice what we are eating (no easy task today), why we are eating, where the food came from, which work was exerted or which pain inflicted to get the food, and so forth. In order to preserve this mindfulness, Ignatius of Loyola suggests that we plan our next meal just after we have eaten. This way we avoid eating gluttonously or without considering who produced the food or whose blood was spilled in such production. The junk food of the senses is not unconnected with the junk food of the spirit.

In order to habituate oneself to live a Christian life, John of the Cross thinks that we have to take aesthetic categories seriously. Too much variety causes ugliness, as in the above piano example. Total ugliness (*total fealdad*) occurs when the soul completely succumbs to desire with no ascetical restraint whatsoever (A, I, 9, 13). I suspect that this idea of "total" ugliness is a limit concept or a regulative ideal for John of the Cross and is not to be taken literally or as a constituitive idea. The incompatibility of alternatives in life makes all of us somewhat ascetical. Life is full of choices between good things, as in choosing to be a dedicated teacher or an honest business-person. Or again, there are numerous good ways to compose music, each of which in a given case excludes other ways. When choosing between positive values there is no uniquely right choice, and, more importantly, some good choices must be renounced. It is silly to aim at *all* the good things in life, so in a peculiar way we are all ascetics who do without some very good things. But some ascetics like John of the Cross self-consciously choose their renunciations and choose them to a greater extent than others.[10]

The renunciations, which John of the Cross chooses to make, blanket all five senses (A, I, 3), an inclusiveness that should not surprise reflective twentieth-century individuals who have noticed how easy it is to succumb to the seductive lures of: (1) the pleasant feel of a calf leather seat in a Mercedes; (2) the smell of expensive perfume or cologne aggressively marketed at Christmas; (3) the taste of Chateau Neuf du Pape; (4) the look of *this* year's fashions—a seduction which should remind us how foolish we were last year; or (5) the siren sound of commercial music—note that it is at times almost impossible not to turn on a car radio. The gate to divine union is narrower than we think (A, II, 7). John of the Cross reminds us that once the ancient Hebrews ate flesh in Egypt they had a hard time appreciating any other food, even manna sent from heaven (D, II, 9).

Distraction is especially a problem because we not only have to come to terms with present perceptions but also with memories of previous ones. Many sights, sounds, smells, feels, and tastes of years gone by have hardly faded. Relying on Matt. 6:24, John of the Cross claims that memory (especially resentment) is a master to which we can easily become enslaved, and no one can serve two masters. Hence, suspensions (*suspensiones*) of memory must occur at the beginning of one's effort to achieve union with God. Although certain powerful images from the past have not faded (that is, they have not lost their intensity), they do change in the sense that they can lead to falsehood (*falsedades*) when intervening events distort what really happened in the past. Because of the destructive nature of resentment, falsehood, and waste of time (*perdimiento de tiempo*), John of the Cross thinks that there is something liberating in the attempt to annihilate (*desnudar*) memory. Perhaps the only positive thing he has to say about memory is that, if accurate, it leads us to humility in that we all have made egregious mistakes in our pasts (A, III, 2–3; S, 33, 1).

Area (B) in the above diagram is meant to indicate that John of the Cross also thought that too much order in one's life, too much asceticism, was destructive of the beauty in solitude (A, I, 8). That is, the well-ordered soul is different from one that exercises totalitarian control over her desires because the soul has a multitude and diversity (*multitud y diferencia*) of affections for God. Animal passion itself is good as long as it does not deter a life of prayer of quiet (*oración de quietud*). Discretion (*discretamente*) is the hallmark of an orderly life (A, I, 9–11, 13).

Chaos in music may lead one to desire order, but repeatedly going up and down the scales is ugly because it is *too* orderly and too predictable. Utter confusion in politics is ugly, but no more ugly than the other extreme. For example, the Italians paid an exorbitant price when Mussolini made the trains run on time. Likewise, an asceticism true to its etymological heritage in athletics is only to be commended if it prepares one to perform well in the big event. Some zealous religious aspirants in John of the Cross's day, and some of his contemporary Carmelites, weakened themselves too much through fasts (D, I, 6), a practice which is to be criticized almost as much as its opposite, gluttony (*gula*).

It must be admitted that John of the Cross views *distracción* (C) as a greater danger than lack of discretion (B). We *often* exhibit *distracción* (C) because of lack of self-control or because of a mistaken conviction that human nature cannot bear asceticism or because of the self-deception or subterfuge we indulge in when we say that asceticism is "positively medieval," and so forth. However, *sometimes* we may discipline ourselves too severely by thinking that our body can bear it. The danger involved in leaning more toward lack of discretion (B) than *distracción* (C), as John of the

Cross does, is that one may present very good reasons why not to overeat, say, without giving good reasons why we should eat at all. If I am not mistaken, however, John of the Cross is up to the challenge. In chapter five, we will consider the distinction between instrumental and intrinsic good in John of the Cross. Here I would like to notice that food, for example, is good instrumentally and intrinsically. Food tastes and smells and looks good precisely because it is part of the divine creation, that is, it is intrinsically good; *and* it is good because it leads to healthy bodily activities like meditating. A wonderful quotation from Nikos Kazantzakis's novel *Zorba the Greek* illustrates John of the Cross's attitude well, I think, with Zorba's boss providing the clue to John of the Cross's own position:

> Tell me what you do with the food you eat, and I'll tell you who you are. Some turn their food into fat and manure, some into work and good humor, and others, I'm told, into God. So there must be three sorts of men. I'm not one of the worst, boss, nor yet one of the best. I'm somewhere between the two. What I eat I turn into work and good humor. . . . As for you, boss. . . I think you do your level best to turn what you eat into God. But you can't quite manage it, and that torments you.[11]

Neither Zorba's boss nor John of the Cross are as indifferent to food as some superficial interpretations of them would suggest.

Too much order or ascetical rigor in one's life is also bothersome to John of the Cross because it leads to drudgery (*trabajo*), spiritual boredom (*tedio espiritual*), and a waste of time. It should be noted that drudgery and boredom are aesthetic categories that are only understandable as deviations from beauty. Most bothersome about lack of discretion (B), however, is the fact that it indicates insufficient self-esteem (A, III, 13, 25; D, I, 2). As before, the more likely outcome, especially for beginners, is that they will not sufficiently deny themselves (D, I, 7). But there is today, and certainly was in John of the Cross's day, a tendency in discretion (B) toward sloth and tedium (*acidias y tedios*) in the ascetic life; sloth because it is possible to allow one's routine to make life too easy. John of the Cross is a tireless opponent to anything that smacks of Homer's land of the lotus eaters, even an ascetic rigor which produces a soporific effect by allowing one's routine to make one's decisions for one, to produce *tedio espiritual*. That is, it is possible for *ennui* to trump solitude. John of the Cross only admires the soul that has been tempted, tried, and proved (D, I, 13–14).

I repeat the point if only because John of the Cross, in particular, and Christianity, in general, are often the subjects of caricature regarding asceticism, especially by those who only notice John of the Cross's hyperbole in the condemnation of *distracción* (C): there is nothing wrong with serving the appetites; rather, there is something wrong with serving the appetites only or with allowing the appetites to have hegemony, as in the man who eats before digesting what he previously ate (M, letters, 7). Pleasure itself is caused by the desire for things that at least appear good; and even if the object of desire is not really good, the phenomenon of pleasure itself is not to be anathematized (M, letters, 12).

A final point needs to be made regarding John of the Cross's criticisms of asceticism (B). The key transition in the thought of John of the Cross is that from meditation to contemplation, a movement which I will later treat in detail. Here I would like to call attention to the fact that meditation, as opposed to contemplation, relies on sensory images, say imagining Jesus at table with his friends. Asceticism (B) in effect would squash the methods of meditation (*modos de meditaciones*), which are necessary for beginners, at least; these are methods which aim at enamoring and feeding the soul through sensation (A, II, 12).

Sandwiched in between asceticism (B) and *distracción* (C) is John of the Cross's preferred view. Three scholars who lend indirect support to this claim are: Gerald Brenan, William James, and Bede Frost. Brenan[12] admits that contemporary readers can get a feeling of claustrophobia when they experience the intensity of John of the Cross's ascetic fervor, but Brenan also notices that there is nothing punitive in John of the Cross's *askesis,* as some contemporary individuals might assume. Even in John of the Cross's famous doggeral:

> To reach satisfaction in all
> > *Para venir a gustarlo todo*
> desire its possession in nothing.
> > *no quieras tener gusto en nada.*
> To come to possess all
> > *Para venir a poseerlo todo*
> desire the possession of nothing.
> > *no quieras poseer algo en nada.*
> To arrive at being all
> > *Para venir a serlo todo*

> desire to be nothing.
> > *no quieras ser algo en nada.*
> To come to the knowledge of all
> > *Para venir a saberlo todo*
> desire the knowledge of nothing.
> > *no quieras saber algo en nada.*
> To come to the pleasure you have not
> > *Para venir a lo que no gustas*
> you must go by a way in which you enjoy not.
> > *has de ir por donde no gustas.*
> To come to the knowledge you have not
> > *Para venir a lo que no sabes*
> you must go by a way in which you know not.
> > *has de ir por donde no sabes.*
> To come to the possession you have not
> > *Para venir a lo que no posees*
> you must go by a way in which you possess not.
> > *has de ir por donde no posees.*
> To come to be what you are not
> > *Para venir a lo que no eres*
> you must go by a way in which you are not.
> > *has de ir por donde no eres* (A, I, 13).

there is no use of *nada* which is not connected with *todo*. Solitude, silence, *desnudez,* poverty, emptiness, forgetfulness, detachment: none of these words have painful associations for John of the Cross. As a matter of fact, even in John of the Cross's prose works, and especially in his poetry, these words have an aura of happiness and peace.

Likewise, William James[13] holds that John of the Cross's ascetic spirit is "undiluted" and that he existed rather than flourished in the sixteenth century, presumably because undiluted asceticism does not allow one to flourish. Yet James admits that he is driven into vertigo regarding John of the Cross and other Spanish mystics because he must acknowledge that they showed "indomitable spirit and energy" and that they were prevented from engaging in "over-abstraction from practical life" because of their strong intellects. And Bede Frost[14] emphasizes that John of the Cross was not primarily concerned with detachments from things, but with detachment of spirit at the center of the soul. This is where the Word is hidden, as we will see in chapter five, but few find union with God because they do not know how to get to the center.

Spiritual centeredness (A) is distinctive because of its balance of unity-in-variety, order-in-multiplicity, and, as we will see in the tension between hopeless profundity (D) and superficiality (E), in its intensity of experience. Two contraries cannot exist in the same subject, as John of the Cross often reminds us (for example, A, I, 4), but two complementary poles can be brought together, indeed they must be brought together if they are to function well, as in the famous dominant theme and its subtle variations in the first movement of Beethoven's fifth symphony. The soul needs to be recollected (*recogida*) in itself so as to preserve the center from centrifugal forces like asceticism (B) and *distracción* (C). This requires a certain degree of diligence and eagerness (*diligencia y gana*) or else, like uncovered hot water, which dissipates its heat, or unwrapped spices, which lose their pungency, the soul will lose its intensity at the center (A, I, 10).

The difficulty in maintaining intensity in the spiritual life is partially caused by the interior darkness of the soul, a darkness which conceals the soul's advance (A, II, 1); it is much easier to plot the progress of a diet or count the number of pull-ups one can perform. John of the Cross is always careful to keep wisdom (the Greek *sophia*) distinct from technique (the Greek *techne*), a distinction ignored by the self-help and spirituality books in shopping mall bookstores. A multiplicity of methods or techniques or computations (like counting prayers or good works, etc.) are not needed on the road to God, only true self-denial (*negar de veras*). A necessary, although not sufficient, criterion for testing the veracity of self-denial is that it leads one to the realization that "the greater spiritual state" is equivalent to "greater interiority." But if one was always on the way toward interiority one would never arrive; John of the Cross encourages one to notice the interior (spiritual) success one has already achieved in the religious life (A, II, 7, 12).

Reiterating the need for sensory stimulation, John of the Cross holds that certain places may be conducive to solitude, such as the mountains were for Jesus (Matt. 14:23), or, perhaps, as a corner of the house at daybreak may be today (A, III, 39–40). However, it is not "holy places" that make one holy; spiritual sobriety and temperance (*sobriedad y templanza*) must always act as guides (D, I, 6) because they, more than any particular place, bring tranquility (*tranquilidad*) and solitude (D, I, 13).

John of the Cross takes seriously the cliché that God humbles in order to exalt. At the beginning of the quest for God, human beings can only see their own misery, as in the above cataract example. But the enkindling of the soul by divine love burns off impurities which distort our vision. Or better, the enkindling of divine love in the center of the soul is like a log on fire which initially is dried by the heat, then has the impurities on its bark burned off; but eventually the *core* of the log catches fire. Better still, the enkindled soul is like iron in the forge (D, II, 6, 10, 13).

Mystical wisdom, which is called secret (because the soul hides within itself), in a certain way flatters individuals, but it also lays on the individual in solitude the burden of realizing that failure to achieve union with God can only be due to itself (*la perdición del alma solamente le viene de sí misma*—see Ossee 13:9). But John of the Cross has confidence that it is not likely that those who intensely desire union with God (that is, those who run swiftly to God) will fail to achieve it. According to John of the Cross, rest and quietude (*sosiego y quietud*) and purity appoint the spiritual homes of those who desire God (D, II, 16–17, 20, 24).

The riches, delights, and satisfactions of God, thinks John of the Cross, are never absent from us. But in order to find them in the hiding places of the soul, two steps must be taken: (1) there must be a departure from things in a reflective asceticism; and (2) there must be self-forgetfulness (*misma por olvido*). By self-forgetfulness John of the Cross means love of God (S, 1, 8–9; S, 1, 20). John of the Cross's view seems to be that in condemning asceticism (B) he is also condemning too little self-respect if only because human beings are part of the divine creation. One must have a healthy sense of self in the first place before one can realize that to be self*ish* is to fall victim to an illusion. (An illusoriness to be treated in detail in chapter four.) Individuals die but God endures. When the soul is in a healthy solitude, it realizes that it is naturally and radically centered in God (*natural y radicalmente tiene el alma su vida en Dios*). John of the Cross paraphrases Acts 17:28 to the effect that in God we live and move and have our being as temporary parts in an everlasting whole (S, 8, 3). Put quite simply (and I will defend John of the Cross against the charge of pantheism in chapter four), the soul's center of gravity (*centro*) *is* God (S, 11, 4).

This quietude and tranquility in God (*sosiego y quietud en Dios*) is compared to the solitary sparrow perched on the highest branch, with beak toward the wind of God. This "solitary sparrow" hears the oxymoronic silent music (*musica callada*) of sounding solitude (*soledad sonora*). Although I will treat John of the Cross's use of language in chapter five, here I would like to emphasize that it is against the background of solitude, he thinks, that significant sounds and utterances can occur (a la Mahler). Hence the dominance of the electronic media takes away the precondition for mysticism (compare S, 14, 24–27). Try finding a quiet place, say, in a college dormitory, or, what is increasingly difficult, in a library or a movie theater or even a church.

John of the Cross offers little hope for union with God in a chatty life-style where the soul cannot recollect (*recogerse*) itself in its deep interior hiding place, a rich cache created by the soul's withdrawal (*ajención*). Like the inner wine cellar where the efforts of the vinedressers are improved, John of the Cross thinks that human cares and work can only be improved through solitude (S, 16, 6; S, 16, 10; S, 19, 6; S, 26, 3; S, 27, 7). Merely being alone is not enough to preserve virtue, rather one must be alone in what he calls the inner chamber of God's love (S, 31, 4; S, 33, 7). Or again, solitude is like a watered garden enclosed by a fence which, as in Robert Frost's famous poem, makes good neighbors. The purpose of this fence is to separate one's daily labors with others from one's own spiritual sabbath, thereby establishing some elbow room for one's spiritual life. Indeed, John of the Cross sometimes refers to this enclosure as a fort (S, 36, 2; S, 40, 3).

The equation of "interior" and "spiritual" in John of the Cross does not preclude there being different centers in the soul of varying levels of profundity. Even rocks are "centered" in their inanimate way (L, prologue; L, 1, 9; L, 1, 11). And animals are centered as moral patients in the sense that they perceive the world from a particular point of view which they value, as when a cow tries to avoid immanent danger. Human beings, however, have layers of centers, like concentric circles nested in each other, such that it makes sense for John of the Cross to quest for the soul's deepest center. Like rocks we are always centered in some particular place; like plants we are nutritively centered in some biosphere, breathing air, and so forth; and like animals we are centered in our sentient concerns. Only human beings, however, can consciously be aware that their deepest center is in God (L, 1, 12). It is *this* center in holy solitude, according to John of the Cross, which can create happiness in the individual even when the body is ill (M, sayings, 76; M, letters, 30).

Against Superficiality

The vertical axis, which runs through the above diagram, should now be sufficiently explained. Next I will turn to the horizontal axis, but only briefly because I will save an extended treatment of sublimity, which leans in the direction of hopeless profundity (D), for chapter four. The solitude, which John of the Cross defends, is not only a mean between too much order and too much disorder, but it is also a mean between experience which is hopelessly superficial, on the one hand, and hopelessly profound or sublime, on the other. Just as *distracción* (C) is more bothersome to John of the Cross than lack of *discreción* (B), so superficiality (E) is more bothersome to him than hopeless profundity (D). That is, John of the Cross's position in the center of the above diagram nonetheless leans somewhat in a northwesterly direction. It is hard to imagine him having any sympathy whatsoever for a cocktail hour spirituality.

What exactly is bothersome about superficiality (E)? For John of the Cross it is (what we might call) a "category mistake" to think that the imitation of Christ (especially the passion) is compatible with sweetness (*dulzuras*) or a syrupy sentimentality. Having a spiritual sweet tooth (*golosina de espíritu*) makes one flabby and overly concerned with exteriority, hence one is predisposed to vanity (*vanidad*); or to pretensions and rank (*pretensiones y mayorías*), as in academe; or to idle recreations (A, II, 7, 11). For example, although John of the Cross is not necessarily opposed to the cult of the saints, he is opposed to any melodramatic decoration of statues or art works depicting the saints, for this amounts to little more than a childish doll dressing (*ornato de muñecas*) or, even worse, to the worship of idols (*ídolos*) (A, III, 35).

Some degenerate into superficiality (E) because they have as their goal in religion *personal* peace, rather than union with God (D, I, 2). Hence it is not surprising that they do not find the peace they desire. Instead they find a thousand envies and disquietudes (*mil envidias e inquietudes*). It is a mistake to *primarily* look for comfort in life because this desire indicates a certain selfishness. *If* comfort comes, according to John of the Cross, it is as an indirect consequence of one's desire to have union with God (L, 2, 28). As one of John of the Cross's poems has it:

> Do not think that he who lives
> *No penséis que el interior*
> The so precious inner life
> (*Que es de mucha más valia*)
> Finds joy and gladness
> *Halle gozo y alegría*
> In the sweetness of earth
> *En lo que acá de sabor*

> P, Commentary Applied to Spiritual Things

Those with the aforementioned spiritual sweet tooth tend to adjust trials to their own (psychological) selves rather than, as John of the Cross would suggest, adjust themselves to the trials (M, maxims, 22).

Even if one avoids trivializing the spiritual life by superficiality (E), one can still err in the opposite direction of hopeless profundity (D) by not noticing that love is something delicate (D, II, 9). Although not as great a danger as superficiality (E), John of the Cross nonetheless indicates that hopeless profundity (D) is a danger because taking God seriously can easily harden a person and strip him of his sense of humor, as in Jansenism or Puritanism. Although there is little evidence of humor in John of the Cross's writings, accounts from those who knew him always mention this part of his character. The life of solitude should not only make one more secure, but also more delightful, and this because to withdraw from the world is to become mild (L, 1, 19; L, 2, 17; L, 2, 26). Relying on Saint Paul (2 Cor. 12:9), John of the Cross agrees that it is when we are powerless (in terms of our desire to impose our will on others) that we are most strong (in our love for God). That is, despite his condemnation of superficiality, there is nothing harsh about John of the Cross's doctrine.

Psychological and personal traits like mildness, delicacy, and patience are the most often cited in descriptions of John of the Cross's life. His asceticism not only did not put calluses on his psyche, but it appears to have softened him in the sense that it predisposed him toward the virtue of receptivity (see chapter three). He even goes so far as to say that love of God is delightful (*sabrosa*) and, surprisingly, sweet (*dulce*). I assume that he refers here to the sweetness, say, of water in a mountain stream rather than to the unhealthy bombardment of sugar children often receive in their lunch boxes (L, 2, 30; D, prologue).

The Dark Night

Thus far in this chapter I have avoided the phrase "dark night of the soul," for which John of the Cross is most famous. I have done this in order to introduce what I take to be a dominant theme in his writing, solitude (*soledad*) as the result of temperance (*templanza*), without preconceptions regarding the dark night, which some inaccurately equate with a histrionic, "sturming und dranging" melancholia.

First I will discuss some commentators on the dark night and then some of John of the Cross's texts. F. Brice rightly notes that night for John of the Cross simply means detachment, a word with which we should now be familiar.[15] But there are two phases of detachment John of the Cross has in mind, the night of sense and the night of spirit, with the former better known than the latter. The night of sense consists in detachment from things through ascetic discipline and can be compared to the fading light of dusk as the objects of the world gradually vanish from sight.

The night of spirit is a more complex (because more interior) phenomenon, consisting of darkness at midnight, when detachment has seemingly left us all alone and all is lost; and of the approaching of dawn, when contemplation begins (A, II, 2). Contemplation, or what is commonly called "mystical theology," consists in the inflowing of God into the soul, an inflowing that is possible only when the soul is empty of other concerns. Although there is a singleness of purpose in the soul, which experiences the dark night, like sunlight concentrated through a magnifying glass, there is nothing world-negating about the dark night. It is quite possible to "leave" the world yet not leave it, in the sense that the soul "dwells" where it loves more than where the body takes it. (Think, for example, of the high school sports star who is only happy at forty-five when he thinks of his glory days.) To the extent that one loves God one can dwell "outside" the world. This loving desire is like fire because the more it consumes the more it demands, creating an exponential growth that makes it possible to progress quickly in the spiritual life once one enters the night of spirit.

Thus, as Deirdre Green emphasizes,[16] far from being negative in a pejorative sense (indeed there is a great deal of *nada* in John of the Cross), the dark night is a creative process whereby an ever-present, yet hardly noticed, light is made obvious because of the dark void (*vacío*) that surrounds it. And Kieran Kavanaugh[17] emphasizes not only the creative sense of the dark night, but also its pragmatic character. John of the Cross wants to point out the safest path through the night for those who have not traversed it before. God, comparable to the sun, is ever-present in the soul, which in turn is comparable to a window; when the window is smeared with dirt the sunlight is occluded, as when *pleonexia* smears the *psyche;* in the measure that the window is cleaned, the sunlight illumines the window; if the window is extremely clear, it appears to be the sunlight itself (hence the allegation made by some regarding pantheism). All of this sounds a bit mechanical, as if merely through hard work unity with God could be achieved. Although this puts the matter a bit crudely, it must nonetheless be admitted that there is a certain workmanlike approach (in this case, window washing) that John of the Cross likes.

In actuality, as we will notice in chapter six, in both phases of the dark night the soul exerts its own effort and receives God's influence. Meditation, in particular, relies on the activity of a human being, specifically on the reflection on specific ideas and images for the purpose of acquiring knowledge and love of God. Bede Frost[18] is correct to alert us to the fact that this activity in meditation carries itself over with its own momentum into the beginnings of contemplation. Likewise, the activity of a human being detaching himself from things carries itself over into the activity of detachment of spirit, the latter of which has its object the recovery of (divine and natural) wholeness, as we will see in chapter four. One can still be selfish even if one is detached from things. For example, without detachment of spirit one's religiosity could degenerate into the mercenary belief that the object of religion is to possess *personal* salvation in heaven. Once again, it is detachment from the *desire* for things, even "things" like heaven, rather than detachment from things, that is of primary concern to John of the Cross.

The emphasis I have given, along with that of the commentators I have cited, to the *activity* of the soul in John of the Cross is meant, as Frost notices, to dispel the assumption that mystics merely avoid evil and then wait to be zapped by a divine lightning bolt. In actuality, John of the Cross thinks that mystical contemplation is not the result of a straight line to God, but consists in arduous work, arduous because even the most spiritual life is punctuated by periods of dryness and because resting content with detachment from the senses without trying to achieve detachment of spirit is like clearing a garden of weeds by merely cutting off the tops. There is no reason to despair of all the work to be done, however, when one realizes that to even start the ascent to spiritual heights is already to have a glimpse of the goal. It is only when one seeks the wrong sort of comfort in religion, according to John of the Cross, that one fails to achieve that goal.

Thus far I have spoken of two phases of the dark night, but it would perhaps be more accurate to speak of two facets. The two facets are interwoven one with the other. There is something of detachment in union with God and there is some sense of union with God even in the beginning of the night of sense. To deny that the night of sense and the night of spirit are co-existing states is to

run the danger that the former could exist all by itself, hence it
would be a purely negative process of its own. Asceticism in that
case would degenerate into "mere" asceticism. That is, the significant
differences between discursive meditation and contemplation should
be thought of as differences in degree rather than kind, with meditation emphasizing the activity in the active-passivity of the spiritual
life (A, I, 13), and contemplation emphasizing the passivity in such
active-passivity, as we will see in chapter six.

The soul's journey is dark not only because it must detach
itself from the desire for things (and hence leave it especially inse-
cure in a culture which values people to the extent that they possess
things) and because it must rely on faith rather than knowledge,
but also because the point of arrival for the dark night is God.
Obviously some objects are visible even in the darkest night, just
as some objects (that is, God) are dark even in the brightest day
(A, I, 1–2; A, II, 1). In chapter three, we will consider *why* God is always somewhat beyond our grasp; here I am primarily concerned
with why the dark night is a narrow road, albeit an essential road
if one wants to travel from meditation to contemplation (D, prologue;
D, I, 1, 8).

Because the dark night dries up appetite, some people confuse
it with melancholy; but dryness (*sequedad*) of appetite is perfectly
compatible with a solicitude regarding God and in no way implies a
lukewarmness (*tibieza*) regarding God (D, I, 9). John of the Cross
was an inveterate and lifelong enemy of melancholy and brooding,
which are really species of selfishness. Even after escaping from
jail, he came out talking about God, *not* about his own sufferings or
about the viciousness of his persecutors. The dark night causes
precise knowledge of self and of one's own misery (*conocimiento de sí
y de su miseria*), he thinks, but this is a type of suffering which is
really a cure. As in the aforementioned wood example, there is a
positive, healing function provided by spiritual dryness at midnight
in that impurities in one's *psyche* are burned away (D, I, 11–12; D,
II, 10).

Strange Islands

As I mentioned in the Introduction, chapters one and two of
this book constitute a unity-in-difference. In chapter two, we will
be concerned with whether the road of solitude (*camino de la
soledad*) leads to quietism and with the issue of whether it pre-

cludes liberating *praxis*. I will argue that it does not lead to quietism, nor does it preclude liberating *praxis;* in fact, I hold that solitude enhances liberation. But I defend these claims in full awareness
of John of the Cross's view of human beings as strange islands
(*insulas extrañas*) who are, in a way, cut off from communication
with others and removed from the common knowledge of things.
Human beings function as islands, however, in their *nocturnal*
tranquility, when the work of the day is done (D, II, 25; S, 14, 8;
S, 14, 25). Or better, the hope is that one could carry this nocturnal
tranquility through the day *as* one works. But in no event is solitude supposed to replace activity in the world.

To say that human beings are "strange islands" is to say that
they are, ultimately, empty (A, II, 6). They become *aware* of this
emptiness through faith (which leads them to realize how limited
their knowledge is), hope (which leads them to abandon the possessions of memory), and love of God (which leads them to realize how
empty the affection is for all that is not God). To say that human
beings are strange islands is *not* to defend solipsism or selfishness.
For example, those who do not love God, according to John of the
Cross, assume that God does not love them, hence they often feel
rejected and abhored (*aborrecidos y desechados*). Herein lies the fine
line John of the Cross is walking regarding his thoughts on solitude.
On the one hand (D, II, 7), it is a type of selfishness to assume that
the world mirrors (or ought to mirror) oneself, and, on the other
hand, it is in fact correct to assume that solitary human beings are
something like Leibnizian, windowless monads. One cannot literally
see into the interior life of another. But if it is true that human
beings are more like mirrors than windows, it is only the highly
polished mirrors of those who have gone through the dark night
who give even remotely accurate images of the divine. Our phantasies cloud our mirroring abilities (A, II, 16), such that to see God
through others is to see God darkly.[19]

The island metaphor takes one a long way toward understanding John of the Cross's idea of solitude, but it can be overemphasized.
Solitariness is holy,[20] he thinks, because it is the most efficacious
path to meditation and imaginative reflection (*el camino de
meditación y discurso imaginario*), a path which continues on to
the hiding places of contemplation (L, 3, 43; L, 3, 53; D, II, 23).
There the soul realizes, if it had not done so already, that it never
really was alone, that its solitariness is an illusion. John of the
Cross is confident that the soul, which possesses nothing to hinder
the presence of God, will *in fact* be visited by God (S, 10, 6). That is,

the path to meditation and then to contemplation *cannot help* but bring joy (S, 20, 9; S, 22, 3).

If one believes, as John of the Cross does, that the spirit of God is in the veins of the soul (a metaphor which helps to work against the charge of dualism in John of the Cross, as we will see in chapter three), then one can understand why he believes that to be put in solitude is to be placed in a state of listening (*escucha*) or receptivity with respect to God. Idle tranquility (*osciosa tranquilidad*) or inner idleness (*ociosidad*) is not laziness, but an opportunity for spiritual listening (*escucha espiritual*). In effect, John of the Cross is distinguishing between meditative solitudes, on the one hand, and the loftiest solitudes (*altísimas soledades*) of contemplation, on the other (L, 3, 8; L, 3, 35; L, 3, 38; L, 3, 63). Just as frequent combing of one's hair gives it luster, the frequent examination in meditation of thoughts, words, and deeds gives proficiency to the soul (M, maxims, 26, 79), he thinks. If one seeks such religious perfection in meditative reading, one will find it in contemplation in:

> . . . the profound silence of his senses and his spirit, which he possesses for the sake of this deep and delicate listening. God speaks to the heart in this solitude (*el profundo silencio que conviene que haya en el alma según el sentido y el espíritu, para tan profunda y delicada audición. Dios que habla al corazón en esta soledad* (L, 3, 34).

CHAPTER 2

Action

Nor have I any other work
   Ni ya tengo otro oficio,
Now that my every act is love.
   Que ya sólo en amar es mi ejercicio.

> St. John of the Cross, "The Spiritual Canticle"

. . . .

I took off my feast-day clothes
   Dejé los trajes de fiesta,
And put on my working ones. . . .
   Los de trabajo tomaba. . . .
The strangers among whom
   Gozábanse los extraños
I was captive rejoiced.
   Entre quien cautivo estaba.

> St. John of the Cross, "A Romance on the Psalm,
> By the Waters of Babylon"

Introduction

It should not surprise us that one of the greatest figures in the history of Western mysticism can edify us even today regarding solitude. It will be the harder task of this chapter to indicate that he can do the same regarding *praxis*. Or more precisely, there are better thinkers to consult if one is primarily interested in ethics or in the theology of politics, but there might not be a better thinker

35

to consult if one wants to get clear on the relationship between contemplation and action.

My procedure will be to start this treatment of the practical side of John of the Cross's thought with a consideration of his own life and times so that his thoughts on *praxis* will be seen as grounded in his own personal experience and cultural heritage. Then I will detail John of the Cross's place within the Carmelite order and the order's efforts at reform, efforts which constitute John of the Cross's handling of the tension between solitude and action. With his own life and his life's work as a background, I will proceed to use John of the Cross for the purpose of criticizing contemporary capitalist and Marxist ideologies. That is, the hermeneutical approach I am taking in this book is a two-way street: I am using the tools and insights of contemporary thought in order to uncover features in John of the Cross's thought that have previously been unnoticed or underemphasized *and* I am using the thought of John of the Cross to notice features (some of them defective) in contemporary thought and culture.

In this effort at ideology critique, I will make explicit what John of the Cross thinks are the real riches in life and what constitutes freedom within his mystical theology. Finally, I will consider the practical ramifications of viewing John of the Cross as a spiritual soldier, sage, and saint. By the end of this chapter, the unity-in-difference mentioned in the introduction, wherein John of the Cross indicates to us what it means to be a contemplative individual-in-society, will be complete.

Life

John of the Cross was born in 1542 at Fontiveros in Castile, twenty-four miles from Avila. His father was Gonzalo de Yepes, who came from a family of wealthy silk merchants from Toledo. This fact should alert us to the rising tide of bourgeois culture in sixteenth-century Spain, but a tide which was partially held in check by several factors: an impoverished class, the aristocracy, the church, reform within the church, and so forth. His mother, Catalina Alvarez, however, was a poor weaver. When the two were married, the Yepes family rejected Gonzalo for having wed beneath himself, a rejection which was so complete that when he died Catalina and her children were left penniless. To have the Yepes door slammed in their faces literally left them homeless, a condition in which much of John of the Cross's youth was spent. That is, when we see John of the Cross draw the distinction between voluntary and involuntary poverty we should note that he was qualified to draw this distinction by firsthand evidence of the latter.[1]

It should not surprise us that a homeless mother should have one of her children, Luis, die. John of the Cross was lucky enough to find a home in a hospital, where he worked tending victims of syphilis. At *el hospital de las bubas* (tumors) John of the Cross excelled, his tendance of the sick being a lifelong occupation for him, and he was sent by those who had, in effect, adopted him to a grammar school where he also excelled, such that he advanced to the Jesuit school at Medina del Campo, where he spent four years. It was here that John of the Cross first experienced the liberating effect of words, specifically the words of his native language used in literature; it was here that John of the Cross first experienced a world beyond that of grinding poverty.

At the age of twenty, John of the Cross entered the Carmelite order, whose internal reform of the Catholic church, in particular, and of Spanish culture, in general, will be discussed soon. It is significant that John of the Cross did not join the Jesuits. Although Ignatian spirituality no doubt greatly influenced him, it is doubtful if the muscular version of Christianity exhibited by the Jesuits was to John of the Cross's liking. In fact, after joining the Carmelites he was tempted by the religious life of the Carthusian monks, who were even more removed from an *overtly* active life than the Carmelites.[2] One of the tasks of this chapter is to locate Carmelite *praxis* between the extremes of too much or too little action, and to locate the proper reasons for action in John of the Cross's thought. By way of introduction to these issues, it is helpful to notice Kavanaugh's claims regarding the Discalced Carmelite life in John of the Cross's day, which

> . . . was predominantly contemplative, but the active apostolate was by no means absent. The contemplative element comprised the recitation of the Divine Office in common, with Matins recited at the hour of midnight; two hours of mental prayer daily; and conventual Mass. The Rule and Constitutions called likewise for fasts and total abstinence from flesh meat; poverty in the type of dwelling, clothing, and food; enclosure and withdrawal from the world. They were also to go barefoot, and thus were soon referred to as the *Discalced* Carmelites. Their active work consisted mainly of preaching and of hearing confessions.[3]

After entering the Carmelites, John of the Cross was sent to the university at Salamanca, which by that time had surpassed the university at Paris as the greatest university on the continent. Although it takes a great deal of intellectual effort to understand John of the Cross and to appropriate him for the purposes of contemporary philosophy of religion, theology, and the religious life, John of the Cross himself was an intellectual only in the sense that he used his studies in systematic theology at Salamanca to develop his own version of mystical theology.

The Carmelites themselves took their name from Mount Carmel (which means "garden" in Hebrew) in Palestine, a mountain which was frequented by Elijah in the Old Testament, and which floated over various solitaries in Judaism and Christianity over the centuries. In 1185, a Greek monk named Phocas found Christian monks on Mount Carmel, who appeared to have been part of a tradition of Christian monks on the mountain going back for quite some time, a tradition which came to a halt in the thirteenth century when the Saracens sent the primitive Carmelites into a diaspora. The Carmelites eventually became a recognized religious order throughout Europe, although the rigor of the primitive Carmelites became attenuated by the time of the sixteenth century.[4]

The reform of Teresa of Avila of the Carmelite order relied primarily on a band of interior conquistadors, a band recruited by her personal solicitations, which were apparently quite difficult to resist. John of the Cross was dissuaded from joining the Carthusians by Teresa of Avila herself, who had, as a spiritual mother, adopted the much younger John of the Cross if only to work him to the bone for the rest of his life in the work of the reform.

No treatment of the social world of John of the Cross and Teresa of Avila would be adequate without the mention of the latter's Jewish roots. After the nobles and the higher clergy, the Jews had been the wealthiest and most influential people in Spain, a status which, when combined with anti-Semitism, led to the pogroms of the late fourteenth century and to the "reconciliation" of many Jews to Christianity in the Inquisition.[5] Teresa of Avila's ancestors were among these. In fact, because her ancestors were, like John of the Cross's, Toledan silk merchants, there are reasons to suspect that John of the Cross may also have had Jewish roots.

Teresa of Avila's reform of the Carmelite order was occasioned by her eventual response to the abuses of convent life. Convents had become places where community gossip gathered and where gallants were given encouragement by nuns clad in jewels. The convents were precursors of the salons, where the idle rich conversed about art and literature.[6] It is important to note, however, that Teresa of Avila's response did not consist in quietism, as we will see. Even when Teresa of Avila was dying she was sent off (in fact, she was carried) to start a new foundation; reform was, and is, hard work.

John of the Cross's role in the reform of the Carmelite order consisted in spreading the reform to men. As Brenan notices, there is a certain charm in small beginnings of heroic enterprises, as in Saint Francis of Assisi's work at the chapel at Portiuncula (now literally swallowed up by a massive church) or in John of the Cross's simple friary at Duruelo.[7] It is hard for us today to understand the political and social importance of establishing a convent or monastery or friary.[8] In the sixteenth century these were believed to be something like powerhouses that radiated spiritual (and material) benefits to the whole neighborhood. Although John of the Cross did not have the talent or interest to make political alliances, he did indirectly affect, and in a very practical way, the social world of his time.

The Calced, unreformed Carmelites obviously resented the Discalced reform, their astringency, and their emphasis on interiority. The unreformed reacted to the Discalced with a defensiveness characteristic of religious dogmatists of any age, but of that age in particular: they jailed John of the Cross in a six by ten foot cell, with only a small window for light, and they left him in the cold of winter and the suffocating heat of summer to think about his mistakes so as to repent. Frequent scourgings over a nine-month stay in jail were also supposed to help him see the light. Their effect was the exact opposite. What is instructive about John of the Cross's stay in jail is that, although he was, as he put it, swallowed by a whale and then vomited up on an alien port (M, letter, 1), he did not leave jail as a bitter cynic, but as an even more careful tender of the poor and sick.

After a life-threatening escape from jail, John of the Cross spent eight months at El Calvario where, despite the austerity of his diet and of the living conditions there,[9] he spent what were perhaps the happiest days of his life. Eventually a sort of rapprochement with the Calced Carmelites was reached, making it possible for John of the Cross to hurl himself into the reform movement at various places: Baeza, Granada, then Segovia. Baeza, with its flourishing wool and silk industry, was like most Spanish cities of the day in that it had both incredible wealth and incredible poverty, a gap not yet closed even in advanced capitalist countries.

John of the Cross's involvement *in* the world is very much evident in several controversies that arose within the Discalced ranks while he was at Segovia. One issue regarded whether priors should be elected or appointed by the general of the order. John of the Cross held strong views in favor of the former. His attempt at democratization of religious authority included opposition to repeat terms for those in positions of leadership, for fear that repeat terms would pose to leaders a dangerous temptation to establish systems of patronage. He held the Platonic view that leaders should be reluctantly cajoled into office by those who voted for them. Those who ambitiously aspire to office, he thought, too easily become obsequious to authority. It is ironic that John of the Cross himself was forced against his will to serve repeat terms as definitor of the order.[10]

Brenan estimates that John of the Cross traveled six thousand miles in two years (on foot, without shoes) overseeing twelve priories and several convents under his care. It is no wonder that he had no interest in religious frivolity, as in the supposed wounds of Christ which appeared on a certain cause célébre in Lisbon, Maria de la Visitación. (The wounds were eventually proved to be fake.)[11] This is not to say that he was adverse to popular piety and a peasant's faith. He liked manual labor and insisted at every foundation that he help lay bricks or sweep the kitchen. In fact, he *could not* see others labor without wishing to assist. At the various towns surrounding the Carmelite priories and convents, he was confessor to both university professors and the townspeople; he ministered to both the *aldeanos* and the *rústicos*.[12] And he never failed to speak strongly on the need for justice and charity. John of the Cross's *relatively* quick canonization after his death was due not to his friends in high places (at his death he was in disfavor with higher authorities in the order, as we will see), but to the overwhelming veneration the people of towns and farms throughout Spain had for him.

It seems that John of the Cross was a successful spiritual director because of his concentration on the spiritual needs of individual persons rather than on oracular pronouncement or on a rigid spiritual method that might be alleged to be valid for all.[13] Further, John of the Cross's poverty of spirit must have been somewhat contagious.[14] F. Brice describes his poverty of spirit as follows:

... if he had been poor in material possessions only, and not in spirit, his soul would have been rich as far as desire was concerned. Thus it is evident that true poverty consists in detachment, for it is not a question of lacking things or of destitution since this implies no poverty of spirit so long as the soul desires material riches.[15]

That is, even poor people (in some cases, especially poor people) can be rich in desire. Deirdre Green notes that:

... it is not the presence or absence of worldly possessions that marks the degree of spirituality in a person, rather the attitude toward them. So long as the *craving* for the things of the senses remains, the soul is not empty; but the absence of desire, or of the direction of the selfish will towards fulfillment of sensual appetites, brings about emptiness and freedom of the soul, "nakedness of spirit," even if there may be an abundance of possessions.[16]

But because John of the Cross's thought constitutes a theology of experience, not of concepts, he offered a real possibility of spiritual growth to the poor and uneducated. Union with God was made possible, he thought, through love rather than through intellectual probing. It is perhaps this sanjuanistic intimacy, similar in many ways to the "deification of the human" in Eastern Orthodoxy, that has traditionally made the secular Carmelite life the most popular secular order in the Catholic church after that of the Franciscans.[17] It was not only John of the Cross's intimacy, however, which made him appealing, but in addition his personal way of indicating that he understood the sufferings of others. The often noticed (as in Ernest Hemingway) Spanish fascination with Christ's passion and death is present in John of the Cross, but not in a morbid way. Bede Frost emphasizes John of the Cross's belief that "the need of the world" is to satisfy the reticulative desire for wholeness, a desire which is gathered together and intensified in Christianity through the passion.[18]

That is, there is something liberating about the passion, according to John of the Cross, and something universal in its appeal. (Think, for example, of the sympathetic version by Miles Davis of *soledad* and of the *via dolorosa* in "Sketches of Spain"; here the pain of growing up black in the St. Louis area meets the Spanish commiseration with, and edification by, Christ.) Although one obviously has a duty to stay in touch with current events (for otherwise one's charity may lose its efficacy), it is important to notice that morbidity is much more likely when considering the horrors and vulgarities of everyday life than it is in considering Jesus's passion. Reading the newspaper can be morbid. There are some events, like the passion, which are, as William Wordsworth put it in "Intimations of Immortality," "too deep for tears." Tears are trifles, according to John of the Cross, when the object of our consideration is the place of suffering within the overall scheme of things, as we will see in chapter four (M, letters, 3).

And, as before, John of the Cross was not unfamiliar with suffering. The leader of the Discalced in John of the Cross's later years, Doria, became angered when Teresa's successor, Ana de Jesus, lobbied the pope to appoint John of the Cross as the superior to Discalced nuns. Doria, who was jealous of John of the Cross's popularity, exiled him to Peñuela, the most isolated of Discalced houses, near where he died in 1591 at the age of forty-nine after a painful illness. John of the Cross went to Peñuela (which was to have been a temporary stop before his exile to Mexico) without protest, although at Carmelite meetings he continued until the end to resist despotism and to champion the secret ballot. Having been the victim of persecution, he wished to guarantee free speech and to eliminate the fear of persecution in others.[19] Regarding Doria, Brenan notes the following:

> Perhaps it is not going too far to see in the contrast between his system of government and that advocated by Juan the same antithesis as that which existed during the Spanish Civil War between the Communists and the Anarchists. The former desired power above everything and overreached themselves in their endeavor to obtain it, whereas the latter wished to destroy power and substitute for it a set of moral values or principles.[20]

The Primitive Carmelite Ideal and the Reform

With some knowledge of John of the Cross's life and of the Carmelite order as a background, we are now in a position to consider the more subtle issues surrounding action in the contemplative life. There is a basic distinction that must be made between the ancient monastic tradition of the West (as in the Carthusians, among others) and the Carmelites. The latter signify a transition from monasticism to a contemplative order of preaching friars. The first Carmelites had done something original: they established a loose knit community of hermits (common in the East) with an occasional, informal apostolate. Although they were contemplatives, they saw that an apostolate was a normal and legitimate overflow from their life of prayer. Any works were permitted which were organically connected to the contemplative life and which did not hinder contemplation. The preaching apostolate was the most obvious sort of action for the early Carmelites, but preaching brought with it the temptation to go to the busy cities to live where the people were.[21] That is, the first Carmelites were both hermits and prophets, mystics and preachers, albeit with a precedence given to the former element in each of these two pairs.

Just as the forty years in the desert came to be regarded as the golden age of Israel, so the recovery of the primitive spirit of Carmel symbolized a return to fidelity, community, solitude, and the destruction of inequalities. There had been contemplative orders before, and there had been active orders in the service of schools, hospitals, parishes, and missions. But the attempt to have a contemplative order with an apostolate poses special difficulties not found in these other orders. The Carmelite apostolate is to actively lead others to contemplative solitude; it is an apostolate of interior prayer; it is a type of teaching regarding that which is hidden. But no one can give something that he does not have.

As in chapter one, the Carmelite ideal is a mean between extremes. On the one hand, it is a rejection of too much activity, of the wrong sort of activity, and of activity done for the wrong motives. It is a rejection of frenetic activity for its own sake, and of violent activity for any reason. It is easy for us to see the appeal the monks on Mount Carmel had for the spiritually shipwrecked survivors of the second crusade who discovered them. They discovered not a cenobitic life where monks recited the psalms in common, but true solitaries-in-fraternity; that is, they discovered true hermits. But even at this early date the Carmelite monks maintained a hospice in Jerusalem. After the fall of Acre in 1291, when the last Carmelites in the East were exterminated, the Carmelites in the West, although they initially settled in out of the way places, eventually settled in towns where extreme or inappropriate activity was a constant danger. In fact, in order to gain a solid footing in the West and in order to placate the overtly active clergy, the Carmelites had to accentuate themselves as friars (not monks) who *did* something. Saint Simon Stock is credited with solidifying the order as an apostolic institute, such that eventually houses of study were established at the major universities, including Oxford, Cambridge, Paris, and Salamanca.

On the other hand, the Carmelite ideal is a rejection of the rejection of *praxis*. As the apostolic activity of the Carmelites increased, there was an understandable reactionary movement that pleaded for the return to monasticism, at the very least, if not to quietism. This reaction often invented a primitive Carmelite ideal of its own choosing, an imaginary ideal which would have attenuated apostolic activity practically to the point of nonexistence. Within the Discalced reform there was a reactionary wing, exemplified by Doria and the friars at Pastrana, which leaned toward this extreme even as it favored centralized control over the order. And it was this extreme wing within the Discalced reform that hounded John of the Cross until his death.

It is obvious to any contemporary reader that John of the Cross avoids the first extreme. It is one of the theses of this chapter to establish the less obvious fact that he also avoided the second extreme. Thomas Merton describes the Carmelite ideal as:

> . . . a kind of "prophetic" union of solitude and apostolate. When this balance is disturbed, when the shift is made too far in one direction or the other, then the primitive spirit is lost. That is to say that when too much emphasis is placed on apostolic action, the primitive spirit is of course weakened and eventually destroyed. But that does not mean that the return to the original ideal is a mere matter of abandoning the apostolate and embracing a solitary life that is primarily ascetical and austere. It seems likely that the apostolate, when kept in its right place, *remains the true guarantee* of the original purity of the ideal. For a Carmelite, the apostolate in its own way encourages contemplation, just as contemplation is the source of a genuine apostolate. To abandon the apostolate altogether in what we might call a kind of "left wing deviation" would result not in a purification of the contemplative spirit, but rather its stultification in the rigidity of an artificial, formalistic cult of solitude and asceticism for their own sakes. . . . The problem was very sucessfully solved by St. John of the Cross.[22]

Because of Doria's brutality there might be a tendency to discredit the second extreme more than the first. Hence it is worthwhile to emphasize the strengths of those who flirt with quietism even if they do not succumb to it. One example is Nicholas the Frenchman, a thirteenth-century Carmelite who authored a work titled *The Fiery Arrow*. Here we have a view that places exclusive attention on solitude. (It should be noted, however, that even in the most

quietistic version of monasticism there is an apostolate in the sense
that monks pray for the betterment of the world; hence they can
perhaps legitimately point out that only the solitary has confidence
in the efficacy of prayer in that only he uses it in an unmitigated
way.) No doubt there are some actions that are best done on in-
stinct, as in rescuing a drowning child from a pond. But when
developing a *plan* of action there is no danger in lining up one's
motives and thinking carefully about what one is trying to accomplish. Nicholas's view seems to have been that the Carmelite transition from East to West, from a limited apostolate to an ambitious
one, was too rapid. Hence, it is not too surprising that even three
centuries later there were still efforts at reinventing a primitive
Carmelite ideal that eliminated *praxis*.

It is part of John of the Cross's genius that he can do justice
both to those who exclaim "Return to the desert!" *and* to those who
require a prophetic eremitism. In John of the Cross there is the
primacy of solitude and contemplation, not in spite of or opposed to
action in the world, but for the sake of it. Poised between Doria, on
the one hand, and Gratian, on the other (who tried to instill in the
Carmelites a missionary zeal to convert souls in America, a move
opposed by John of the Cross), John of the Cross transcended them
both. He

> ... included in himself all that was good in either of them:
> who was an austere lover of solitude, but more prudent than
> Doria because he knew that solitude itself could become a fetish,
> an object of immoderate attachment. He knew that the love of
> austerity could become a mere "penance of beasts." He fully un-
> derstood and carried out St. Teresa's apostolic ideals without be-
> ing swept away by the volatile enthusiasms of a Gratian. He it
> was who embodied in himself the true prophetic spirit of Carmel,
> and it is remarkable that of the three, he was the one who was
> externally the least fiery, the least impressive, the most obscure.
> Of the three he was the most silent, the most retiring, the truest
> solitary, the greatest contemplative. But also, at the same time,
> he was of the three the greatest apostle, the one who had the
> surest and deepest effect on other people. These were not souls
> whom he had hunted out with the busy zeal of an aggressive
> convert maker: they were people who had been brought to
> him. . . without his knowing how they came to him. And they were
> transformed.[23]

Although John of the Cross implies that even solitude can become
a fetish, there is always some need in the contemplative life for a

desert, even if it be a chapel or a path in the woods. One goes to the desert not to prepare for *praxis,* in that contemplation has no ulterior purpose besides itself and its contribution to God; rather the contemplative acts in order to complete what one has learned in solitude.

For some critics *praxis* has come to mean something grand or histrionic, as in armed revolution, hence for them there is something trivial in John of the Cross's activities. But it should be noted that the work of John of the Cross and Teresa of Avila constitutes nothing short of the Spanish reformation. Fernand Braudel, in his massive study of the age of Philip II, makes it clear that Spain in the sixteenth century was militantly Catholic at least partially because it was recently Catholic, however odd that sounds. The wilder parts of the mountains still hid some Moors and, as has been noticed, the Jews had just recently been "reconciled" to Catholicism.[24] Protestantism per se was a foreign transplant in Spain, and Spain was a tree that did not lend itself easily to grafting.

But for at least five reasons, including two major ones, John of the Cross can be seen as a structural equivalent to a Protestant reformer *within* the Catholic church. First, the Protestant criticism of Catholicism that it had largely abandoned scripture was not without substance, as Catholics have come to admit. But as Brenan notes,[25] no Protestant reformer ever quoted Scripture more than John of the Cross. As a matter of fact, the omnipresence of scriptural citations in John of the Cross, in contrast to his relatively few citations of systematic theologians, is one of the biggest surprises for first time readers. John of the Cross is said to have memorized vast chunks of the Bible, including much of the Old Testament. Second, as we will see in chapter five, John of the Cross's attacks on idolatry in Catholicism are as severe as those of almost any Protestant reformer.[26] And third, like the Protestant reformers (as in Luther's belief that one is saved through faith alone) John of the Cross believes that a human being cannot be saved by what he *does.*[27] One is "saved" by union with God which, as we have seen already and will see again in chapter six, involves an element of passivity with respect to God. I have tried to emphasize in this chapter, however, that John of the Cross does not share some of the Protestant reformers almost total disdain for "good works"; John of the Cross does not disdain good works, even if he does carefully demarcate what they are.

Points four and five are related and are far more substantial than the previous three. The former point is that John of the Cross, like some of the Protestant reformers (George Fox comes to mind), emphasizes interior prayer. There were some in the sixteenth century, like the Dominican theologian Melchior Cano, who thought that the greatest heresy of the day was the tendency toward interior prayer. This tendency, along with Teresa of Avila's Jewish descent, made the Carmelite reform suspect in some quarters. One of the most significant reasons for the success of the reform was Teresa of Avila's charm and her calculated submissiveness to men.[28]

At this point I would like to treat the relationship between John of the Cross and quietism, a word I have used loosely until this point as a convenient straw man. John of the Cross openly defends the prayer of quiet, which is a type of contemplation where one has an intimate awareness of the presence of God. He would not, however, defend quiet*ism,* which is an exaggerated type of interiority which has both plagued and stimulated Christianity from its beginning. The most famous quietists have been the thirteenth-century monks on Mount Athos called the "hesychasts" (literally, the quietists) and the seventeenth-century thinker Molinos. Quietists like Molinos tend to separate completely mystical theology from any intellectual apparatus, including systematic theology. This leaves one's highest aspirations open to sentimentalism; it denigrates entirely the preparatory value of *discursive* meditation; and it can lead to a reprehensible moral outcome in that it leaves no opportunity for, and no incentive to, practice the virtues. On all of these counts John of the Cross is innocent of the charge of quietism. (John of the Cross's approach to rationality will be treated in the next chapter. Here I would only like to note once again that he was in fact interested in systematic theology and philosophy *to the extent that* they were propaedeutic to mystical theology.)

The particular variety of quietism with which John of the Cross was confused was a group called the *"Alumbrados"* or "Illuminists," who emphasized an interior, spiritual version of Christianity over a ceremonial one. Although John of the Cross was not a quietist, one can see why some people would confuse him for one, just as Socrates, the greatest opponent to Sophism, was thought by some to be a Sophist. Teresa of Avila was perhaps the first person to direct John of the Cross to several recent books on interior prayer by Francisco de Osuna, Bernardino de Laredo, and Garcia de Cisneros. In fact, Osuna's 1537 work titled *Tercer Abecedario Espiritual* was the first work on mysticism published in Spanish. This work perhaps introduced John of the Cross to the idea of recollection (*recogimiento*), whereby one must empty one's mind so as to make room for God: *Este no pensar nada es pensarlo todo.*[29]

Teresa of Avila and John of the Cross read Osuna, despite the fact that he was attacked by the Inquisition in 1524, and they were no doubt positively affected by his belief that a letting go (*dejamiento*) leads to an optimism in religion. In fact, Juan Antonio Llorente, who had access to the files of the Inquisition, states in *Historia critica de la Inquisicion en España* (1818) that John of the Cross's own case was at least sent to the Inquisition even if John of the Cross was not actually tried. John of the Cross's similarity to some of the Protestant reformers regarding interiority can also be seen when it is considered that in 1559 the Council of Trent put on the index many works on mysticism and translations of the New Testament.[30]

The fifth point, which lends support to the claim that John of the Cross's *praxis* consisted in the significant action of reform (of the Carmelite order, of Catholicism, and, by implication, of Spanish culture in general), is his criticism of the imperious, the pretentious, and the gaudy in religion, a criticism to be treated in detail in chapter five. But it is important to notice that John of the Cross developed this criticism *within* the Catholic church. Frost notes that in the case of quietism it is easy, once the criticism of certain practices in institutional religion gets started, to develop contempt for institutional religion in general.[31] Further, the quietists tend to think that religious services are for beginners only, whereas John of the Cross had a continued appreciation for the simple, dignified, yet mysterious quality of public prayer in the Mass.[32]

There has always been something of a tension in Christianity between systematic theology and mystical theology, and John of the Cross preserves this tension, albeit with an emphasis on the latter. New Testament antinomianism is one sort of reaction, as is sanjuanistic mysticism, to a sterile, mechanical, and overly institutionalized religion, as Colin Thompson emphasizes.[33] Some contemporary thinkers may wonder not about John of the Cross's criticisms of institutional religion, but rather about his willingness to stay within the institution at all, especially when it is considered that he actually received physical torture within the church. An *apologia* for John of the Cross would have to consider several factors, including his distaste for abstractions and his conviction that religious truth is best achieved through edifying *experience*. Consider the difference between religious studies as a discipline or philosophy, on the one hand, and theology, on the other. There are many advantages in favor of the former as opposed to the latter. For example, in philosophy one can pursue the truth objectively without being de-

flected by irrelevant considerations of authority and tradition. But
this strength can easily turn into a weakness. If one's allegedly
disinterested approach to the truth is not anchored in some historically grounded assumptions, and not concretely connected to *real
people* with whom one shares a history, and to whom one must
respond when one makes an intellectual mistake, then one's "objec-
tivity" can easily prostitute itself to the first caller, whether the
caller be an aristocratic bias or the sheer weight of capital. (Marx
makes this very point.)

However frustrating (even painful) community may have been,
John of the Cross was committed to it. He submitted to the church
as we today might submit to "experts." In neither case is a slavish
obsequiousness to be praised. John of the Cross does sometimes
refer to *los filósofos* or *los teólogos* of the tradition in general, and
sometimes to individual thinkers (Boethius, Dionysus, Saint Gre-
gory, Saint Augustine, Saint Francis of Assisi, Saint Bernard, Saint
Thomas Aquinas). But these citations very seldom do any intellectual work for John of the Cross, as William James would put it, in
that they merely provide the matrix out of which John of the Cross
attempts to make his own contribution to religious truth. Further,
because of the untoward moral implications of quietism and because of the vagaries of individual "revelations" (for example, the
aforementioned fraudulence of Maria de la Visitación), John of the
Cross thought that the church provided a needed counterbalance to
private cults of spirituality and to "solitude" used as a ruse for self-
indulgence.[34] Human persons themselves are the origin of many
"divine" locutions (A, prologue; A, II, 22, 29).

It must be admitted that any defense of the institutional church
runs the risk of embarassment if the church uses its tradition or its
power for the purely defensive purposes of the institution itself.
John of the Cross was willing to run this risk, just as he was
willing to run the risk that public expressions of religion would
water down solitude or distract one from solitude. That is, if John
of the Cross was pulled toward quietism, he definitely stopped
short of it. He approved of the church as long as it fostered love as
opposed to lukewarmness (*tibieza*), mere formality (*cumplimiento*),
force (*fuerza*), or blind habit (A, III, 19). He is what Paul Tillich has
called a *"baptized* mystic."[35] Thompson puts the matter well:

> At least San Juan's mysticism, arising from his participation in a
> worshipping community, avoids the temptation of discounting the
> institutional, organized side of religion. The most serious accusa-

tion against him is that if some of his statements, taken in isolation, are stretched to their logical conclusion, they come perilously
close to implying an individual way to God which does not need at
its higher levels the normal forms of organized religion.[36]

Because John of the Cross did not leave us anything like Teresa
of Avila's *Foundations,* he seems to be somewhat oblivious of many
of the features of his age, as in the rise of nation-states, the loss of
the Netherlands, and the Spanish attempt to master the New World.
But he could hardly have been ignorant of these events, nor is it
likely that he was apathetic in a pejorative sense about them (indeed
there is a great deal of *apathes* in John of the Cross). As director of
formation for the reform of the Carmelites, he found the place from
which he could act authentically, religiously, and efficaciously in
the world.[37]

Ideology Critique

Any contemporary attempt at evaluating, or even at describing, John of the Cross's *praxis* should come clean regarding the assumptions made in the evaluation. Intellectual Marxists, or, as
they are now called, "critical theorists," have done tremendous work
in alerting contemporary readers to the assumptions of bourgeois
ideology which infect the reading of texts. Unfortunately, critical
theorists have not usually used the same razor sharp tools when it
comes to their own Marxist ideology. *My* assumption will be that
there is much to be learned from both liberalism and Marxism, and
that a reading of John of the Cross with one eye each on the
strengths of liberalism and Marxism will be productive in the effort
to determine the proper place of a religious individual-in-society in
the contemporary world. That is, John of the Cross's mystical theology will help us to appreciate both the strengths and weaknesses of
both liberalism and Marxism.
The best place to start the effort of ideology critique from a
sanjuanistic perspective is with the thorny issue of the scope of
John of the Cross's concern: Was his mystical theology meant for
an elite few or for the masses? There is nothing wishy-washy about
saying: "both." We should be reminded of the fact that all Christians
are called to contemplation, to achieve that perfection appropriate
to human beings, but this is a far cry from claiming that all are
called to attain the highest stages of the night of spirit.[38] Because

each soul is valued by God there would be little sympathy in John of the Cross for either the view that a human being is an increment of capital or that a human being is primarily a member of a class. This caring egalitarianism is evident in the subtitle to *The Ascent of Mount Carmel,* where John of the Cross hopes that his remarks will be valuable both for beginners and proficients. His goal is:

> . . . to explain all these points, so that *everyone* who reads this book will in some way discover the road that he is walking along, and the one he ought to follow if he wants to reach the summit of this mount (emphasis added—A, prologue, 7).

God is diffused through the world, as I will emphasize in chapter four, diffused along its highways and byways and on its common table (L, 1, 15). The New Testament epistles themselves were written, as John of the Cross no doubt noticed, for the poor mass of converts to Christianity.

A consideration of three different types of union will illustrate both the egalitarian and inegalitarian dimensions of John of the Cross's thought. The most fundamental union with God consists in the solidarity human beings have with God as parts of the divine creation; without this union we would *all* fail to exist. Although not all experience the union of grace that occurs to those who actually hear about God and make some small steps toward God, almost all are in this category, too. But the third sort of union of mind and will with God, the sort of union usually referred to in John of the Cross, is relatively rare. A great part of John of the Cross's *praxis* is to convert "Christians" to Christianity, to help people move from the second to the third sorts of union. Countless numbers of people have started out well in religion, reached a certain plateau, and then had their religious quest fizzle out gradually. John of the Cross often speaks boldly about religion in order to combat what appear to be the greatest enemies of religion in nominally Christian cultures: complacency, insipidity, and the transformation of profundity into vulgarized and minimalized truths.[39]

John of the Cross was not only a mystic but also a mystigogue who, like a Socratic midwife, aided in the birth of solitude in those who were merely "practicing Catholics." Why do so few attain the third sort of union? Not because God wishes there to be few, but because only a few have learned how to make room for God.[40] It is sad enough to see many people failing to advance to God; even sadder, according to John of the Cross, are those who actually move backwards by engaging in useless and exotic religious exercises (now actually paid for with money, often enough at quite a price):

> They resemble children who kick and cry, and struggle to walk by themselves when their mothers want to carry them; in walking by themselves they make no headway, or if they do, it is at a child's pace (A, prologue, 3).

If one of the major causes of complacency in religion is the lack of good spiritual direction, contributing causes include a lack of courage (ánimo) to break from one's "wealth," and an unwarranted assumption that some small attachment to things or some small character flaw will go away by itself or that it can conveniently be disposed of at some point in the future (A, I, 11; A, III, 20).

According to John of the Cross, it is unclear why God does not raise (eleva) all to contemplation if they desire it (D, I, 9). Perhaps because they do not *really* desire it. Contemplation presupposes some habitual predispositions, hence most are not uplifted. One may have a fleeting desire to climb a mountain, but if one does not exercise and if one drinks too much alcohol the desire is somewhat flippant. Most circumstances in life make contemplation unlikely.[41] In Eccles. 38:24ff., we learn that a certain leisure is required for religious perfection: How can one become wise if one works the plow from dawn to dusk? When will one meditate? Union with God, for John of the Cross, can occur in *this* life, hence developing the material preconditions for, and the principles of distributive justice conducive to, leisure are no triffling matters.[42]

Because of the difficulty in obtaining the highest sort of union with God, John of the Cross thinks that those who are normally considered advanced Christians are really beginners, and vast stretches of John of the Cross's writings are not meant for beginners. These "advanced" Christians, he thinks, need the astringent medicine he offers. Even "good" people sometimes find the poor loathesome; John of the Cross's response is to shock them by describing in bold terms what union requires. John of the Cross also wrote in bold terms regarding what one can expect in the dark night so that he would exclude no one who had gone through the dark night before.[43] Although perfection (John of the Cross seldom uses the word *perfecto* or its cognates) is lonely, union (*unión* or its cognates), by way of contrast, requires community with God and with neighbor. The latter is John of the Cross's primary concern. Even his concentration on religious experience indicates this point.

The roots to this word (*ek peri entia*) point to one going outside of oneself to the beings around us.

If it seems to some that John of the Cross is "too negative" or that he is tearing down the spiritual life, it is because some readers incorrectly assume that John of the Cross is talking exclusively to beginners (A, III, 2). He is quite explicit that only a few actually achieve union because only a few reach the greatest intensity of the interior life; and this because only a few are really willing to undergo strong purgation, to undergo the dark night (D, I, 14; S, 26, 4; L, 1, 24). Hence, as we will see again in chapter four, only a few are really fit for experiencing sublimity (*subida,* literally a climb), even if all are fit potentially (L, 2, 27). As before, there is a pragmatic bent to John of the Cross's thought in that above all else as a spiritual director he wants religious seekers to make progress. One of the virtues of speaking boldly, as John of the Cross does about the spiritual life, is that one can more quickly and easily eliminate error (a la Popper) and move on to a closer approximation of religious truth. Karl Rahner catches well the spirit of John of the Cross when he explicitly lists boldness (*parresia*) as one of the Christian virtues as long as boldness is supplemented by severe attempts at refutation of the inadequate features of one's daring proposals.[44] (Consider, for example, John of the Cross's careful, life-long exploration of the startling aphorism: To come to possess all desire the possession of nothing.)

It is obvious that John of the Cross was not explicitly about the business of critiquing liberal or capitalist ideology. But it is equally obvious that his thought runs directly against the tendency in capitalist countries to materialize Christianity and to reduce it to the status of a mere accessory to pleasure, financial security, or nationalism. Further, John of the Cross would no doubt be quick to notice that in capitalist cultures the rich often lament their poverty.[45] It is one thing to have distractions in culture, it is quite another to systematize the distractions such that they actually become essential to the success of the economy.[46] There is something perverse about an economic system in which if most of the people led simple, moderate lives, the system would likely collapse for lack of "demand." And there is something questionable, at the very least, about an economic system which encourages self-interest, if not selfishness, and merely tolerates charity, or which reduces charity to self-interest through the mechanism of a tax break. For example, Mr. Smith, the Adam of capitalism, once said that it is not from the benevolence of the butcher, the brewer, or the baker that we expect our dinner, but from their regard to their own interest. For these and other reasons it is odd that the relationship between capitalism and Christianity is assumed by many to be less problematic than the relationship between Marxism and Christianity. Even if capitalist self-interest benefits others materially, as in many (but not all) instances it does, it is difficult to see how it does so spiritually.[47]

It should not be assumed at this point that I am trying to slip in through the back door a defense of Marxism. Rather, I am claiming that in light of the fact that there has recently been much effort in Latin America at taking Marxism from its supposed atheism and showing some compatibility with Christianity, perhaps the next wave of interest in Christian economic theory will move away from the supposed marriage made in heaven between capitalism and Christianity. One can imagine these two movements meeting in the middle somewhere, such that the Christian might come to realize that he had previously bartered away his Christianity for either the trinkets of Adam Smith or the revolutionary fervor of Karl Marx. At that point the stage would seem to be set for a complete rethinking of a Christian life in modern economic society. John of the Cross, I allege, aids in this effort in several ways.

There are obviously some points of compatibility between John of the Cross and capitalism: capitalist countries have generally been strong defenders of freedom of religion, and the liberal presuppositions of capitalist culture preserve a sense of individual liberty compatible with (albeit different from) sanjuanistic solitude. But equally obvious are points of compatibility between John of the Cross and Marxism, as in John of the Cross's belief that the point to mystical theology is not to theorize about the spiritual life but to change it. In fact, over thirty years ago Alasdair MacIntyre called for a "dark night of the soul," an "ascesis of poverty and questioning, which must renew our politics."[48] The interaction between the thought of John of the Cross and Marx is most prominent in Marx's notion that a human being is one who suffers, and because he is aware of his suffering a human being longs passionately for the object of his desire.[49] The trick is to do justice to the similarities between John of the Cross and Marx without failing to notice their important differences, as in the fact that the object of John of the Cross's desire, God, is nothing at all like Marx's.

Kenneth Leech rightly notices a fourfold pattern in both John of the Cross and Marx consisting of alienation, the unmasking of illusion, illumination through upheaval, and the importance of struggle. Also common to both is the movement away from self-centeredness toward communion.[50] Indeed, contemporary followers of John of the Cross could learn a great deal from critical theorists and liberation theologians regarding how to spot alienation as a social as well as a personal reality, and how to spot the structural or institutional character of evil.

In the final analysis, however, John of the Cross's view of the world is just as hostile to Marxism as it is to capitalism. (Luckily it is not the job of this book to defend a third alternative between the two, although I personally have always been attracted to a Michael Harrington-like socialism.) John of the Cross's *praxis* is not Marxist in that he thinks that the Christian does great works *as a consequence of* service to God. That is, a person is not the sum of his actions, as in the pistons of an engine. Christian Marxists (for example, the liberation theologians in Latin America or in North America and Europe) tend to materialize Christianity as much as theologians under the siren call of capitalism, albeit with the goal of generating liberating *praxis*. Frost rightly labels John of the Cross as a defender of the mixed life, where one has no hesitation (à la Hamlet) to act so as to eliminate injustice, but, in order for one's actions to be commendable (or efficacious in the long run), they must flow from a spiritual center.[51] The ideal, as before, is not to generate an unbridgable gap between contemplation and action, but to have Martha and Mary become one, to have action grow organically out of contemplation. What one hears whispered in dark contemplation one can proclaim from the rooftops (Matt. 10:27).

Action that does not radiate from the center runs the risk of squandering the substance of human activity. John of the Cross would have us simplify our exterior activity so that it does not exceed the limits of our charity. He thinks that we should rid our activity of any pertness and presumption that tend to make our "charity" a type of self-gratification. John of the Cross, Marx, and Thoreau are all opponents of pious do-gooders. The last alerts us to the (sanjuanistic) idea that:

> There are a thousand hacking at the branches of evil to one who is striking at the root, and it may be that he who bestows the largest amount of time and money on the needy is doing most by his mode of life to produce that misery which he strives in vain to relieve.... Philanthropy is almost the only virtue which is sufficiently appreciated by mankind. Nay, it is greatly overrated; and it is our selfishness which overrates it.[52]

That is, Marx is not the only critic of superficial bourgeois schemes to eliminate destitution. John of the Cross's contribution to the

effort to get beneath the surface of poverty, to get to its root, consists in the belief that contemplation must not be sought as an aid
to action, rather the most commendable and the most enduring
action derives from contemplation.[53]

Real Riches

It would not only be inaccurate to claim that John of the Cross
was not a creature of his age, it would also play into the hands of
those who lampoon mystics for their ethereal experiences floating
above the *lebenswelt*. Nonetheless, I am trying to show in this
chapter that John of the Cross's thought provides a ladder for us to
partially transcend liberalism and Marxism and to view both from
a higher religious plateau. To know a mental limit as such is to
partially transcend that limit. For example, all of a dog's thoughts
are doglike, but dogs do not know this. Human beings talk about
"mere" human knowing, which indicates that they can at least
imaginatively place themselves in the shoes of a superhuman
knower. Likewise, human beings now know that they are *partially*
determined by political and economic ideology, hence because of
this knowledge they can liberate themselves somewhat from ideological thinking. John of the Cross's treatment of possessions offers
insight into what it means to give oneself over to things no matter
what political ideology one finds oneself in; and his treatments of
poverty, freedom, and work are likewise at least partially trans-
ideological.

John of the Cross's penchant for boldness (that is, for putting
his case on the verge of overstatement without falling into it) is
nowhere more obvious than when he claims that we should burn
our attachment to worldly possessions (A, I, 2–3; also see Tobias
6:18–22). His use of "burn" pushes us toward overstatement, whereas
"attachment" stops us short. His sense is that possessions turn into
idols, which make us weary (*cansan*) when we venerate them, and
which put us in a Sisyphean predicament. For example, given the
calculated changes in fashion every season, dressing in style is
necessarily a Sisyphean project akin to emptying the ocean with a
sieve. Fashion by its very nature is a deceit in its claim of an
absolute right in favor of the present over the past. There is a
certain infidelity in the claim that this year's suits will be youthful
and supple, when last year the advertisers claimed anything but
the proposition that oldness and stiffness were the vogue. As Roland

Barthes puts it, "Fashion's aggressiveness, whose rhythm is the same as that of vendettas, is thus disarmed by a more patient image of time."[54] Like Barthes, John of the Cross refers to attachment to possessions in violent terms, like the torment (*atormentan*) of a person in prison or chained in a (Platonic) darkened (*oscurecen*) cave (A, I, 4, 6).

It must be admitted that John of the Cross is primarily worried that attachment to possessions will make one less capable of union with God. But he is also very much aware of the implications of many possessions for social justice issues, as in the biblical motto (Matt. 7:6) that we should not take from children so as to give to the dogs, that is, to our whims. In a way, he thinks, all creatures are as crumbs from God's table, but this metaphor should not get away from us to the point where we would deny children a dignified meal at their parents' table (A, I, 6). He also quotes Isa. 9:20 favorably: "He will turn to the right and be hungry, and eat toward the left and not be filled."

John of the Cross was not concerned with Manichean purity or with a denigration of bodily desire because of the body's inherent evil. Appetite is not evil, but it *is* blind and in need of direction. Just as one small crack can ruin a pitcher (A, I, 8, 11), so a cracked *psyche* can unleash untold devastation (think of Ted Bundy, the serial killer). One simply cannot traverse the narrow path to God with many attachments to possessions. Such attachments not only breed avarice, they also prove self-defeating on purely utilitarian grounds: the imagination of gold, he claims, gives to gold a more excellent structure than it has (A, I, 12; A, II, 7, 12). In sum, the maniacal thirst for goods is: (1) impious, in that many in effect make gods out of money and temporal goods (*hecho para sí dios del dinero y bienes temporales*); (2) selfish, in that it leads to vainglory (*vanagloria*); and (3) unjust, in that attachment to possessions eventually leads to disesteem of neighbor (*desestime del prójimo*). Even the memory of possessions can have these three consequences (A, III, 19, 22; D, I, 7).

The ebullience of John of the Cross, his *elan,* his zest for life is evidenced in his belief that to be empty of the attachment to possessions is to be full of hope, primarily, but also of faith and love. Poverty of spirit (*pobreza de espiritu*) yields contentment (*contento*), which is analogous, I take it, to Greek *hedone*. That is, John of the Cross is claiming that the contemplative life leads not only to Aristotelian *eudaemonia* but also to *hedone,* not only to human fulfillment but also to a pleasant life. Another bold claim, no doubt, but not an idle one in that it was tested by the homelessness, time in jail, and so forth, experienced by John of the Cross in his own life (D, II, 21; S, 1, 9; S, 1, 14; A, III, 7, 11, 15). And even if it is possible to have poverty of spirit while experiencing material wealth, it is usually the case that poverty of spirit requires *at least* intermittent diminishment of material wealth (see Matt. 13:44).

John of the Cross primarily embodies what Albert William Levi calls the ideal of the philosopher or theologian as saint, and second-arily as sage.[55] He does not instantiate the ideal of court intellectual (as in Descartes) or scholar (as in Kant or Tillich). For him the drink of highest wisdom makes one forget possessions (S, 26, 13), except the "possession" (*tener*) of God. And *this* sort of possession comes in an ascending order: possession of God through God's gifts, then through union, and finally through spiritual betrothal and marriage (L, 3, 1–2), to be discussed later.

John of the Cross was not the sort of cleric whose detachment made him incapable of dealing with the practical world. From his letters (for example, M, letters, 4), we learn that he was involved in the details of purchasing and maintaining houses for the friars. His claim that to possess God in all one should not possess anything in all (M, letters, 17) has as its scope one's *personal* possessions, as opposed to the possessions of one's dependents. Detachment from things as a personal motto allows one to appreciate, to the extent that one can, the present qua present so that one is not continually confronting tomorrow's concerns (M, precautions, 7, 11). John of the Cross oxymoronically defends the belief that today's riches are the lasting ones. There is too much useless labor (*trabajo*), he thinks, in planning for future contingencies, a uselessness which can be mitigated by a strong defense of the theological notion of "sabbath" in one's day to day living (A, I, 4, 7).

When one does not carry the sabbath with him, when one is not concentrated on God, one rejoices in what deserves no joy (as in a victory for one's college team, despite the corruption of college athletics), one hopes for what will bring no profit (*aprovecha*—as in the hope for adulation from others), and one mourns for that which should make one rejoice (as in mourning for a solitary person enter-ing the dark night). John of the Cross's pervasive concern for the virtues and vices associated with various emotions like joy, hope, and grief underlines the fact that he is a virtue-based ethician in the tradition of Plato and Aristotle and their Christian followers throughout the middle ages (A, III, 6). Joy (*gozo*), for example, is analyzed by John of the Cross into two types: it can refer to a subjective feeling of personal elation (analogous to Aristotle's pleasure—*hedone*), and it can refer to an objective condition of being in the correct relationship with God quite apart from one's personal mood (analogous to Aristotle's happiness—*eudaemonia*). The former is quite legitimately caused by many phenomena, like simple, but good, food, and illegitimately so by myriad vanities: riches, titles, status, even by having children (say through concern for male lineage), or by getting married (as in the discreet charm of yuppie weddings). Joy as pleasure is at the core of the claim in Eccles. 7:5 that the heart of the fool revels in joy, but the heart of the wise in sadness. Joy as *eudaemonia,* however, can be brought about by having children *because* they glorify God or by getting married *because* of love. Real joy in creatures is produced, he thinks, once we dispossess them and do not require them to give us pleasure; such dispossession of creatures also allows us to have a clearer knowledge of them (A, III, 17, 18, 20).

We often hobble back, thinks John of the Cross, to superficial joy because of the trifles (*impertinencias*) we sell ourselves for; he was acutely aware of how distorted our judgment can be through gifts (A, III, 19) of compliments and petty assurances. But the heavenly manna, he thinks, only appears when the flour is gone. That is, all the assurance we need that life is good and that we are loved can be found in an elemental meal, which supplies both the substance and the savor (*sabor*) we need. Finding comfort in luxury is like pasturing on a slippery mountain of enticements that do not satisfy. Those who eat a great deal are often the most hungry (A, I, 5–6). And those who take excess joy in food usually end up with a lack of charity for others (A, III, 25—as in the eating of beef, which, as we now know even if John of the Cross did not, comes from a cow who eats over ten pounds of grain so as to produce only one pound of meat).

Grace and elegance only give apparent joy for the (obvious) reason that they fade; John of the Cross rather seeks joy by rising to the divine fortress to plunder the riches there (A, III, 21; D, II, 18; S, 3, 5). The point to this chapter, however, is to concretize John of the Cross's thought, even his blatantly devotional thought. The wild beasts of the world, war and hardship, are not unconnected with the distinction between the two joys. The joy of contemplation, the more permanent sort of joy, tends to ameliorate a warlike spirit by keeping before us the vastness of the world, such that the addition or subtraction of possessions, colonies, and influence are like the inflowing or outflowing of a small stream into the ocean (S, 3, 6;

S, 20, 11). In our acquisitive (and not accidentally, violent) culture
it is important to notice along with John of the Cross that profit
(*aprovecha*) is an ambiguous term. In addition to the obvious meaning of excess capital after expenses are paid, it can also have
sanjuanistic meanings dealing with the riches of precious, saintly
souls; the discovery of what we want when desires are denied; the
refreshment brought about by the solitude after labor—see Matt.
11:28; and the perfection which occurs when we "have" nothing
(M, letters, 7; M, sayings, 15, 18, 51).

The ease with which one can appropriate John of the Cross for
the purposes of criticizing capitalist ideology, and the ease with
which one can learn from John of the Cross in that critique, cannot
be used to establish the case for Jesus as a *political* liberator. John
of the Cross would seem to be opposed to this interpretation. He
does, however, believe that the poor can be liberated (Ps. 71:12 and
87:16), as is indicated by the fact that Jesus himself was both
materially poor and poor (*pobre*) in his daily labors (A, I, 3; A, II,
19). This distinction between material or involuntary poverty and
voluntary povery of spirit becomes obvious in John of the Cross
when he warns mendicants not to beg at the door of the materially
poor. *Their* poverty is nothing to be happy about; nor is there anything histrionic in claiming that those in involuntary poverty are
often trodden underfoot in blood (M, letters, 3; S, 23, 6), as the
recent history of American involvement in Central America has
made obvious. John of the Cross is never able to forget the involuntary poor, no doubt partially because he rose from their ranks
(M, letters, 19).

John of the Cross encourages material poverty only to the extent that it is conducive to a healthy spiritual poverty. Or better,
we are all like poor orphans, in a way, in that we all will vicariously
experience the death and sufferings of others, but the religious
aspirant is made *aware* of his spiritual poverty by avoiding the
thousand spiritual and temporal "necessities" which impinge themselves on us (*mil necesidades espirituales y temporales*), a multitude
which can only be overcome with patience over the course of a life
(M, letters, 10, 16, 19). By *internalizing* a craving for money and
things, and by craving a better tomorrow from a material point of
view (Matt. 6:31–34), we end up stealing from ourselves, and there
is no worse thief, he thinks, than the one inside the house. Spiritual poverty, however, like *nada,* gains for us all; no one is poor, he
thinks, who walks with God (M, letters, 19, 20, 27).

Freedom

It should now be obvious that for John of the Cross one is not liberated through material possessions. In order to zero in on his own notion of freedom, I would like to distinguish three senses of the term. Perhaps the most obvious sense of the term is freedom from external constraints, as in being released from jail or in having the ability to buy food if hungry. Although this freedom is immensely important (John of the Cross *escaped* from jail and ran away!), it is important as a necessary but not sufficient condition for human well-being. A second sense of freedom refers to free will or the ability to choose among alternatives. This is what the medievals called "*libero arbitrio.*" Once again, this freedom is important as a necessary but not sufficient condition for human well-being; further, free will is a necessary condition for the highest freedom of all. This third and highest type of human freedom is what John of the Cross usually refers to when he uses *libertad, desocupación,* and so forth, or their cognates, words which Kavanaugh insightfully translates as "liberation." This highest freedom does not so much refer to the ability to choose but to choose *well,* to be liberated from the tendency to choose poorly.

An exclusive or predominant concern for freedom from external constraints can, strangely enough, be a sort of slavery, according to John of the Cross, as in "liberating" oneself from labor by buying some household device and then depending utterly upon it; when the device breaks one is left in a "desperate" situation. Advertisers make much of this phenomenon. Likewise, *libero arbitrio* is not true freedom for John of the Cross because merely having the ability to choose among alternatives can leave one in a state of spiritual destitution if one chooses poorly.[56] The liberating effect of choosing well presupposes liberation from habitual tendencies that pull at one against one's will (A, I, 4, 11). To be liberated from misery and submission (*sujeción*) one must be empty; that is, liberation presupposes the dark night (A, I, 12, 15).

The superiority of spiritual freedom to freedom from external constraints is illustrated by the fact that when the latter is taken away, the former can perhaps endure; one can (albeit with difficulty) be free even while oppressed, as John of the Cross learned in jail. There would be something reprehensible in this claim only if John of the Cross implied that being oppressed was a matter of indifference. But he neither states this nor implies it since he seems to have admiration for any Moses liberating his people from oppression (A, II, 19, 22).

The higher reaches of freedom normally presuppose a certain amount of leisure time, that is, a certain amount of freedom from external constraints. The true and principal freedom (*verdadera y principal libertad*) consists in a pacified and silenced (*sosegado y acallado*) state in which one is not fettered, for example, by gnawing hunger for food (A, II, 9, 19). Thus, the highest freedom, he thinks, is both a freedom from and a positive freedom. It is a freedom from vanities, temptations, imperfections, sensuality, and from enslavement to one's old self (*libra de sí*), and *eventually* even from discursive meditation. It is also a freedom of spirit (*generoso bien del alma*) or soul (*el alma libre*). The two are the same, however. A free soul is one that has liberated itself from the fatigue of ideas; liberty of spirit consists in freeing oneself from being concerned about one's enemies (A, I, 4; A, III, 23, 29; D, I, 8, 10, 13; D, II, 16, 22). (If we apply these sanjuanistic views on freedom to John of the Cross himself, however, we notice that only a heroic figure like John of the Cross—or Gandhi or Martin Luther King—can obtain the highest freedom while being stripped almost entirely of freedom from external constraints.)

John of the Cross's theory of freedom is connected not only with the unity-in-difference discussed here in the first two chapters of the book, chapters which detail John of the Cross's conception of an individual-in-society, but also with his mysticism, to be discussed later in chapter six. He says that:

> When the soul frees itself of all things and attains to emptiness and dispossession concerning them, which is equivalent to what it can do of itself, it is impossible that God fail to do His part by communicating Himself to it, at least silently and secretly. It is more impossible than it would be for the sun not to shine on clear and uncluttered ground (L, 3, 46).

To be liberated from disturbance and torment, and from a weak operation of the soul, which is analogous to the captivity in Egypt, is to achieve the liberating effects of union with God (S, 22, 1; S, 24, 5; L, 3, 38). Therefore, causing psychic disturbance in others, say through everyday bureaucratic tyranny (*tiranizas*), may be to deprive them of something of supreme importance (L, 3, 59; L, 3, 61).

Underemphasis of "freedom from" in John of the Cross could lead to the view that he was a quietist. Hence it is important to emphasize the value he saw in hard work (*lo trabajoso*) as well as the value he saw in spiritual leisure, which is made possible by hard work. His hope is that the contemplative fruits of spiritual leisure would be carried back into one's work so as to enrich the process as one gears up for more spiritual leisure. So despite the apparent idleness of the free soul in spiritual leisure, it is well employed (*bien empleada*) in contemplative occupation (A, I, 13–15). Among the works infused with the effects of contemplation are works of charity, on which John of the Cross puts the following remarkable emphasis:

> ... one act done in charity is more precious in God's sight that all the visions and communications possible—since they imply neither merit nor demerit—and how many who have not received these experiences are incomparably more advanced than others who have had many (A, II, 22).

It should not surprise us at this point that John of the Cross quotes positively the book in the New Testament furthest removed from quietism, that of James 2:20: without works of charity, faith is dead. He is particularly interested in works of charity done in community with others (he also quotes Matt. 18:20) so as to better combat the cunning of self-love (A, I, 4; A, II, 22, 24; A, III, 16).

Works of charity are essential parts of sanjuanistic liberation, but only if they are not done in a superficial way, as when their spiritual motivation is lost, or when they are not done out of love for God. John of the Cross's scepticism regarding "good works" is, as we have noted, superficially similar to Luther's, but this scepticism can more accurately be described as an opposition to phariseeism and as an emphatic affirmation of the cliché that virtue is its own reward (A, III, 27–28). He says that:

> ... most of the works publicly achieved are either faulty, worthless, or imperfect in God's sight, because people are not detached from these human respects and interests (A, III, 28).

Liberating charity occurs when one hides one's good works from others as much as possible, and even from oneself, as in the rarely exemplified injunction in Matt. 6:3 that the left hand should not know what the right is doing. John of the Cross's reasoning here is quite straightforward: if one is motivated in one's charitable works by satisfaction, the works will cease or slow down once the satisfaction ceases. The wise person is concerned both with the substance and profit (*substancia y provecho*) of works (A, III, 28–29).

There is little said in an explicit way by John of the Cross about the implications of his thought for the education of youth, but he does make it clear that those reared in luxury have a tendency to run away from anything rough, like the road to liberation. That is, John of the Cross favors the inculcation of traits conducive to perseverence (*perseveran*) and the robust life as long as one does not get so attached to *praxis* that one feels guilty when in "inactive" solitude (D, I, 7, 10–11). The active life does not have to harden one into thinking that life is a jungle of competitive activity. Dignified labor can actually soften one toward God, he thinks, make one sympathetic to one's neighbor, and help one to develop patience (D, I, 13):

> The more intimate and highly finished the work must be, so the more intimate, careful, and pure must the labor be; and commensurate with the solidity of the edifice is the energy involved in the work (D, II, 9).

The confusion one has when one starts a new trade is similar to the initial darkness in the spiritual life. But energy is needed in the quest for freedom in that the one who *starts* the quest for God at rest will not succeed. The quest starts in the practice (*ejercicio*) of the active life of virtue (D, II, 16; S, 3, 3). Within the active life of virtue, John of the Cross makes no distinction between one's job, on the one hand, and charitable works done after hours, on the other. Christian *agape* is both intrinsically good and good on utilitarian grounds, he implies, such that if one works with a spirit of love one's effects (*efectos*) will be great (*grandes*) in whatever one does. Sanjuanistic work is not, as it is in capitalist (and Marxist) economies, a commodity whose value is found solely or primarily in what one is paid (or in what one contributes to the state or party); work should literally be, as another cliché has it, a labor of love (D, II, 20; S, 9, 7).

There is much activity in life which is unliberated, either because it consists in unprofitable work (*muchos oficios suele tener el alma no provechosa*) or useless pastime (*pasatiempos inútiles*). At such times of at least apparent uselessness, it is legitimate to withdraw from the active life (*vida activa*) altogether, at least it is legitimate to do so if one is motivated by an abundance of charity.

Jesus reproved Martha (Luke 10:39–41), he thinks, not because she led an active life, but because she did not realize that the greatest *work* is love (S, 25, 2; S, 28, 7; S, 29, 1). Withdrawing from the active life is no panacea for confusion, however. In both the overtly active and contemplative areas of our lives (*la vida activa como en la contemplativa*), the soul must practice love (*ejercitar el amor*) in order to succeed in these areas. The contemplative has not lost or really left the world just because he is no longer seen on the common ground of diversion and recreation (*solaz y recreación*), hence he also needs to be reminded that contemplation presupposes the practice of love (S, 29, 2; S, 29, 5–6).

It is reprehensible, according to John of the Cross, to exhort the contemplative to turn more fully toward action, or to burden him continually with busywork (S, 29, 3). John of the Cross is clear about this in the following passage, which reminds us of the above quote from Thoreau regarding the thousand people hacking away at the branches of evil:

> Let those, then, who are singularly active, who think they can win the world with their preaching and exterior works, observe here that they would profit the Church and please God much more, not to mention the good example they would give, were they to spend at least half of this time with God in prayer, even though they may not have reached a prayer as sublime as this. They would then certainly accomplish more, and with less labor, by one work than they otherwise would by a thousand. . . . Without prayer, they would do a great deal of hammering (*martillar*) but accomplish little, and sometimes nothing, and even at times cause harm (S, 29, 3).

John of the Cross tells us that he could go on forever on this topic, indicating that the alleged opposition between contemplation and action concerned him a great deal (S, 29, 4).

One's sole occupation (*negocio*) *as a contemplative* is to receive God; other active occupations in the world are perfectly acceptable as long as one never loses oneself entirely in the work. The soul can do a great deal and achieve a sort of liberation by doing "nothing." Freedom of spirit is precluded by an occupied (*ocupado*) heart (S, 29, 8; L, 1, 9; L, 3, 47–48). To vacate one's heart does not require that one renege on one's duty (*obligado*) to perform one's job well in life, whatever that job may be. As a virtue-based ethician John of the

Cross maintained an adherance to simple *civitas*. But liberating solitude does require that in some sense one withdraw from the labor (*trabajoso*) of the senses (L, 3, 56; L, 3, 65).

If a religious seeker keeps in mind that purity of conscience is greater than many works, and that one good work done in secret is greater than a thousand done by a peacock looking for attention, then he can really make his work efficacious as well as tred steadily along the path to liberation. Prefiguring Kant, John of the Cross thinks that doing things with a good will is superior to doing a great deal. But, once again, this should not be taken as an *apologia* for doing nothing. God does not want, he thinks, sluggish (*haraganas*) or cowardly (*delicadas*) souls (L, 3, 67; M, sayings, 12, 20, 56, 69; M, letters, 17).

Soldier, Sage, Saint

In this last section of the chapter, I would like to determine what sort of spiritual seeker (and finder) John of the Cross was. In this effort, I will be using Robert Neville's helpful categories: soldier, sage, and saint.[57] But in order to prepare the way for an application of these categories, I would like to make a bit more explicit how John of the Cross sees the relationship between the individual and community.

Self-love (*amor propio*) is dangerous, according to John of the Cross, because it deceives our judgments regarding others and it encourages us to coax others to flatter us (*adulación*), as in making fashion "statements" in return for praise. And we have noted before the connection John of the Cross sees between the loss of humility toward self (*humildad para sí mismo*) and the loss of charity (*caridad*) toward others (A, II, 6; A, III, 22–23). Although John of the Cross in the sixteenth century would have been somewhat naive about the effect of political and economic *structures* on human society, he is nonetheless correct that a failure to encourage the virtue of charity in individuals will ensure social chaos in almost any political arrangement:

> The extent and enormity of the disaster. . . is patent. . . we hear everyday of many murders, lost reputations, insults, squandered fortunes, rivalries, quarrels, and of so many adulteries, rapes, and fornications, and of fallen saints so numerous that they are com-

pared to the third part of the stars of heaven cast down to earth
by the tail of the serpent [Apocalypse 12:4] (A, III, 22).

That is, in *any* culture there will be a need for works of mercy
(*obras de misericordia*), urbanity (*política*), and good manners (*buena
índole*), in particular, and virtue (*virtud*), in general (A, III, 27).

We have seen that implicit in John of the Cross are various
insights that support the effort to critique contemporary ideologies
and various insights regarding the virtues needed to have a just
society. Good manners are not enough, however. (In fact, Mary
Magdalene, he thinks, was correct in showing bad manners.) Good
customs (*buenas costumbres*), the closest sanjuanistic equivalent to
just political and economic structures, are also needed (A, III, 27;
D, II, 13). The custom of allowing personal profit is not in itself
immoral, for John of the Cross, even if it is difficult to see how it is
compatible with Christian *agape*. The desire for personal profit is
detrimental, he thinks, both to the humility, which is the root of
love of neighbor (*amor del prójimo*), and to the courage needed to
enter the dark night (A, III, 38; D, I, 12; D, II, 15).

There is something of a self-fulfilling prophesy connected with
the encouragement of self-interest. The self-interested person soon
assumes that everyone else is self-interested, too, just as the thief
thinks everyone else steals and the malicious person thinks everyone
else bears malice. Self-interest is in tension with religion if only
because love of God already indicates a type of community between
two persons; in fact, the Christian trinity itself is a type of community (S, 36, 1; L, 4, 8). God dwells in all souls, John of the Cross
thinks, but in the self-centered person only as a stranger. By denying
ambition (*pretensión*) this strangeness can be ameliorated (L, 4, 14;
M, sayings, 75).

It is tempting to suggest at this point that the origin of ambition
lies in the transitional period between the stability of human identity
in the Middle Ages and the social mobility of modern individualism,
the very period in which John of the Cross lived. According to this
hypothesis, the shift from a rigid, hierarchical system of human
identity to the unstable, existential "system" (elaborated in the
seventeenth century by Descartes and sedimented in capitalist
economy) "explains" the rise of the ambitious individual. That is,
the move from attributed identity to achieved identity provokes
ambition, as well as the existential burden of bad faith, whereby a
person is unable to return to a primally authentic identity and is

nonetheless haunted by guilt for not returning; ambition is a necessary consequence of the breaking of the chain of being and the construction of Renaissance individualism.

Although there is a certain appeal to this theory, as in the suggestion that drunks have done to alcohol what the single-minded have done to ambition, I think that the theory should be rejected. Ambition is something far more pervasive in human history that this theory suggests (Plato's and Aristotle's *philotimia* often gets translated as "ambition"), and it is more dangerous than Rotarian optimism. John of the Cross's opposition to ambition is deeper even than Shakespeare's, who only seems to have been opposed to ambition if it exhibits a will to transcend the constricting self provided by one's birth (as in Macbeth's case) such that a talionic punishment is required. Ambition for John of the Cross prolongs the very notion of Self longer than, and defends the notion of Self more energetically than, it should be preserved and defended.

What is unique about John of the Cross, in particular, and perhaps also about the Carmelite ideal, in general, is the attempt to acknowledge the primacy of the contemplative life while doing full justice to the (ambitionless) social dimension of Christianity. John of the Cross's clear emphasis on community and on the belief that one who does not love neighbor cannot love God, should now be firmly established (also see M, other counsels, 9; M, letters, 13). In the final analysis, however (and this claim will be important to remember when we get to Neville's categories), whenever a conflict develops between solitude and action John of the Cross leans in the direction of the former. Perhaps the line from John of the Cross, which best indicates this tension in his thought, and his preservation of both poles in the tension, albeit with a preference for one pole, is the suggestion that we ought to have equal love *and* equal forgetfulness for all (M, precautions, 5). In order to maintain a forgetfulness for all even as we love them we must regard all as at least partial strangers (M, precautions, 6).

John of the Cross is full of suggestions as to how to preserve solitude without avoiding our duties in the world: let others handle business matters when possible, do not notice the moral inadequacies of others when at all possible, try to maintain an equilibrium when in the face of those who are least tolerable to you, ignore gossip at all costs, and so forth (M, precautions, 8, 13; M, counsels, 2, 3, 8). Even devilish people are to be thought of as artisans, he thinks, for they, too, are trying to prove or sculpt one's sainthood (M, precautions, 9, 15).

And sainthood *is* John of the Cross's ideal. Neville isolates three models for the spiritual seeker, each of which would hold an attraction for John of the Cross, but none as much as the saint. The religious *soldier* is the one who notices above all else that in spiritual matters license is the opposite of freedom:

> "Free spirits," variously swayed by their senses and passions, by ringing appeals and visions, may be free in many ways; but they are not free in spirit. Psychic integrity is the root of spiritual freedom, and psychic integrity begins in discipline. Spiritual discipline is paradoxical, however. At first it looks like the building of an improved and more integrated self. . . . The seeker discovers the paradox soon enough. Jesus warned: "One who grasps at self will lose it, but one who rejects self on my account will gain it" (Matt. 10:39; see also Matt. 16:25). This principle is echoed in the Hindu emphasis on detachment, in Buddhism's denial of the substantiality of the self, and in Taoism's injunction to be one with the tao.[58]

That is, spiritual discipline requires and leads to the abandonment of the self! This is as obvious in John of the Cross as it is in the examples cited by Neville.

The heroic development of spiritual soldiers, like the Jesuits or the Methodists, is not foreign to John of the Cross's own development, as we have seen with respect to his asceticism and his dogged efforts at reform. The spirited part of his soul, the third part of the soul in Plato's tripartite division in the *Republic,* was quite healthy. He had a certain soldierly strength of will, as evidenced in his ability to marshall all of the inherited and acquired components of his experience into a public expression. This ability was most evident in his success at learning from his time in jail and his further ability to share with others this experience. It was his belief that one needs to assert a soldierly purification of one's self before one can abandon that self in the dark night.

John of the Cross also exhibits some of the characteristics of the spiritual seeker as *sage:* "The most prevalent way of having knowledge is to use it to manipulate objects for parochial purposes; this causes a distortion of our knowledge of the whole."[59] The sage has as his goal the synoptic vision of the whole. Instead of possessing knowledge, and John of the Cross would agree with Neville here, the knower is possessed. There is a paradox here analogous to the soldier's building a self so as to lose it. "The more of God and the world which one possesses, the less one is a separate possessor. . . . The sage at the end finds that his or her knowledge as possession is empty and that the knower is not him- or herself but God."[60] As we will see in chapters four and six, this is very close to John of the Cross's own controversial view. John of the Cross's status as sage should also be emphasized if only to provide a counterbalance to those who would focus exclusively on his affectivity and not on his (Platonic) concern for wisdom.

My thesis here at the end of this chapter is that John of the Cross is all three: soldier, sage, and especially saint. Consider the mutually implicative status of these three designations in Neville:

> Which is best? To have a good will, a profound understanding, or a pure heart? To the extent that any one heroic trait can be perfected without the others, it is a mixed blessing. Without knowledge and worthy passions soldiers may be as effective in evil as in good. Without strength of will sages are ineffective, and without desires consonent with what they know to be the good they are subject to that tragic pride in their own virtue by which the wise so often fall. For all their perfected impulses, saints without toughness and thorough understanding are saps.[61]

It has been my contention in these first two chapters that John of the Cross not only perfected his impulses, to use Neville's phrase, but also exhibited a very practical toughness and understanding; his understanding will also be discussed in the next chapter. There is a primacy to John of the Cross's sainthood, as opposed to his spiritual soldiering and his sagacity, in that his most distinctive contribution to Christian spirituality seems to be the way in which he seduces us to *want* the things truly worth having in life:

> Persons are not fixed facts but *movements* of facts. More specifically: persons are movements from one arrangement of facts to another. The limits of rearrangement are set by the nature of the earlier set of facts; they can be rearranged in only a limited number of diverse ways. . . . Seduction is the chief curriculum by which society civilizes its young to want the things truly worth having.[62]

Part of John of the Cross's genius is to make us acutely aware of how particular individuals here and now can change their lives.

The soldier inspires us by offering a heroic model mostly lacking in the modern age, and to see John of the Cross as soldier is to further move away from the close connection some people see between mysticism and quietism:

> The temptation of singleminded paths is to attain apparent suc-
> cess by disengaging us from the historical crises of our own lives.
> Westerners who devote themselves wholeheartedly to Indian yoga,
> for instance, often survive the crises faced by the rest of us by
> withdrawing from them; but this leaves their discipline forever in
> the practice stage.[63]

John of the Cross as reformer (and Thomas Merton as social com-
mentator, especially as an opponent to the Vietnam War) stands in
sharp contrast to such single-mindedness.

Proper sagacity in our age may be even harder to come by than
spiritual heroism. Neville offers us some clues here as well regarding
how to understand John of the Cross:

> To be a sage, one cannot help being sensitive to the implausibility
> of much of traditional wisdom. On the other hand, it is the special
> feature of sage knowledge that it engage its object in the most
> direct and vital fashion.[64]

John of the Cross's *selective* use of tradition and of systematic theology is an instructive instance of Neville's very point. My hope is
that this book is another instance; there is much in John of the
Cross, despite my appreciation of him, which is *so* historically contingent that it can only be understood today with difficulty (for
example, his fascination with the devil).

A saint in our age should be more philosophical than in others
(think of sagelike saints like Thomas Merton, Martin Luther King,
or Gandhi). Academic philosophy (and, to a lesser extent, theology)
in our century has been derelict in supplying the synoptic vision
that society needs and that someone other than manipulators in
the electronic media should supply. With the fragmentation of life
it seems that an unphilosophical saint in our age is "likely to have
attained purity of heart by denying the very engagements with
experience which make life human today."[65] Reason in its integrity
is the thinking process by which one guides *life*.[66] Hence, once one
abandons the idea that reason is equivalent to *techne* one can see
how John of the Cross provides thoughtful models of a sagelike, an
artistic, and a saintly life. These are models that act as alternatives
to the other more popular sorts of life which nonetheless provide
something valuable to contemporary culture: the political life, the
"productive" life, or the scholarly life. Thompson sums up well what
John of the Cross's contribution could be to contemporary concern
in philosophy and theology for *praxis*:

History has been deeply scarred by the violence and destruction
men have worked on one another, and the healing of their alienation continues to escape them. One way is to pass laws to make
people do what they ought to do. But it may be that a better way
of attracting men to live in peace and for love is the way San Juan
first used when he wanted to express the wonder and glory of the
mystical union between man and God. Instead of spelling out in
detail how the world may be set to right, it may be that the better
way is to show them images of haunting beauty, which can play
upon their minds and feelings, and draw them to the good not
reluctantly, but gladly. Then, when they begin to understand and
feel the call of love and become committed to its increase, then the
details may follow as the beauty once glimpsed takes root and
bears its reconciling fruit.[67]

CHAPTER 3

Gender

The wounded stag
Que el ciervo vulnerado
Is on sight on the hill. . . .
Por el otero asoma. . . .
Our bed is in flower,
Nuestro lecho florido
Bound round with linking dens of lions. . . .
De cuevas de leones enlazado. . . .
In the inner wine cellar
En la interior bodega
I drank of my Beloved. . . .
De mi Amado bebi. . . .
The bride has entered
Entrado se ha la esposa
The sweet garden of her desire. . . .
En el ameno huèrto deseado. . . .
And now the turtledove
Y ya la tortolica
Has found its longed-for mate.
Al socio deseado.

St. John of the Cross, "The Spiritual Canticle"

. . . .

I entered into unknowing,
Entréme donde no supe,
And there I remained unknowing,
Y quedéme no sabiendo,
Transcending all knowledge. . . .
Toda ciencia trascendiendo. . . .

73

An understanding while not understanding. . . .
> *De un entender no entendiendo. . . .*

This knowledge in unknowing. . .
> *Este saber no sabiendo. . .*

That wise men disputing
> *Que los sabios arguyendo*

Can never overthrow it.
> *Jamás le pueden vencer.*

St. John of the Cross, "Stanzas Concerning an Ecstasy"
. . . .

That the lover become
> *Que se haga semejante*

Like the one he loves.
> *El Amante a quien quería.*

St. John of the Cross, "The Incarnation"
. . . .

Among some animals
> *Entre unos animales*

That were there at that time.
> *Que a la sazón allí había.*

Men sang songs
> *Los hombres decían cantares,*

And angels melodies.
> *Los ángeles melodía.*

St. John of the Cross, "The Birth"

Introduction

It should now be clear how the first two chapters of this book hang together like centripetal and centrifugal forces in equilibrium. In this chapter, I will analyze in detail this curious phenomenon: how *apparent* opposites energize the thought of John of the Cross. In this effort I will primarily consider his dipolar theism, that is, his effort at synthesizing the best in both systematic theology and mystical theology, and the best in what have been traditionally conceived to be male and female divine predicates. Emphasizing dipolarity in John of the Cross, however, is not the same as claiming that he was a "dualist." In fact, I will argue that John of the Cross was *not* at all a dualist in that the centripetal and centrifugal forces in his thought (in this case, soul and body) are indeed in equilibrium and are part of one fundamental reality.

That is, John of the Cross believes in one God who can be viewed (indeed must be viewed) from at least two different perspectives, including a perspective which includes suppressed feminine predicates, and in one human nature, which can be viewed from the perspectives of either soul or body without treating either soul or body as separate (Pauline or Cartesian) substances. The apparent opposites that energize John of the Cross's theory of human nature surface in the forms of rationality (traditionally conceived as a male trait) and loving affectivity (traditionally conceived as a female trait). By the end of the chapter, I hope to be in a position to indicate what I think John of the Cross can contribute to contemporary concern over male bias in religion.

Several asymmetrically valued pairs have been detailed by Caroline Walker Bynum: male/female, intellect/body, active/passive, reason/emotion, order/disorder, supernatural/natural, and so forth.[1] These values are asymmetrical in that "the inferior sex" is associated with the latter, disfavored term in each pair. It is my hope to give equal weight to each element in these pairs. This in itself may be indicative of a slight male bias because, as Bynum notices, the very desire to make use of dichotomous gender images is more often exhibited by men than by women. But, as we will see in the next chapter, I plan to locate these pairings within a larger, unified whole. (That is, John of the Cross's notion of divine inclusiveness returns, in a way, to something like the Great Mother tradition.) Bynum herself seems intent on describing God in both traditionally male and traditionally female terms; the point is that we should not view these pairs as contradictory (as opposed to complementary) nor should we favor one term at the expense of the other. As we will see, John of the Cross would be at least somewhat compatible with Bynum's concern for polar equality, as when he engages in a mythical gender reversal in his poetry, a reversal that is typical of male mystics: by personifying the soul as feminine John of the Cross symbolizes renunciation and conversion, whereas when a woman mystic speaks of herself in traditionally male terms she is symbolizing elevation.

Jurgen Moltmann is instructive regarding the roots of male bias in religion, a bias which must be uncovered in order to understand John of the Cross.[2] The earliest testimonies of religion appear to be matrifocal; the mystery of life and hence of the divine were originally worshipped as the "Great Mother." Both the cult figures of the paleolithic age and of the religions of the early civilizations in Greece, Persia, and India were matriarchal. Belief in the

Great or World Mother entails the notion that the world is a great organism, a macanthropos, who gives birth to and nurtures individual human beings. One of the theses of this and the following chapter is that belief in the world as an organic (maternal), divine whole does not necessarily entail primitive myths, for example, myths regarding an entrance to heaven through the divine cranium or to hell through the anus mundi. Here in chapter three, I will develop John of the Cross's approach to gender, an approach which will be treated again and completed in chapter four regarding his thoughts on nature. Chapters one and two hung together as an example of unity-in-difference; chapters three and four hang together as complementary approaches to John of the Cross's thoughts on God.

A key transition in the history of religion occurred when the World Mother came under attack. For example, the creation narratives of the Old Testament are largely polemics against the Canaanite matriarchal cults and are attempts to establish the patriarchal cult of Yahweh. (Gerda Lerner, however, is correct to point out that in the earliest texts Yahweh's gender identity was either unspecified or exhibited through both male and female aspects. But eventually Yahweh became associated in a strong way with a father God.)[3] And in Greek mythology an attenuated version of the World Mother can be found in Mother Earth. But when the father sky gods (Uranus, Zeus, Yahweh, God the Father, etc.) took charge of the universe, a dualism easily developed where heaven and earth, divine and mortal, supernatural and natural, and (most importantly for my purposes here) male and female were pitted against each other, to the detriment of the latter element in each of these pairs. The point I am trying to make here is that the Judeo-Christian-Islamic tradition has historically, but perhaps not necessarily, been tied up with patriarchal monotheism, with the hegemony of a male, heavenly, supernatural God.

As is well known, however, the feminine principle never died out in Christianity. For example, the belief in the cosmos as an archetypal person was transformed, through the mediation of Stoic cosmology, into the mystical body of Christ, who is the head of the universe. This view preserved (albeit in a diminished way) a sacramental view of (mother) nature, as evidenced in the burial rituals where the dead are returned to the womb of the earth. Or again, salvation history was advanced in Christianity through the marriage of God with holy mother church.

In this chapter, I will first detail John of the Cross's dipolar theism, and then his opposition to dualism as evidenced in his defense of both rationality and love. Throughout the chapter, I will bring contemporary feminist concerns to bear on John of the Cross's texts, as well as bring John of the Cross's own thoughts to bear on contemporary feminist concerns. I allege that the dialogue between the two will be quite fruitful.

Dipolar Theism

John of the Cross would agree with the goal of traditional Christian philosophers and theologians, that is, logical analysis is in the service of a higher end. But he implies that the systematic theologian's conception of God is internally incoherent. One of the major complaints John of the Cross seems to have with systematic thought (in philosophy and theology, as opposed to biblical theism), as I will show, is that it either explicitly or implicitly identifies God as active and not passive. St. Thomas Aquinas's unmoved mover is the most obvious example of this tendency, but in general systematic theologians see God as a timeless, supernatural (male) being that does not change. The inconsistency lies in also claiming that God knows and loves. For example, if God knows, God must be a subject on the analogy of human subjects. And if God is a subject who knows, God must be affected by, by passive with respect to, the object known, and have properties traditionally classified as feminine.

It is precisely this failure to make clear how God could be a God of love that leads to what Constance Fitzgerald calls a "feminine impasse." And it is significant, I think, that for Fitzgerald the best guide we have to avoid this impasse is the dark night of John of the Cross.[4] Fitzgerald is also wise to point out that to "desexualize" God altogether runs the risk of deism. Rather, by emphasizing the sanjuanistic experience of a personal God in contemplation one can learn to appreciate, according to Fitzgerald, the positive aspects of passivity as opposed to the subordinate type of obsequiousness often associated with feminine passivity. It is true that by seeing male and female divine predicates as complementary we run the risk of continuing the tradition of viewing women as mere helpers to males, but this is not a necessary consequence of complementarity.

It will be to our advantage to get as clear as we can on what we mean by the term "God." I will use the term to refer to the supremely excellent, or all-worshipful being. This definition resembles somewhat Saint Anselm's "that than which no greater can be conceived." Yet the ontological argument is not what is at stake here. Even if the argument fails, the preliminary definition of God as the supremely excellent being, the all-worshipful being, or the greatest conceivable being seems unobjectionable. To say that God can be defined in these ways still leaves open the possibility that God is even more excellent or worshipful than our ability to conceive. This allows us to do justice to mystics like John of the Cross who legitimately fear that that by defining God we are limiting God to "merely" human language. All I am suggesting is that when we think of God we must be thinking of a being who surpasses all others, or we are not thinking of God. Even the atheist or agnostic would admit this much. When the atheist says, "There is no God," he is denying that a supremely excellent, all-worshipful, greatest conceivable being exists.

When the contrasting predicates excellent-inferior are applied to God, an invidious situation develops. If to be invidious is to be injurious, then this contrast is the most invidious one of all when applied (both terms) to God because God is only excellent. God is inferior in no way. Period. To suggest that God is in some small way inferior to some other being is to no longer speak about God but about some being that is not supremely excellent, or all-worshipful, or the greatest conceivable. Systematic theologians have assumed that all contrasts, or most of them, when applied to God are invidious.

Let us assume from now on that God exists in that John of the Cross was never intellectually or emotionally fettered by the possible nonexistence of God. In this sense his was a very Catholic age. But what attributes does God possess? Here John of the Cross quite legitimately had some doubts. Consider the following two columns of attributes in polar contrast to each other:

one	many
being	becoming
activity	passivity
permanence	change
necessary	contingent
self-sufficient	dependent
actual	potential
absolute	relative
abstract	concrete

Systematic theologians have tended toward oversimplification. It is comparatively easy to say "God is strong rather than weak, so in all relations God is active, not passive." In each case, the systematic theologians have decided which member of the contrasting pair is good (the traditionally male terms on the left) then attribute it to God, while wholly denying the contrasting term (the traditional female terms on the right). Hence, God is one but not many; permanent but not changing, and so forth. This leads to what can be called the "monopolar prejudice." Monopolarity is common to both traditional systematic theology and pantheism, with the major difference between the two being the fact that systematic theology in Christianity has admitted the reality of plurality, potentiality, and becoming as a secondary form of existence "outside" God (on the right), whereas in pantheism God includes all reality within itself. Common to both systematic theology and pantheism is the belief that the above categorical contrasts are invidious. The dilemma these two positions face is that either the deity is only one constituent of the whole (systematic theology) or else the alleged inferior pole in each contrast (on the right) is illusory. I will show that John of the Cross avoided these errors.

It seems that for John of the Cross this dilemma is artificial. It is produced by the assumption that excellence is found by separating and purifying one pole (the supposedly male terms on the left) and denigrating the other (the supposedly female terms on the right). That this is not the case can be seen by analyzing some of the attributes on the right side, and by analyzing, as I will try to do, certain passages in John of the Cross which attribute passivity and other traits traditionally conceived as feminine to God. At least since Saint Augustine most systematic theologians have been convinced that God's eternity meant not that he endured through all time but that he was outside of time altogether and did not, could not, be receptive to temporal change. Saint Thomas Aquinas identified God, following Aristotle, who was the greatest predecessor to systematic theology, at least in its scholastic variety, as unmoved. Yet both activity and passivity can be either good or bad. Good passivity is likely to be called sensitivity, responsiveness, adaptability, or sympathy. Insufficiently subtle or defective passivity is called wooden inflexibility, mulish stubbornness, inadaptability, unresponsiveness, and the like. To deny God's passivity altogether is to deny God those aspects of passivity that are excellences. Or again, to altogether deny God the ability to change does avoid fickleness, but at the expense of the ability to lovingly react to the sufferings of others. For John of the Cross this is too great a price to pay.

The terms on the left side of the above diagram have both good and bad aspects as well. Oneness can mean wholeness, but it can also mean monotony or triviality. Actuality can mean definiteness, but it can also mean the lack of potentiality to respond to others. What happens to divine love when God, according to Thomists, is claimed to be *pure* actuality? God ends up loving the world, but is not intrinsically related to it, whatever sort of love that may be. Self-sufficiency can, at times, be selfishness.

The trick when thinking of God in sanjuanistic terms, I allege, is to attribute to God all excellences (left *and* right sides). In short, excellent-inferior or good-evil are invidious contrasts, but one-many, being-becoming, et al., are non-invidious contrasts. Unlike most systematic theology and pantheism, John of the Cross's theism is dipolar. To be specific, within each pole of a non-invidious contrast (for example, permanence-change) there are invidious elements (inferior permanence or inferior change), but also non-invidious, good elements (excellent permanence or excellent change).

John of the Cross does not believe in two gods, one unified and the other plural, and so forth. Rather, what are often thought to be contraries are really mutually interdependent correlatives, as Charles Hartshorne indicates:

> The good as we know it is unity-in-variety or variety-in-unity; if the variety overbalances, we have chaos or discord; if the unity, we have monotony or triviality.[5]

Supreme excellence, if it is truly supreme excellence, *must* somehow be able to integrate all the *complexity* there is in the world into itself as one spiritual whole. The word "must" indicates divine necessity, along with God's essence, which is to necessarily exist. And the word "complexity" indicates the contingency that affects God through creaturely decisions or feelings. But in the view of most systematic theologians, God is solely identified with the stony (male) immobility of the absolute, implying non-relatedness to the world. The point to John of the Cross's mystical theology, however, is that there is no reason why we have to see God as an unmoved, permanent, unfeeling being who possesses various properties traditionally associated with maleness, as systematic theologians have usually done. That is, the problem is not so much with systematic theology per se as with the *way* in which systematic theology was done until John of the Cross's day, indeed with the way in which it is still often done.

God in abstraction, God's being, may in a way escape from the temporal flux, but a living God is related to the world of becoming, which entails divine becoming as well if the world in some way is internally related to God, as John of the Cross thinks. The systematic theologian's usual alternative to this view suggests that all relationships to God are external to divinity, once again threatening not only God's love, but also God's nobility. A dog's being behind a particular rock affects the dog in certain ways, thus this relation is an internal relation to the dog. But it does not affect the rock, whose relationship with the dog is external to the rock's nature. Does this not show the superiority of canine consciousness, which is aware of the rock, to rocklike existence, which is unaware of the dog? Is it not therefore peculiar that the male God of traditional theology and philosophy of religion has been described solely in rocklike terms: pure actuality, permanence (as in Luther's "A mighty fortress is our God"), only having external relations, unmoved, being not becoming?

It might be wondered at this point, as perhaps John of the Cross did, why traditional systematic theology has been so popular among theists even though it has so many defects. There are at least four reasons, none of which establishes the case for traditional systematic theology: (a) It is simpler to accept one pole and reject the other of contrasting (or better, correlative, non-invidious) categories rather than to show how each, in its own appropriate fashion, applies to an aspect of the divine nature. Yet the simplicity of calling God "the absolute" can come back to haunt the systematic theologian or philosopher of religion who succumbs to male bias if absoluteness precludes relativity in the sense of relatedness to the world. (b) If the decision to accept monopolarity has been made, it is simpler to identify God as the absolute rather than to identify God as the most relative. Yet this does not deny divine relatedness, nor that God, who loves all, would therefore have to be dependent on all. That is, God may well be the most dependent of all as well as the most absolute of all, in the sense that, and to the extent that, both of these are excellences. God is absolute and dependent in different aspects of the divine nature; analogously, I retain my identity through all of the changes in my life. (c) There are emotional considerations favoring divine permanence, as found in the longing to escape the risks and uncertainties of life. But even if these considerations obtain, they should not blind us to other emotional considerations, like those which give us the solace which comes from knowing that the outcome of our sufferings and volitions makes a difference in the divine life which, if it is all-loving, would certainly not be unmoved by the sufferings of creatures. (d) It is seen as more easily made compatible with monotheism. But the innocent

monotheistic contrast between the one and the many deals with
God as an individual, not with the dogmatic claim that the divine
individual itself cannot have parts or aspects of relatedness to the
world. In short, the divine being becomes, or the divine becoming
is. God's being and becoming form a single reality:

> There is no law of logic against attributing contrasting predicates
> to the same individual, providing they apply to diverse aspects of
> this individual.[6]

But the remedy for "ontolatry," the worship of being, is not the
contrary pole, the worship of becoming, as some interpreters might
suggest:

> God is neither being as contrasted to becoming nor becoming as
> contrasted to being; but categorically supreme becoming in which
> there is a factor of categorically supreme being, as contrasted to
> inferior becoming, in which there is inferior being.[7]

The divine becoming is more ultimate than divine being in dipolar
theism only for the reason that it is more inclusive. To be agent and
patient is in truth incomparably better than being either alone.

I should note again at this point that it is not systematic theology itself or philosophy of religion itself that is the problem, but
rather the *way* in which male bias has affected systematic theology
and philosophy of religion. The texts I will cite from John of the
Cross's mystical theology are instructive regarding how systematic
theology and philosophy of religion could change their course. I
should also note that in this chapter I am not trying to advance
any thesis regarding whether or not women have a distinct nature
from men or regarding whether a possibly distinct feminine nature
is due to nature or culture. Rather, I am only suggesting that
monopolar theism distorts our view of God by eschewing a whole
class of divine predicates, a class which has (not coincidentally)
traditionally been viewed as feminine.

To claim that John of the Cross is a dipolar theist is to suggest
that he was, *to a certain extent,* positively influenced by the
Thomistic tradition. He agrees with that tradition that God remains
immutable forever (*immutable para siempre*), but the meaning of this
claim (A, III, 21) is not immediately clear. Does it mean that God is
an unmoved mover who is immune from creaturely influence *or* does
it mean that God is *always* amenable to such influence (as in the

Great Mother tradition), as opposed to our temporary and intermittent ability to be influenced by others? I will show that there is massive evidence in John of the Cross in favor of the latter interpretation. Further, John of the Cross agrees with traditional systematic theology that God is simple and unified (L, 3, 17), but, again, what does this mean? That God is not affected by the diversity in the world *or* that God receives *all* of the diverse information from the world and harmonizes it into a uni-verse? The latter, I allege. In any event, when we concentrate on God's gifts to us rather than on God, we often leave the divine nature itself unexplained (M, letters, 12).[8]

There are several passages in John of the Cross where both of the above poles are brought together. Consider (S, 32, 1), where it is suggested that:

> The power and the tenacity of love is great, for love captures and binds God Himself. Happy is the loving soul, since she possesses God for her prisoner, and He is surrendered to all her desires.

Note, on the one hand, terms like "power" and "tenacity," and, on the other, terms like "love" and "surrender." Likewise, John of the Cross claims that:

> It is a property of perfect love to be unwilling to take anything for self, nor does it attribute anything to self, but all to the Beloved. If we find this characteristic in base loves, how much more in love of God (S, 32, 2).

Here we see that John of the Cross conceives of divine love (that is, perfect love) on the analogy, albeit remote, of human love. God is *changed* by those God loves, even if God takes nothing from the person loved, in the act of surrender (again, see S, 32, 1). John of the Cross's God is, like Plato's,[9] a dipolar God whose gaze provides a warmth and beauty and splendor like the rays of the sun (S, 33, 1).

All Christians can agree with John of the Cross that God is wise and good and unique, in that the greatest conceivable being could not possibly be ignorant or evil, nor could the greatest conceivable being have a rival, for having a rival would eliminate God's status as the perfect being. But when John of the Cross attributes to God a property like grandness, he is also quick to notice God's humility. Indeed when God in effect says, according to

John of the Cross, "I am yours," humans can legitimately deem themselves, in a way, God's equals, as we will see. God, for John of the Cross, is just *and* merciful, powerful *and* loving, strong (*fuerte*) or sublime *and* delicate. The list could go on at some length (L, 3, 2; L, 3, 6).

It must be admitted that most systematic theologians have also attributed these contrasting predicates to God, but inconsistently because they "reduce" (or "harmonize") them at a higher level to divine immutability. The difference between John of the Cross and most systematic theologians, I allege, is not that John of the Cross refuses to consider meta-level predicates, but that he worries that meta-level abstractions will occlude the fact that God is a loving person to whom one can be related. All systematic theology and philosophy of religion involves abstractions, but John of the Cross makes a dogged effort in his descriptions of God to keep his abstractions as concrete as possible, hence his tendency, which I have tried to document throughout this book, to mix abstract concepts and poetic images.

John of the Cross's dipolar theism is consistent with and amplifies the energizing contrasts in his thought, which we noticed in the first two chapters of this book, for example, the contrasts between light and darkness (both of which have good and bad connotations in John of the Cross), or between *todo* and *nada,* or, as Colin Thompson correctly notes,[10] between God as transcendent and God as immanent/personal. The fact that John of the Cross's dipolar theism is directly connected with gender issues becomes obvious in the following remarkable quotation:

> It should be known, then, that God nurtures and caresses the soul, after it has been resolutely converted to His service, like a loving mother (*amorosa madre*) who warms her child with the heat of her bosom, nurses it with good milk and tender food, and carries and caresses it in her arms. But as the child grows older, the mother witholds her caresses and hides her tender love (*tierno amor*); she rubs bitter aloes on her sweet breast and sets the child down from her arms, letting it walk on its own feet so that it may put aside the habits of childhood and grow accustomed to greater and more important things (*cosas más grandes y substanciales*). The grace of God acts just as a loving mother by re-engendering in the soul new enthusiasm and fervor in the service of God. With no effort on the soul's part, this grace causes it to taste sweet and delectable milk and to experience intense satisfaction in the per-

formance of spiritual exercises, because God is handing the breast
of His tender love to the soul, just as if it were a delicate love
(D, I, 1).

In fact, no earthly mother's love or brother's love can equal God's
maternal and fraternal love (S, 27, 1).

The tension between John of the Cross and systematic theology
as traditionally conceived is largely due, as Frost notices, to the
fact that John of the Cross's thought is built on the conviction that
God is a person. It is comparatively easy to *say* that God is a person, as systematic theologians have usually done, but it is quite
another thing to develop a theory regarding the divine predicates
where one can *consistently* say that God is a person. John of the
Cross's emphasis on the divine person(s) also puts him in tension
with what Frost calls the "pseudo-mysticism" of those who make
God an impersonal natural force, for in that case God would be
inferior to human persons. The danger, however, as we will see in
the next chapter, in such pseudo-mysticism lies not so much in its
falsity as in its partial truth.[11] In some sense God *is* a natural force
for John of the Cross.

Divine receptivity and change are evident throughout John of
the Cross's writings. That is, he supplies ample evidence that God
has the (traditionally feminine) attributes listed on the right side
of the above diagram. When prayer does not please us, it may well
be *pleasing* to God; further, God can be *displeased* with us, say if we
desire flashy visions of the divine (A, II, 21). God's emotional life
includes *desire,* say the desire to exalt us; in fact, John of the Cross
thinks that God is pleased when we are exalted. This pleasure is at
least partially due to the fact that God, who is always the preeminent
being, has no need to be exalted (S, 28, 1). God, for John of the
Cross, desires (*quiere*) that we rejoice with the divine more than
with other human beings; God desires to be united with us and to
be transformed through mutual love (L, 1, 25; M, letters, 7). That
is, love never reaches perfection until the lovers are so alike that
they are *transfigured* (*transfiguran*) by unitive love (*amor unitivo*).
This *mutual surrender* (*dos entregas*) of God and the human soul
can be found nowhere, as far as I am aware, in monopolar, systematic
theology (S, 11, 12; S, 16, 11; S, 27, 2).

Despite the passion of Jesus, and the belief in Jesus as divine,
few systematic theologians have been willing to suggest, along with
John of the Cross, that God can be *humbled,*[12] a humility which

makes intelligible to us how God could be *merciful* (*piedad*) and how God could attain a *liberality* (*liberalidad*) devoid of covetousness (A, III, 20; S, 13, 1). God is humble enough to be *wounded* by the human soul's love for the divine (S, 35, 7). God, for John of the Cross, is so *gentle* that there is something reprehensible in fearing God or in fainting before God as if "He" were a despot (L, 4, 12). If a person is seeking God, that person can receive sanjuanistic courage in learning that God is *seeking* him even more (L, 3, 28). God's *surrender* to us in loving union, and the goods which ensue from that union, are the glories of the divine life (see John 17:10), according to John of the Cross (L, 3, 79; L, 3, 82).

Systematic theologians did religion a tremendous favor by eliminating some of the anthropomorphic excesses found in popular religion and in biblical theism. But in the effort they ran to the other extreme, whereby their "God" became the grandest of abstractions, a God immune from temporal change and influence, and a God who could be described in personal terms only at the price of consistency. John of the Cross reintroduces us to a personal God who can alternately be described by what have traditionally been considered "male" *and* "female" (like receptivity, gentleness, surrender, etc., as detailed above) predicates. But he does this without engaging in anthropomorphic orgies. John of the Cross's writing is deceptively simple in the tradition of mystical theology at its best. The careful reader, however, learns to see through this devotional disguise to the dipolar logic of perfection buried beneath.

Against Dualism

Monopolar theism very often is connected with a metaphysical or cosmological dualism. Perhaps the easiest way to account for this connection is to trace the roots of monopolar theism back to Aristotle. Although Plato developed a dipolar categorial scheme (where form is contrasted to matter, etc.), his cosmology is ultimately a psychical monism, where the World Soul holds the cosmos together as a *uni*verse. Aristotle, however, developed a single categorial scheme of embodied form. Paradoxically, from this emphasis on embodied form Aristotle ultimately constructed a more vicious dualism than any ever envisaged by Plato, in that Aristotle's divinities are *completely* self-sufficient entities, unmoved, and separated from all change and embodiment. The influence of Aristotle's gods, I allege, extends to Thomas Aquinas and, in fact, to much contemporary philosophy and theology. (I will argue in the next chapter that John of the Cross's theism is far closer to Plato's than to Aristotle's.) Once Aristotelian dualism was accepted by theists, it was easy in religion to associate "maleness" with the rational or spiritual and "femaleness" with the natural or bodily. Therefore, metaphysical dualism has been interpreted by many contemporary feminists as a concealed type of sexism. My thesis in this section of the chapter is that although there is a tension in John of the Cross between (supposedly male) rationality and (supposedly female) loving emotion, John of the Cross never allows this tension to become so severe that he had to resort to dualism to explain human nature.

I am not claiming that John of the Cross does not flirt with dualism; indeed he does. Nor am I claiming that he completely avoids male bias; he does not. But I am claiming that he did a better job of avoiding male bias in religion than most systematic theologians and that contemporary individuals interested in gender issues in religion could learn a great deal from John of the Cross. It should be remembered that John of the Cross inherited heavily sexist baggage from the history of Judaism and Christianity, and from the Aristotelian and Manichean ideas that greatly influenced Christianity. The practice of celibacy, for example, is at least partially to be explained in terms of its ascetical benefits, but also at least partially in terms of the common belief that sexual activity put one in contact with both "body" and "woman," both of which were assumed to be deviations from spirituality.[13]

But despite John of the Cross's flirtations with dualism and his *partial* attachment to sexism, or perhaps because of these factors, he is worthy of consideration regarding gender issues. Consider Monica Furling's contemporary comments regarding the nineteenth-century Carmelite nun, Thérèse of Lisieux, in particular, and regarding all saints of a previous age, in general, including John of the Cross:

> What is sometimes difficult for a twentieth-century reader is a sense that motives which once seemed above suspicion—self-denial, bodily mortification, a life lived "for others"—may contain hidden gratifications, covert claims for glory and power, masochistic solutions to intolerable situations, which for us destroy the sense of wonder. Whether we like it or not—and there is, in most of us, a tendency to enjoy making heroic projections—we find ourselves becoming critical about sanctity, spoiling the idealised pic-

ture with psychological questions which detract from the sense of perfection and awestruck admiration once accorded to the saints. We note their childhood difficulties, neurosis, their inability to adapt to normal adult life, their illusions and defenses. It is a kind of reductionism which, at first sight, seems to leave us poorer, bereft of the example of those who once seemed to show us how life should be lived. At first sight, but not at second perhaps. In many ways the women and men who have been called saints become more, not less, remarkable and lovable, when we see their frailty more clearly. We begin to see that their courage and heroism lay in their exploration of the human condition, and their originality resided in knowing the extremes of mind and spirit, as Columbus's lay in exploring the world geographically.[14]

John of the Cross's explorations of the relationship between the spiritual and the bodily do *not* "sweep away, not only the grosser business of the flesh, but all art and music and literature, all the expansions of grace and beauty."[15] Any reader of John of the Cross's poetry would know this. Nor does John of the Cross, as I will show, hold the allegedly "Platonic" view of a soul sharply distinguished from the body and imprisoned by it, as Thompson alleges.[16] But Thompson is correct in noting that John of the Cross never teaches that the body is evil, a belief that should legitimately be feared by an opponent to dualism. That is, it is correct to dispute the notion that God gave us bodies only to deny them.

I think it is a mistake, however, to hold, along with Karl Barth, that the whole idea of negation is wrongheaded. He says, and I assume that he has John of the Cross in mind, that:

> In a purely formal sense no one, not even a Spanish mystic, has ever really looked away from himself and beyond himself, let alone transcended himself in a purely formal negation.[17]

Barth's point seems to be that in addition to John of the Cross teaching a denial of the body, a claim which I will dismantle presently, he teaches a type of self-centeredness. There is a sense in which we are never free of self, nor ought we to be in that our existence is given to us by God, as Thompson notices in his critique of Barth.[18] But there is another sense in which the whole point to Christianity, according to John of the Cross, is to redirect one's energy away from the self and toward God, a redirection which also militates against Barth's interpretation.

John of the Cross's *nada* is often a hyperbolic term which, *if* taken literally in every instance, could lead one to believe that he was a dualist. A more accurate reading of John of the Cross's corpus, however, and a more judicious reading of "*nada*," leads one to the conclusion that John of the Cross was not so much interested in a negation of creation as a reevaluation of it. As we will see in chapters four and five, no one who despised natural bodies, including the eroticism of natural bodies, could possibly have written *The Spiritual Canticle.*[19]

It is crystal clear in John of the Cross that the two parts of the human person constitute one fundamental reality (*dos partes son un supuesto*) such that, even if there are temporary, sensual rebellions of one against the other, each part shares what the other one receives (D, I, 4). Kavanaugh's translation of *supuesto* as the Latin *suppositum* (for example, D, II, 1), rather than in any equivalent in English, is no doubt meant to remind us of John of the Cross's roots in Aristotelian/Thomistic hylomorphism. John of the Cross was, in fact, influenced by hylomorphism, but, as we have seen, he was more consistent than either Aristotle or Saint Thomas Aquinas in his refusal to adopt a monopolar theism (which leads to a metaphysical dualism). As we will see in the next chapter, just as the soul is the form of a human body—the two together constituting the *supuesto*—so also the divine literally in*forms* (*informada en el divino*) the natural world (D, II, 9). That is, John of the Cross is a more consistent hylomorphist than either Aristotle or Saint Thomas Aquinas because the divine for Aristotle and Saint Thomas Aquinas completely transcends matter (*hyle*).

The appetites do not really war against the spirit (*ninguna guerra haga al espíritu*) in John of the Cross, rather each part of the person is nourished by spiritual food from the one *supuesto*. The intermittent battles between the spiritual and the bodily can, in fact, be pacified (*sosegar*), but only if, through the longings of a simple and pure love, one enters the night of sense (A, I, 15: A, II, 1; D, II, 3). Metaphysically the body (and the lower part of the soul) is literally con-formed (*conformidad*) to the soul, just as the universe conforms to divine influence (S, 20, 4). As Frost notices,[20] the human soul and the human body depend on each other so integrally that a dead body is not really a *human* body, but a relatively formless lump of matter.

The battles between the spiritual and the bodily are likely to flare up when feelings are unbridled by reason or when eroticism is not brought within the context of the overall goals in life. For example, the soul (*ánima*) of some individuals is more easily affected by bodily activity than that of others; likewise, some with acutely sensitive psychic abilities can more easily gain or lose bodily health (A, III, 16; D, I, 4). The soul is not a prisoner in the body, according to John of the Cross, even if there are some obstacles to a peaceful union of soul with body (*la unión del alma con el cuerpo*), obstacles found throughout temporal and natural reality (L, 1, 29). But it would be a mistake to try to eliminate bodily urges altogether in that *sensual, sensualidad,* and *sensitiva* are words used by John of the Cross to refer to realities that are basically good. Sensible consolations, it should be remembered, can be especially important in the meditative beginnings of the spiritual life. Although sensual delights (like trances and visions) are not essential parts of the spiritual life, they do help to illustrate the unity of human nature.[21] Frost sums up well the sanjuanistic view:

> To understand St. John, then, we have to resist the tendency to think of soul and body as two separate entities in some way joined together, side by side, as it were. . . the soul. . . determines human nature to be the unity that it is. So, too, we must resist the even commoner idea of the soul as a part of our nature exclusively designed for the purposes of religion in something of the way in which each organ of the body has its particular function. This modern misconception is peculiarly dangerous as it tends to make the soul little more than an *ensemble* of the emotions, and to forget that its highest faculties and activities are those of the intellect and the will. . . the highest aim of religion is to save and recreate the mind.[22]

It is a good thing to be, as we are, *in*carnate; unfortunately, we are often merely carnal.

Because the soul must, at times, resist bodily inclinations there is a danger that we will be lulled into the belief that the body is merely a temporary stopping place for the soul, a belief made somewhat intelligible by the fact that when sensory appetites are quenched (think of the desire for food or sex) the mind is free to pursue (and find) the truth (D, I, 12–13). But John of the Cross is careful in these instances to qualify claims that can run away toward dualism: the soul *seems* (*parecía*) to fly away from the body (S, 13, 2), and in the ascetical life the soul must *in some fashion* (*en alguna manera*) abandon the body (S, 13, 4). These qualifiers keep John of the Cross's bold defenses of asceticism from falling over into dualism.

John of the Cross's opposition to dualism and his simultaneous defense of soul against the urge toward materialism is very much evident in the following quotation:

> ... the soul lives where she loves more than in the body she animates (*ánima*); for she does not live in the body, but rather gives life to the body, and lives through love in the object of her love (S, 8, 3).

The paucity of negativity in John of the Cross toward the body is also evident in the fact that by sixteenth-century standards he hardly ever talks about sin; he much more frequently refers to appetite. There is a place for sin, even original sin, in John of the Cross, but not because the body is inherently evil or because seduction by "the feminine" is necessarily bad. For example, original sin for John of the Cross seems to refer to the fact that we can make mistakes all by ourselves without the aid of degenerate historical or cultural or economic institutions.

That is, John of the Cross is in no way a precursor to seventeenth- and eighteenth-century Jansenism. The type of piety that developed out of Jansenism was inflexibly rigorist and characterized by the belief that human (mother) nature was corrupt, and hence most *eros* was corrupt. *This* sort of rigor is not at all compatible with John of the Cross's asceticism, nor with the sweetness and familiarity with which he addresses God in his writings. The divorce between the spirit and the flesh found in Jansenism is not necessary to, or even conducive to, contemplation.

Rationality

In this and the following section of the chapter, I will explore the two poles within the unified soul (*alma*): the mental and the affective, or, in traditional terms, the male and the female. I would like to reiterate, however, that in no way am I assuming that women are less rational than men (in fact, in twelve years of teaching I have never noticed less of a capacity for logical argumentation in women), nor am I assuming that men are less capable of loving affectivity than women.

Perhaps it is best to start a discussion of rationality in John of the Cross by noting that there is no necessary opposition in his thought between faith and reason. When both terms are properly understood, faith is not only consistent with, but actually is included in the latter. If "faith in God" refers to a belief that God exists, or to having a theoretical conviction that God exists, then one can easily see that "to believe" is equivalent to "to *think* with assent." To a large extent John of the Cross borrows from the scholastics the idea that faith includes at least three parts: knowledge (*notitia*), assent (*assensus*), and trust (*fiducia*). And it is important to note that John of the Cross was not willing, like Luther, to subordinate the first two parts to the third.[23] Regarding faith John of the Cross was no reformer.

By rationality John of the Cross does not refer merely to technical skills or problem-solving abilities, to what the Greeks called *techne*. Nor does he refer merely to Greek *episteme* (scientific knowledge). Rather, as we have seen, he has something much broader in mind, like the Greeks' *sophia,* which consists in thinking about, and gaining some understanding of, one's place in the overall scheme of things in the universe. And it is important to notice that wisdom has traditionally been personified as feminine, as opposed to *techne*. Wisdom consists in understanding how the particular and the universal relate. It must be admitted that mysticism is opposed to rationality *if* rationality is construed exclusively or primarily in terms of *techne* or *episteme*. John of the Cross is clear that we should not busy ourselves with particular knowledge (L, 3, 48). He would have had a hard time acknowledging as truly rational the winners of a game of Trivial Pursuit. Rather, prudence or wisdom in the cognitive order, in conformity with faith,[24] shows signs of health only when it directs its attention to God (S, 2, 6).

It is in fact rationality (*entendimiento*) that brings Christian wisdom (*sabiduría*), an oxymoronic (and Socratic) wisdom in ignorance whereby the wise person is the first to admit nescience in comparison to God (S, 2, 7; S, 26, 13). But for a human being to eschew rationality is to give up on the one feature of human existence that distinguishes it from an animal's life, hence the removal of the cataracts of ignorance facilitates the transition from the animal man or woman to the spiritual person (L, 3, 75).

The unity of soul-body in John of the Cross is mirrored in the unity of activity exerted by rationality-love. But John of the Cross gives conflicting evidence regarding which of the two has the upper hand, evidence which at least indicates the integral connection between rationality and love. At times John of the Cross suggests that it is impossible to love without first understanding what is loved (for example, S, 26, 8; L, 3, 49), but at other times he suggests that one must love God before one receives knowledge regarding God (S, 38, 5). Further, when John of the Cross refers to the rational person's thirst for God, one can see a primacy in rationality if one emphasizes "rationality" and a primacy in love if one emphasizes "thirsts" (L, 3, 19). Or again, the primacy of rationality is apparent when John of the Cross suggests that the light of knowledge also generates heat, that is, the heat of love (L, 3, 49). But the primacy of love is indicated in the following consideration: for John of the Cross it is better to understand a little but to love a great deal than to understand a great deal but to love a little.

There is little need to resolve this issue, however. The important things to notice are that: (a) (traditionally male) rationality and (traditionally female) affectivity are partners in John of the Cross's anthropology; and (b) rationality plays a far greater role in his thought than many assume. Regarding rationality and affectivity it should be said that John of the Cross sees a cooperative project between love and will, on the one hand, and knowledge and intellect, on the other (L, 3, 49). And it should be said that rationality for John of the Cross is, in a way, the receptacle for all objects (A, III, 1), or, to put the point in contemporary terms, there is no such thing as theory-free observation or theory-free affectivity.

One obvious historical reason (actually, a self-fulfilling prophecy) for associating rationality with maleness is the fact that throughout most of Western civilization women were not permitted to attend universities, nor even to become literate. Frost is instructive in noting that neither John of the Cross nor Teresa of Avila distrusted the intellectual life. In fact, the latter wanted to establish Discalced houses for men in part to get *learned* spiritual directors. (It should be remembered that the accurate formulation of Teresa of Avila's famous aphorism is that it is only *when praying* that one should love much rather than think much.) The style of mystical theologians like John of the Cross and Teresa of Avila is certainly different from, but *not necessarily* opposed to, that of systematic theologians.[25]

It is only when rationality is equated with *techne* that it is likely to lead to religious mediocrity. That is, John of the Cross avoids two extremes: the "intellectualist" stance, which rakes together information for its own sake or which alleges to have found an algorithm for the spiritual life, and the "spiritualist" or quietist stance, which shows an indifference to, or opposition to, rationality altogether.[26] In between these two extremes lies John of the Cross's judicious use of reason in defense of what I have called "dipolar theism." He believes in the otherness of God (but not an "absolute" otherness, as Frost alleges), the necessary existence of God, and the constancy of God, on the one hand, and the loving passivity of God, on the other. The latter indicates, according to Frost, that John of the Cross kept his feet on the ground (that is, on mother earth) even as he soared.[27]

One of the key features of John of the Cross's project was to call attention to the relationship between God and rational creatures. In fact, the spiritual life is itself rational human nature raised to the highest state. Human nature is perfect in its own way, but because of *entendimiento* it is able to abstract from particulars and rise to the universal. It is clear in John of the Cross that such a rise is always conditioned by the nature of the knower, that objects are known according to the mode of the knower. Hence religious knowledge binds rationality as well as the feelings to God. Frost rightly emphasizes this aspect of John of the Cross when he says that:

> No one has ever more completely exposed the emptiness of that emotional slush of the feelings which runs riot today under the name of Christianity than he does, especially in the early chapters of *The Dark Night,* no one comes nearer. . . in showing that a "spirituality" which is not rooted in the mind, is the most dangerous of delusions.[28]

That is, the desire to "know" through supernatural means like visions, voices, or trances is far more presumptuous than trying to know God through rational evidence. Even contemplative "unknowing" is the perfection of rationality rather than its loss; contemplation, as before, is the perfection of *discursive* meditation. The habits acquired through rationality certainly remain after, if not during, contemplation.[29]

Part of John of the Cross's intellectual achievement is due to the influence of Thomism on him, as in his agreement with the terms on the left side of the diagram in section 2 of this chapter. Regarding the terms on the right side of the diagram, John of the Cross was influenced first and foremost by the personal, changing God of the Bible (who is hardly an unmoved mover!) and by his own meditative and contemplative experiences. John of the Cross's intellectual genius consists in his ability to bring these two poles together into a coherent whole. Further, in the effort to understand this synthesis it would be unwise to ignore the intellectual content of John of the Cross's poems, as we will see in chapter five. Modern culture can be cruel toward the systems of previous ages, as Thompson notices, hence it is no small gain in this chapter to have discovered an unsuspected, intellectual profundity in his thought in the form of his dipolar theism, and this despite the fact that my primary aim has been to focus on the importance of gender in his thought.[30]

I would also like to make it clear that the contrasts that energize John of the Cross's thought should not be confused with violations of the law of contradiction. A contrary or a contrast is not a contradiction. He is usually clear that contradictories are not to be glorified, as in his motto that evil cannot comprehend goodness (L, 1, 23). That is, it makes no sense to bifurcate evil into "evil evil" (a redundancy) or "good evil" (a contradiction in terms). So also "good good" is a redundancy and "evil good" is a contradiction. But the thought of contraries against contraries (*contrarios contra contrarios*) causes him to exclaim: "O wonderful thing!" (¡*oh cosa admirable!*). He cites as one example, in addition to those treated above in section 2 of this chapter, the contrast between hardness and tenderness (L, 1, 22; L, 1, 23; L, 1, 25). Good hardness, I assume, refers to the refusal to give up on moral principles when pressured, a refusal to sell out when the chips are down; whereas invidious hardness consists in a pigheaded refusal to alter one's response to new data or to the recent sufferings of others. Good tenderness, I assume, refers to the pliable and tractable and traditionally feminine qualities of divinity found in John of the Cross's poetry; whereas invidious tenderness refers to gullibleness or softness in the face of evil. I would like to reiterate at this point that the complementarity of traditional male and traditional female divine traits should not be construed to mean that the feminine divine predicates are *mere* complements and have less integrity than the male predicates. Because of the history of asymmetricality it is understandable that scholars like Mary Daly exhibit caution regarding dichotomous thinking, even if the dichotomies involved are eventually located within a larger (omnipresent) whole.[31]

Love

In addition to his emphasis on rationality, there is another, and more well-known side to John of the Cross, a side which is

especially enshrined in his symbolic gender transformation in his
poem "The Spiritual Canticle" and in his commentary on that poem.
Here the soul (*alma*) is personified as feminine and as desiring a
more intense enkindling of love for the bridegroom, God. The easy,
sweet longings of love, however, are found throughout the works of
John of the Cross (see, for example, A, I, 14). Love is not opposed to
rationality for John of the Cross. Love, like rationality, assimilates
like faculties. Like knows like, on the one hand, and the arrows of
love (that is, the actions and motions of love), which come from the
human quiver, strike and attach themselves to God so as to make
human beings like God (A, III, 13), on the other. By love John of
the Cross does not primarily refer to subjective feelings of delight
(*sabor*) or sweetness (*suavidad*), although these are in fact included
in his version of love, but to the drive to elevate the mind to God
(*levantamiento de mente en Dios*).

We can strike God with the arrow of love only because God has
already struck us; God strikes us in a spiritual inflaming that
engenders the passion of love (D, II, 11). The mutually implicative
status of reason and love is indicated by John of the Cross's belief
that the ladder of love to God can be thought about, reflected on,
and categorized into a science of love (*ciencia de amor*), a "science"
which is not a technique but a thoughtful consideration of the
ardent sort of love for God that makes us bold or daring (*atreverse*) in
God's presence (D, II, 18, 20). John of the Cross's loving knowledge
of God is similar to Plato's interpenetration of *eros* (love) and
episteme (knowledge) in the *Symposium*. As Kavanaugh notices,[32]
the mutual causality between love and knowledge allows John of
the Cross to give primacy to each. That is, knowledge is a necessary
but not sufficient condition for mystical wisdom; and love is a necessary but not sufficient condition for the same. When John of the
Cross says that love is a fire that naturally rises upward (D, II, 20),
and that nothing is obtained from God without love (S, 1, 13), some
interpreters are tempted to make love the sole, sufficient cause of
mystical wisdom, but there is not enough textual evidence in John
of the Cross to support this claim.

The point I am trying to establish in this section of the chapter
is that if one concentrates on love in John of the Cross, one does
not have to play into the hands of those who would assume that a
"feminine" tenderness in religion precludes a toughminded commitment to reason. Likewise, as we will see in the next chapter, John
of the Cross's concern for love is anything but selfish; the whole
point to religious love is to help us escape self-centeredness so as to
become theocentric (S, 9, 5). Further, John of the Cross's concentra-

tion on love is not to be confused with a fetish for the histrionic in religion, as if the relationship between the soul and her beloved were to be depicted in a melodrama. It is possible to be struck with love for God instantaneously, but John of the Cross is clear (he refers to Ezek. 16:5–14) that in most instances the soul grows gradually to love God (S, 23, 6).

The soul (again, personified as feminine) can become bold (*osadía*) with respect to God because of the equalizing effects of love. The continual motion of love's urgings encourages the soul to be unified with God, and not to be subservient to her supposed master (S, 33, 2; L, 1, 8). Even though the soul is naturally inclined to love, it nonetheless hurts to love a being who is sometimes hidden. But the contrast between pleasure and pain is a tricky one in John of the Cross. One should not be too quick to "cure" the pain of love's wound if this "wonderful" pain in the end actually heals the soul (L, 1, 13; L, 2, 7; L, 2, 13).

There are hundreds of references in John of the Cross to "love" (*amor*), "spouse" (*esposo*), "beloved" (*amado*), and so forth. But Thompson thinks that it is an open question whether John of the Cross's love is a grasping *eros* in search of a reward or a pure, self-giving *agape*. The issue is important if for no other reason than the fact that some (for example, Anders Nygren) think that Christian *agape,* in order to remain pure, must sweep away all vestiges of the self-interested erotic love found in Greek philosophy. Barth, in his aforementioned remarks aimed against mysticism, seems to agree with Nygren.[33] Paul Tillich, however, was not bothered by some intrusion of *eros* into *agape.*[34] He thought that there was bound to be some element of desire in the will to unite with God. But this is not selfishness; as we will see in the next chapter, John of the Cross is quite willing to lose his self, but not prematurely. No mystical encounter would be possible if a human being were not precious to God; a human being has something to give to God.[35]

John of the Cross's persecutors, anticipating Nygren and Barth, were scandalized by the eroticism in *The Spiritual Canticle,* thus causing its publication to be delayed until after John of the Cross's death. But this eroticism, despite its numerous similarities to Greek *eros,* is different as well in that it avoids the trap of grasping self-love by culminating in an *igualdad de amor* with God. Thompson is correct that:

> *"Igualar"* will mislead us if we think of it as meaning "making equal in *being* with"; we should rather understand it as "removing the distance between."[36] (emphasis added)

Despite the fact that human love can never be as permanent as God's nor as pervasive as God's, John of the Cross's equality of love *does* entail that there is no difference in kind between the soul's love for God and God's love for her.

The similarities between John of the Cross's *amor* and Greek *eros* are most apparent in those passages where love is described in Dionysian terms. John of the Cross's commitment to rationality alerted him to the negative features of Dionysian passion, features which he depicts metaphorically as the drink in the chalice of the Babylonian woman in the Apocalypse. This wine of prostitution is a symbol for the vain joy human beings often exhibit, especially by those of high rank (A, III, 22). But John of the Cross more often notices positive features than negative ones. He compares the soul itself to a vineyard in flower. When a human being is inebrieted (*embriaga*) by God it is due to the force of a spiced and aged wine that has been tested (see Eccles. 9:15). That is, he is not interested in handing a carte blanche to anyone who wants a quick high in religion caused by the effervescence of cheap "wine" (S, 17, 5; S, 25, 7–11).

The virtues themselves are like sweet wine, as is the love of wisdom (*el amor de la sabiduría*), that is, as is philosophy (*philia* for *sophia*). To be inebriated by love of wisdom, John of the Cross thinks, is to be led to a state where one is absorbed (*absorberse*) and transformed (*transformarse*) in God, as we will see in the next chapter. The process of this transformation causes one, in the dark night, to be sick (*langueo*) with love, but eventually it brings on the brightest festivity of love in divine union (S, 7, 2; S, 16, 4; S, 30, 1; S, 37, 5). The human spirit is a swift horse that does not lend itself easily to the hegemony of Apollonian order even if passion must in fact cooperate with reason (L, 2, 13).

John of the Cross and the "Feminine"

Thus far in this chapter we have seen that John of the Cross's thought militates against monopolar theism, a theism which often enough leads to a metaphysical dualism, which in turn usually denigrates qualities traditionally conceived as feminine. We have also seen that John of the Cross is opposed to a mind-body dualism in the human person, a dualism which is usually elaborated, once again, at the expense of certain phenomena traditionally conceived as feminine. In this final section of the chapter, I would like to examine not the divine attributes, nor John of the Cross's approach to the relationship between reason and love, topics which in an indirect but very real way have implications for gender concerns in religion. Rather, I would like to examine the direct contact between John of the Cross and the "feminine."

First it should be noted that a good deal of John of the Cross's life was spent with women religious. As we have seen, he was recruited to the Carmelite reform and dissuaded from joining the Carthusians by Teresa of Avila herself. And almost as much of his time as a spiritual director was spent with women as with men. The dedications to his writings bear this claim out. *The Spiritual Canticle* was written at the request of Ana de Jesus, one of the leading Carmelites. The work was meant to tap John of the Cross's training in scholastic theology, training which was denied to nuns, although John of the Cross was quick to praise Ana de Jesus's fine understanding of mystical theology, understanding gained through love and experience. And *The Living Flame of Love* was written at the request of a certain Doña Ana de Peñalosa. That is, two of his four major works were written for women. The most important of his minor works, the "Sayings of Light and Love," were written for Madre Francisca de la Madre de Dios, a nun at Beas.[37] And most of his extant letters were written to women: Madre Catalina de Jesus, Madre Ana de San Alberto (Prioress of Caravaca), Madre Leonor Bautista, to a group of nuns at Beas, and to young women who wanted to become Carmelite nuns, to Madre Maria de Jesus (Prioress of Cordoba), Magdalena del Espiritus (a nun at Cordoba), Doña Juana de Pedroza in Granada, to a nun suffering from "scruples," and to Maria de la Encarnación (a nun at Segovia), Doña Ana del Mercado y Peñalosa, and to an unnamed nun in Segovia. We have only a few works that are written to men (for example, the "Precautions" were meant for the friars at El Calvario).[38]

It is no wonder, therefore, that John of the Cross was a "feminist" when discussing the divine attributes and the dignity of (mother) earth. I do not want to overstate the case by claiming that John of the Cross totally avoided sexism or that he shared most of the views associated with contemporary feminism. For example, at one point he personifies the lower part of the soul as girlish; that is, phantasies are seductive lures that are not to be trusted (S, 18, 4). At another point he complains about a honey-mouthed, unmanly (*afeminado*) approach to religion; but in the same passage (A, III, 25) he indicates that what really bothers him is a certain vice called "*molicies*." Kavanaugh translates this as "effeminacy," but the primary meaning of this word, and a better translation in this context, I think, is "softness" or "flabbiness." John of the Cross himself notices that the Carmelite nuns were strong soldiers in the fight against spiritual dryness (M, letters, 5). What bothers him is an approach to God, whether exerted by men or women, whose laxity makes one ill-prepared to appreciate the sublime elements in religion.

As before, the dignity of the feminine is most prominent in John of the Cross's symbolic gender transformation whereby the soul (not the body) is personified as feminine. This "woman" detaches herself from things so as to be attached to her lover and enter the spiritual marriage. The soul cannot be molested when it withdraws from the world (pace chapter one) and enters into God (S, 20, 15; S, 22, 2; S, 40, 1). Although human nature itself is also personified as feminine by John of the Cross, he does not personify it in this way so as to blame "woman" for human failings. In fact, original sin was due to Adam, he thinks, an attribution which avoids the sexism and speciesism which often characterize the story of the fall, when a woman and an animal are used to explain man's problems (S, 23, 2; S, 23, 5). It must be admitted that the love relationship between the soul and God is often described in John of the Cross in such a way that God is personified as masculine, but as the remarkable quotations in section 2 above indicate, John of the Cross is also willing to describe God as mother. And even when God is described in male terms, patriarchy is not necessarily involved, as when the equalizing power of love enables John of the Cross to see God as brother (S, 22, 7; S, 24, 5).

John of the Cross was very much a creature of his time in his apparent assumption that women had to be either nuns or mothers; he quotes Rachel (Gen. 30:1) to the effect that she had to have children or she would die. But this in no way diminishes the respect he had for women religious, especially for Teresa of Avila. It is interesting to speculate, although I will not explore Teresa of Avila's texts in order to prove this claim, that Teresa of Avila may have been more of a monopolar theist than John of the Cross. He usually refers to God in intimate, familiar terms (the *tu* form in Spanish), whereas Teresa of Avila, who was forced to "know her place" in sixteenth-century culture as a loyal daughter of the church, usually refers to God as king. The point I wish to make here is that the relationship between John of the Cross and Teresa of Avila is a complex one (too complex to deal with adequately without a detailed analysis of Teresa of Avila's writings), and not a simple one whereby one could assume that the major contributions to feminism in religion come from Teresa of Avila as opposed to John of the Cross.

Carolyn Walker Bynum's study of women mystics in the Middle Ages is helpful in noticing several similarities between John of the Cross and Teresa of Avila.[39] John of the Cross, like women mystics, has a tendency to balance regal and erotic imagery for God, to identify with Jesus's suffering, to deemphasize the devil and the notion of cosmic warfare, to emphasize the communal binding with the mystical body of Christ brought about by mysticism, and so forth. Further, one should remain open to the possibility that John of the Cross's mysticism as well as Teresa of Avila's may in part be due to the fact that mysticism provides a substitute for certain cultural deprivations (as in the effects of sexism on Teresa of Avila) or psychological deprivations (as in the effects of poverty on John of the Cross).

There is obviously a difference in temperament between John of the Cross and Teresa of Avila. The former rarely talks about himself, the latter does so all the time. Perhaps, and this is idle speculation on my part, this is due to the fact that John of the Cross, having been exposed to philosophy and systematic theology, had a greater sense of urgency to fit his personal religious experiences within the context of the claims made in favor of universal reason. Teresa of Avila, however, who was not given the opportunity to study philosophy or systematic theology, would quite understandably feel no such urgency. And perhaps this idle (albeit tantalizing) speculation on my part could even be extended so as to explain Teresa of Avila's much more favorable attitude toward visions and voices and trances. However inadequate this interpretation of their differences may be, it is still a far more generous approach than that found in the (sexist, even if held by some contemporary feminists) suggestion that women are by nature less concerned with the rational and the general than men, and that they are more concerned with the emotional and the particular. In any event, the differences between John of the Cross and Teresa of Avila should not be overemphasized. Regarding the fundamental points of the spiritual life and of the Discalced reform, Frost says the following:

That there was any real conflict between the mind of St. John and St. Teresa upon these points is unthinkable, although the great difference in temperament must be taken into account, and the fact that as a lifelong confessor and director of nuns, St. John knew even more about the spiritual life than did St. Teresa, who

also, as she tells us, suffered for years from both a frequent change
of directors and bad direction, and at one time was very much
influenced by the *Third Alphabet* of Fray Francisco de Osuna, some
of the teaching of which St. John seems, at least, to intend to
refute directly in *The Ascent*. And if St. John is severe on the
childishness of many souls, it is St. Teresa who cries, "Lord, save
us from silly devotions."[40]

Sonya Quitslund does a fine job of exploring the feminist spirituality in Teresa of Avila, a spirituality which sheds light on John
of the Cross's own.[41] Teresa of Avila was both an exceptional woman
and an "extraordinarily ordinary" woman. This oxymoronic designation refers at least to her establishment of non-competitive, non-
dominating modes of relationship among sisters, ordinary relations
which had become extraordinary. She became an extraordinary saint
in part because she was such a perfectly ordinary woman. She
exhibited maternal care for all who were close to her, and she
exhibited, especially in her early years, the typical womanly sins:
she was extremely anxious to please and to be loved, even if it
meant doing things which she disliked. The main difference between
Teresa of Avila or John of the Cross as feminists, on the one hand,
and contemporary feminists, on the other, is that the latter are
more aware of the devastating consequences of these games, and of
the dark side of sexist structures which even infect, as we have
seen, discourse about the divine predicates themselves.

There is evidence that Teresa of Avila was at times bothered by
the fact that all the power was in the hands of men, who often
enough held the virtues of women as suspect.[42] One of her responses
to this predicament was the novel idea of having illiterate nuns
educated. Strange as it sounds today, she recruited John of the
Cross in part for the purposes of women's liberation. He brought an
intellectual quality to an order of women at a time when it occurred
to hardly anyone except Teresa of Avila that women needed intellectual stimulation. Again notice that two of John of the Cross's
four major works were written for women. And they were written
in Spanish, so as to remove the barrier posed by Latin, which was
the language of the universities and of the church hierarchy.

Teresa of Avila was well aware of the danger in thinking that
ordinary experiences were of divine origin, but she was also intent,
according to Quitslund,[43] on turning a woman's weakness into a
strength: the more vulnerable to God's grace, the more open to
mystical experience. It was John of the Cross's challenge to eliminate

this weakness, which we today generally believe is culturally and historically contingent, while preserving the predisposition to contemplation. He more than once indicates that lack of progress in the spiritual life is due to a lack of self-confidence. John of the Cross's own spirituality, as Gerald Brenan notices, is a mixture of an immense tenacity of purpose and a feminine sensibility. The latter is best exhibited in the personification of the soul as feminine in "The Spiritual Canticle," which is one of the few places where John of the Cross writes in the first person singular.[44] Here we have a dialogue between the soul and her beloved, who has deserted her.

> Setting out to seek him, she enquires of the woods and flower-enamelled fields if they have seen him pass. They answer that he went by hurriedly, leaving them clothed in his beauty as he looked at them. . . . If only his eyes, she exclaims, could be reflected in that crystal fount! The eyes appear and she is transported in a *vuelo* or ecstasy. . . . Her lover *is* the mountains, valleys, strange islands, rivers, nights, music, silence and refreshing feast. . . . The lover leads her into his inner wine cellar. . . . She promises to be his spouse and, going out into the fields drunk with love, loses the sheep she had been tending. . . . The lover then speaks and his words denote that the consummation of the nuptials has taken place. After an allusion to the apple tree where her mother (Eve) was lost, in the shade of whose wood (the Cross) he had betrothed himself to her, he conjures the birds, lions, stags, mountains, valleys, river banks, water, airs and wakeful fears of night not to disturb his beloved.[45]

There are obviously many levels of meaning in the poem, which have been ably treated by Brenan and Thompson, among others. What I would like to emphasize is Thompson's contention that John of the Cross *intends* his works to be variously interpreted, as I have noted before. For example, in the context of gender studies in religion we should accentuate the transition from the first five stanzas of the poem, where the action moves quickly, to the next six stanzas, where the action slows down so that we can concentrate on the *inward state of the bride,* a state that is treated most brilliantly in Teresa of Avila's own writings, with which John of the Cross was familiar.[46]

The above quotation from Brenan, to the effect that God in "The Spiritual Canticle" appears in the hills and flowers, forces us to look ahead to the next chapter on "Nature," where we will consider the issue of divine embodiment. Systematic theologians and philosophers of religion have traditionally thought that the mind-body analogy implied a degrading view of deity.[47] God, the monopolarists claimed, is only mind or spirit, not body. They have failed to notice, however, that if this analogy is degrading, the father analogy is no less degrading. Is God to be identified with mud?, it might be asked. The response should be, Does God have a male sex organ? Without that organ what is left of the idea that God causes the world as a father causes a child? Among other mistakes, male bias in religion is based on bad science. The Aristotelian belief that the father provides the form and the mother merely provides the soil led to the belief that the father is the real cause of the child. Now we know better in biology, and the hope is that we will eventually know better in theology. As Hartshorne puts the point:

> The mind-body analogy is not degrading if the father (or parental) analogy is not. And without either analogy there is no good basis for the idea of God as causative of creatures.[48]

All predicates when applied to God involve *some* negativity in that God does not know, love, and so forth, as we do. With respect to divine embodiment, however, systematic theologians have allowed this negativity to run wild, especially with respect to divine embodiment when it includes feminine traits as traditionally conceived, and when it includes the terms on the right side of the diagram above in section 2. In this and the succeeding chapter, I am attempting to determine the degree to which one can sanjuanistically attribute "feminine" and "embodied" predicates to God.

CHAPTER 4

Nature

Seeking my Love
    Buscando mis amores,
I will head for the mountains and for watersides,
    Iré por esos montes y riberas,
I will not gather flowers,
    Ni cogeré las flores
Nor fear wild beasts;
    Ni temeré las fieras,
I will go beyond strong men and frontiers.
    Y pasaré los fuertes y fronteras.
O woods and thickets
    ¡Oh bosques y espesuras,
Planted by the hand of my Beloved!
    Plantadas por la mano del Amado;
O green meadow,
    Oh prado de verduras,
Coated, bright, with flowers,
    De flores esmaltado,
Tell me, has He passed by you?
    Decid si por vosotros has pasado!
Pouring out a thousand graces,
    Mil gracias derramando,
He passed these groves in haste;
    Pasó por estos sotos con presura,
And having looked at them,
    Y yéndolos mirando,
With His image alone,
    Con sola su figura

Clothed them in beauty. . . .
   Vestidos los dejó de hermosura. . . .
My beloved is the mountains,
   Mi Amado, las montañas
And lonely wooded valleys,
   Los valles solitarios nemorosos,
Strange islands,
   Las ínsulas extrañas,
And resounding rivers,
   Los ríos sonorosos,
The whistling of love-stirring breezes.
   El silbo de los aires amorosos.

St. John of the Cross, "The Spiritual Canticle"

I live, but not in myself. . .
   Vivo sin vivir en mí. . .
I no longer live within myself
   En mí yo no vivo ya,
And I cannot live without God.
   Y sin Dios vivir no puedo.

St. John of the Cross, "Stanzas of the Soul that
Suffers with Longing to See God"

Introduction

It should be obvious from the previous chapter that monopolar
theism, which sees God as supernatural, cannot generate anything
like the rich theology of ecology found in dipolar theism. But in
order to understand John of the Cross's thoughts on (mother) nature,
it will be helpful to distinguish three levels of sentiency or feeling,
which will function as heuristic devices. My hope is that through
these devices we will be better able to appreciate John of the Cross's
commitment to doctrines like the mystical *body* of Christ, divine inclusiveness of the world along with divine sublimity, the belief that
the religious life is one of total commitment of one's natural abilities,
as well as the belief that this commitment even makes sense in the
face of the fragmented mess we often make of our lives.

The three sorts of sentiency (S) are as follows. S1 is sentience
at the microscopic level of cells. S2 is sentiency per se, sentiency in
the sense of feeling of feeling, found in animals and human beings,
whereby beings with central nervous systems or something like
them can feel as wholes, just as their constituent parts show prefig-

urement of feeling on a local level. And feeling is localized. Think of a knife stuck in one's finger, or think of sexual pleasure. S2 consists in taking these local feelings and collecting them so that an individual as a whole can feel what happens to its parts, even if the individual partially transcends the parts. That is, a human being is both immanent in his bodily parts (for example, if damage is done to cells in my finger when a hot object is touched then I am hurt) and transcendent of them (for example, even if my finger is amputated I remain a whole person).

S3 is divine sentience. If I am not mistaken, John of the Cross would find agreeable the following four-term analogy:

$$S1: S2 :: S2: S3$$

The universe is a society or an organism (a mystical body) of which one member (God) is preeminent, just as human beings are societies of cells of which the mental part is preeminent. John of the Cross would not find the following four-term analogy an adequate tool in describing the cosmos:

S1: several unrelated microscope slides : : S2: the world as a jumble of parts

Because animal individuals must, to maintain their integrity, adapt to their environment, mortality is implied. But if we imagine God we must not consider an environment external to deity, but an internal one: the mystical body of the World-Soul. This cosmic, divine being-in-becoming has such an intimate relation to his/her body that there must also be ideal ways of perceiving and remembering the body of the world so that the micro-individuals (S2) in the world can be identified. We can only tell when cells in our finger have been burned by the fire; we cannot identify the micro-individuals as such.

John of the Cross's God can be used for the purposes of present philosophizing. For example, if God is omnibenevolent then God cares for the world, hence each new divine state harmonizes itself both with its predecessor *and* with the previous state of the cosmos. This is analogous to a human being or an animal harmonizing itself with its previous experience and bodily state, but with a decisive difference. The human being must hope that its internal and external environment will continue to make it possible for it to survive, whereas God has no such problem in that there is no external environment for God. But the differences between God and human beings (for example, God knows the micro-individuals included in the divine life and God has no external environment) should not cloud the important similarities (for example, the facts that self-change is integral to soul at all levels and that the soul-body analogy used to understand God does not preclude the person-person analogy, which links the divine person with human beings).

The most important similarity lies in the fact that one's bodily cells are associated, at a given moment, with one as a conscious, supercellular singular, just as all lesser beings are associated with the society of singulars called "God." As we have seen, in a way all talk about God short of univocity contains *some* negativity, in that God does not exist, know, love, and so forth, exactly as we do. With regard to the divine body, however, almost all theists have allowed this negativity to run wild. John of the Cross's thought is important to note in this regard in that he avoids this imbalance, as I will show.

John of the Cross offered a striking anticipation of the doctrine of the compound animal individual, even if he ultimately fell short of the principle that individuality as such must be the compounding of organism into organisms. But this is not surprising because cells were not yet discovered. He did realize that in the case of the divine individual, where all entities are fully appreciated, there can be no envy of others or conflict with them in that they are integral to the divine goodness. Less completely are an animal's cells internal to the individual. For example, bone cells in a finger are less internal and less fully possessed by the individual than are the brain cells. These considerations regarding divine inclusiveness also explain why the cosmos could not be held together and ordered by a malevolent God or a plurality of gods, in that these deities are always partly divided within or among themselves, and are incapable of an objective grasp of the world. The cosmos can be held together only by an all-sympathetic coordinator. Erazim Kohak puts John of the Cross's position well:

> Shall we conceive of the world around us and of ourselves in it as *personal,* a meaningful whole, honoring its order as continuous with the moral law of our own being and its being as continuous with ours, bearing its goodness—or shall we conceive of it and treat it, together with ourselves, as *impersonal,* a chance aggre-

gate of matter propelled by a blind force and exhibiting at most the ontologically random lawlike regularities of a causal order?[1]

God is the integrating principle of the world, which is otherwise a concatenation of parts.

The divine body is superior to our bodies because there is nothing internal to it, for example, cancer cells, which could threaten its continued existence. Further, our bodies are fragmentary, as in a human infant's coming into the world as a secondary life-style expressing its feelings upon a system that already had a basic order in its cells; whereas the divine body does not begin to exist on a foundation otherwise established. When an animal dies, its individual life-style no longer controls its members, yet the result is not chaos, but simply a return to the more pervasive types of order expressive of the cosmos. God is aware of the divine body, and can vicariously suffer with its suffering members, as John of the Cross often indicates, but God cannot suffer in the sense of ceasing to exist due to an alien force. Even though individuals can influence God, as fingers can influence individuals, none can threaten God in the way a gangrenous finger can threaten an animal individual.

Not even brain death can threaten God because the soul-body analogy cannot be pushed to the point where a divine brain is posited. As before, the contrast between the brain and a less essential bodily part only makes sense because an animal has an external environment. Consider that the divine body does not need limbs to move about, for it is its own place; space merely is the order among its parts. It does not need a digestive system or lungs to take in food or air from without in that there is no "without." So it is with all organs and appendages outside the central nervous system, which, as we know but John of the Cross did not, is the organ that adapts internal activities to external stimuli, a function which is not needed in the inclusive organism. The only function of the divine body is to furnish God with awareness of, and some control over, bodily members.

In John of the Cross's refined use of the body of Christ analogy, although there is no special part of the cosmos recognizable as a nervous system, every individual becomes, *as it were,* not so much a finger as a brain cell *directly* communicating to God, and likewise receiving influences from divine feeling or thought. In the remaining sections of this chapter, I will be citing textual evidence from John of the Cross in support of the claim that the four-term analogy mentioned above is a fruitful heuristic in the attempt to understand John of the Cross's thought.

Panentheism

If one only emphasizes divine transcendence of nature in John of the Cross, one ends up with the monopolar (traditionally male) God of most systematic theology. I hope I have demonstrated the inadequacies of such a view. I should add, however, that a reverence for a transcendent, *super*natural God not only makes no sense, in that a strictly transcendent God beyond human influence could not receive reverence, but it also leaves the natural world devoid of spiritual significance. That is, monopolar theism is not unconnected with the contemporary ecological crisis. It is to John of the Cross's credit that he was not a monopolar theist. Likewise, if one overemphasizes divine immanence in John of the Cross, he begins to look like a pantheist, and I assume both that there is insufficient evidence in John of the Cross to support such a view and that *if* John of the Cross were in fact a pantheist he could hardly do justice to God as a person. With Camille Campbell and Deirdre Green I claim that John of the Cross was not a pantheist (literally, all *is* God) but a panentheist (literally, all is *in* God).[2] Panentheism is an attempt to do justice to both divine immanence and transcendence. One of the many virtues of panentheism is that it allows one to defend a "creation-centered" spirituality where life, not sin, is seen as primary without losing the traditional virtues associated with divine transcendence, even if such virtues are placed within a larger whole.

In chapter one, I concentrated on John of the Cross's anthropology, where one seeks God in oneself (*a Dios en sí*), but it is perhaps more accurate to say that one seeks oneself literally in God (*a sí en Dios*). This latter seeking (A, II, 7) presupposes the sort of asceticism treated earlier in this book, an asceticism which includes suspensions of memory. To those who object that these suspensions of memory are unnatural, John of the Cross responds by claiming, first, that the forgetfulness of the mystic (analogous to that of the absent-minded professor) only occurs at the beginning of union (that is, mystics should be able to meet all of their practical responsibilities in life), and second, that forgetting to eat, say, at the beginning of union has as its goal the perfection of natural appetites when inclusive union becomes a habit. The strength of the claim that John of the Cross was a panentheist is enhanced when we read him say that we should, in habitual union, not measure God by ourselves, but ourselves by God (A, III, 2; D, I, 7).

A spiritual person who feels that he is included in the divine life, as if in a womb, desires to penetrate (*penetra*) even the deep things (*los profundos*) of God (see 1 Cor.2:10—D, II, 8), as John of the Cross indicates in the following quotation:

> Yet beside this life of love through which the soul that loves God lives in Him, her life is radically and naturally centered in God, like that of all created things, centered in God, as St. Paul says: In Him we live and move and are (Acts 17:28). This was like saying: In God we have our life and our movement and our being. And St. John says that all that was made was life in God (John 1:3–4). Since the soul knows she has her natural life in God. . . (S, 8, 3).[3]

This belief in being included *in* the life of God allows one to understand the biblical dictum (found in both the Hebrew and Christian Scriptures) that one should love God with all one's heart, soul, and strength. If this dictum is taken in a political sense, totalitarianism seems to be implied. It is only when the dictum is taken in an organic sense that it can be acceptable. The value of a cell's life (as opposed to a citizen's life) consists *simpliciter* in its contribution to the health of the whole of which it is a part. Likewise, our value consists in our contribution to the divine whole, *including* the contribution of present well-being. John of the Cross's frequent references to the idea that God is owed all of our heart, soul, and strength (for example, A, III, 16; D, II, 4) should force the monopolar theist to ask *why* we should love God with our whole being if our love ultimately makes no difference to God.[4] Panentheism can explain why such a love is required of us; it can explain Paul's claim in Gal. 2:20 that it is not he who lives but Christ (S, 12, 8); and it can explain the claim of John 1:4 that all that is made has life *in* God (S, 14, 5).

According to John of the Cross, God *vitally* transforms the soul into God when natural imperfections are ameliorated (S, 20, 4). This transformation consists in making explicit and making felt what is usually left implicit; and this explicit transformation is consummated in a spiritual marriage that is (S, 22, 3):

> . . . a total transformation *in* the Beloved in which each surrenders the entire possession of self to the other with a certain consummation of the union of love. The soul thereby becomes

divine, becomes God through participation (*participación*—emphasis added).

Repeatedly John of the Cross makes it clear that the soul not only works for God but *in* God (S, 28, 5):

> So great is this union that even though they differ in substance, in glory and appearance the soul seems to be God and God seems to be the soul (S, 31, 1).

It is God's love for the soul, he thinks, which makes it possible for the latter to feel that it is *in* God and that it is equal to God in the sense that God loves the soul as God loves himself/herself. This is because the soul is in fact part of God (S, 32, 6).

For the panentheist, God is the wholeness of the world, correlative to the wholeness of individual organisms. Any sentient individual experiences and acts as one; the theistic question is whether the cosmos is experienced as, and whether it in some profoundly analogous sense is, a one. An experience of oneself as a fragment is already an implicit affirmation of an integral uni-verse. It should be noted, however, that fragmentariness is not the same as finitude. Human beings are both fragmentary and finite, but God only escapes the former. That is, infinite-finite is another non-invidious contrast that has been inadequately treated by monopolar theists. In *some* sense it is good that God is finite, for it is only a being who can have determinate relations here and now with a particular being who could be the sort of personal lover John of the Cross calls God. And in other obvious senses God is infinite. It is John of the Cross's hope that human beings as fragments can achieve meaning in life by being absorbed (*absorta*) into God's all-inclusive, mystical body (*cuerpo místico*). Consider the following tongue twister:

> That I be so transformed in your beauty that we may be alike in beauty, and both behold ourselves in Your beauty, possessing now Your very beauty; this, in such a way that each looking at the other may see in the other his own beauty, since both are Your beauty alone, I being absorbed in Your beauty; hence I shall see You in Your beauty, and You shall see me in Your beauty, and I shall see myself in You in Your beauty, and You will see Yourself in me in Your beauty; that I may resemble You in Your beauty, and You resemble me in Your beauty, and my beauty be Your beauty and Your beauty my beauty; wherefore I shall be You in Your beauty, and You will be me in Your beauty, because Your very

beauty will be my beauty; and therefore we shall behold each other in Your beauty. . . . All my things are yours, and yours mine (John 17:10). He says this by essence. . . we say it by participation. . . . For His whole mystical body (S, 36, 5).

Once again, neither traditional systematic theology nor pantheism can account for such a passage. The former cannot adequately treat the interpenetration of God and humanity in this passage and the latter cannot account for the clearly distinct personality of God in this passage. Panentheism can account for both, as well as for the extreme sort of divine inclusiveness indicated here.

Because divinity is its own place and has no external environment to move to, John of the Cross affirms the claim that God does not move (L, 3, 11), but this is hardly the Thomistic affirmation of an unmoved mover. Rather, John of the Cross is trying to show that God is moved by the activities, particularly the sufferings, of creatures within the divine life, and that God penetrates the human soul and then absorbs it into divinity by spiritual means (L, 2, 17; L, 3, 63). As we will see in chapter six, John of the Cross sometimes speaks as if God does the absorbing, and at other times he speaks as if the soul must desire to be dissolved (*desatada*) in order to be absorbed into the divine life (S, 37, 1). In any event, he is consistent throughout his writings in believing that the soul can in fact consciously see herself further into God, even if most only see implicitly that they are fragmentary parts of a whole, of a cosmos (S, 36, 11). The soul's operations "are *in* God through its union with Him, it lives the life of God" (L, 2, 34—emphasis added). Or again, "The soul becomes God from God through participation *in* Him and *in* His attributes (L, 3, 8—emphasis added).

Individuals who take religion seriously tend to wonder about what it is that death cannot destroy. It is one thing, however, to say that death is not the end, and another to (selfishly) assume that the "I" will live forever. If religion consists in what we do with our fragmentariness, then John of the Cross was religious because he tried to locate his place as a fragment within an everlasting being-in-becoming who is not a fragment. Hartshorne puts the point as follows:

> We are fragments, but if we are beloved fragments, never to be simply forgotten, that can be enough. To appreciate this, we must stop trying to have it both ways, on the one hand claiming *more* than fragmentary status, as when we assert our (personal) im-

mortality, and on the other hand, claiming even *less* than fragmentary status, as when we attribute all choices to God, as though
we make none at all ourselves.[5]

Although John of the Cross may not have entirely escaped the
belief in personal immortality, it is clear that for him the soul's
happiness consists not in limitless duration of the "I," but in *giving* to
God more than the soul is worth, a giving which is not a forfeit of
something that is rightfully a human being's to possess: the soul *is
made one* with God through participation in the divine life (L, 3,
78–79).

The key tension in John of the Cross's panentheism consists in:
(1) the consciousness of the fact that all creatures have their life
and duration in God, but this is a consciousness that must be
balanced against (2) the awareness of how creatures are distinct
from God, an awareness which prevented John of the Cross from
becoming a pantheist (L, 4, 5). Injustice is done to John of the
Cross when either of these poles in underemphasized. When this
occurs, it is usually the consciousness of the fact (1) which is short-
changed. The evidence in favor of (1), however, is easy to find. John
of the Cross emphasizes that we should prostrate ourselves on the
ground with respect to "self" and that we should delight in the fruit
of forgetfulness of self *so that* we can be united with God (M, maxims, 35; M, letters, 20, 23). The immediate "cash value" of John of
the Cross's panentheism is delivered when he claims that whoever
knows how to die in all will have life in all *now*. He refuses to deliver promissory notes to the effect that union with God must be
postponed to the future. "Outside" of God (strictly speaking, there
is no outside to God), he thinks, everything is narrow (*estrechura*),
and flippant promises to find God in the future are indeed "outside"
God (M, other counsels, 2; M, letters, 12).

Merton claims that there is no need to crown John of the
Cross's subtle treatment of the union of creatures with God by
calling such treatment "Franciscan."[6] The paucity of attention paid
by scholars to John of the Cross's view of nature, a paucity noticed
by Lucien-Marie Florent, is no doubt partly responsible for the
view that within Christianity the Franciscan tradition has a mo-
nopoly on a sacramental view of nature.[7] *That* John of the Cross had
a sacramental view of nature, rather than a denigrating one, there
can be no doubt. The question is, *how* can he hold a belief in a God
who is above and beyond us as well as a belief in a God who is
immanent in all things? Frost asks this question without adequately
responding to it; but Frost is on the right track in suspecting that

an adequate response would have to be along the lines of the claim made in Acts 17:28 that God is the one in whom we live and move and have our being. This "in" can be seen as a corollary to belief in divine omniscience. Omniscience entails the notion that all actualities are in God virtually because that which is known is, in some sense, "in" the knower. In hylomorphism, the soul embraces the whole person, hence to know a soul is to include a person within oneself. The matter is a bit more difficult when it is a human soul attempting to know divine soul, but as Frost suggests:

> . . . the human mind is normally incapable of apprehending or comprehending anything as a whole, its always partial knowledge of the whole of anything is only gained by a process of analysis and reasoning in which the whole under consideration is, as it were, taken to pieces, each part being examined separately and in relation to the whole, viewed from one angle and another, so that finally the separate parts can be built up again with some knowledge of what the whole is in itself. But such knowledge is always incomplete since never can the whole be seen in its wholeness, all at once, completely and perfectly. But the mind does possess the capacity, varying with individuals, of a natural, aesthetic and religious intuition or contemplation in which, however, whilst the whole is more fully embraced, it at the same time loses distinctness, that perception of its parts gained by analytic reflection, etc., is merged into and submerged by a general, all-comprehending view, "confused," as St. John (of the Cross) says. To study a section of country in order to make a map or survey of it is a very different thing, and results in a very different kind of knowledge to that gained by simply contemplating it as a whole, and the latter lacks the detail and distinctness of the former, whilst, on the other hand, it gives a wider, more satisfying and enjoyable knowledge.[8]

It might be asked why, if human beings are already included in the divine life, it makes any difference to become aware of this fact or to try to understand it. John of the Cross's belief seems to be that it is one thing to be absorbed into the beauty of God, but it is quite another to be interiorly transformed by this beauty (S, 11, 10). Or again, it is one thing to be included in divinity, it is another to have this inclusion make a transformational difference in one's life. Contra Francis Bacon, John of the Cross thinks that knowledge is not so much a power to do things, although it is also this, as an intrinsic value (much like aesthetic value) to be appreciated for its own sake. (I will treat this point in much more detail in the next

chapter.) *Knowing* that one is a part of a tremendous whole digni-
fies our lives; knowing that we are but *parts* of that whole teaches
us humility. The latter realization convinces us that as creatures
we are "as" nothing when compared to God (Jer. 4:23), which is
quite different from nihilism; we are ugly *when compared to* divine
beauty (Prov. 31:30). Earthly thoughts are like reptiles *if* they attach us to exteriority and prevent a deeper union with God. As
John of the Cross puts the issue, it makes little difference if a bird
is tied by a thread or a thick cord (A, I, 4, 9, 11). Appetites (for
wealth, adulation from others, security, et al.), both subtle and
gross, often prevent an understanding of panentheism because they
tend to cause the belief that the world is left as a concatenation of
parts, as we have seen Kohak emphasize. And appetites have a
tendency to multiply geometrically like sprouts around a tree, or
like leeches (Prov. 30:15), or like parasites, which eat one's entrails
(think of resentment); they are often (as in Ruben in Gen. 49:4)
poured out like water rather than like wine (A, I, 10).

To enter into a deeper union with God than that which exists
quite naturally regardless of what we do, and to know that
panentheism is true, we must, like Moses, leave all of our possessions
at the bottom of the mountain (Exod. 34:3). Like Hydra's heads,
John of the Cross's metaphors, for the appetites that prevent enter-
ing deeply into God, abound: they are like encircling bees (Ps.
117:12), or like the fetters on a yoked ox, or like being chained to a
pasture like a beast (A, I, 5, 7). As was detailed in chapter one, the
disciplining of one's animal life, along with the positive understanding of what it means to have an animal body, are conducive to a
spiritual life in God (A, III, 26). For example, to understand the
metaphor of the mystical body of Christ one needs to understand
not only "mysticism" and "Christ" but also "body." John of the Cross
is fond of comparing a lonely soul to a wounded animal body, as in
a stag who seeks a remedy for its wound in the refreshment found
high in the mountains. That is, in the dark night of the soul one
exercises all of the virtues *together*, even those associated with the
harmonic functioning of an animal body (D, I, 13; S, 9, 1; S, 13, 9).

Divine Immanence

To claim that John of the Cross is a panentheist is at least to
claim that there is a strong commitment on his part to divine

immanence, in contrast to an almost exclusive concern in traditional (male) systematic theology and philosophy of religion for divine transcendence, or in contrast to an inconsistent commitment to divine immanence in traditional thought. John of the Cross's belief in divine immanence has led Brenan to call his position "almost pantheistic" (especially in the twelfth stanza of S) and to refer to his "so-called pantheism." These are somewhat imprecise ways of putting my very point regarding John of the Cross's pan*en*theism. In this section of the chapter, I will both treat John of the Cross's doctrine of divine immanence and prepare the way for the next section, where I will indicate why a thinker like Frost could be led into thinking that John of the Cross's thought is free from anything like pantheism. That is, my panentheistic interpretation of John of the Cross (along with Camille Campbell's and Deirdre Green's interpretations) can refine the legitimate insights of Brenan and Frost and avoid their errors.

John of the Cross's belief in divine immanence is an understandable consequence of his love of nature. Brenan alerts us to the fact that John of the Cross wrote most of his prose works while at Granada, in view of the Sierra Nevada. Throughout his life he called on all the beauty of created things (*toda la hermosura de las cosas*) to praise God. Toward the end of his life, he would rise before dawn and pray under the willow trees at La Peñuela where the friars had a fifty acre farm or *cortijo*. But he liked to go *beyond* the farm to wild areas, a fact which will become significant in the next section of this chapter on the sublime. The point I wish to make here is that for John of the Cross the whole of creation is the body of the bride (*esposa*) of Christ, hence it made sense for him to write "The Spiritual Canticle" in a *pastoral* idiom where the relevant parties make love among the woods and hills. Yet Brenan sees ambiguity in John of the Cross's view of nature because, on the one hand, God's creation reflects divine beauty and is helpful for beginners in the spiritual life, and, on the other, eventually concern for natural creatures must be purged. This ambiguity can be resolved by criticizing Brenan's assumption that traditional systematic theology and pantheism exhaust the logical alternatives regarding how to view God. If panentheism is a viable alternative to these two positions, then there is no necessary conflict between belief in divine immanence, on the one hand, and belief in divine transcendence, on the other. As before, for example, I am immanent in my body, such that if you cut my finger with a knife you hurt *me*, but I transcend my body in the sense that if you cut my finger off altogether there is no less of me as a person, I still get a whole vote at the polls.[9]

Both Brenan and Frost are correct in trying to defend John of the Cross against the charge of pantheism if what is meant by pantheism is the claim that God is to be *identified* with nature without remainder. Brenan thinks that John of the Cross was dangerously close to pantheism in his thoughts on nature, but that somehow John of the Cross avoided pantheism. I am trying to specify this "somehow." Frost's position is a bit more confusing. He admits that John of the Cross's view of the created universe is a sacramental one, that is, it is a view which preserves the real presence of God in nature such that there is no "mere" matter in nature. But he is skittish about the possibility that John of the Cross's religiosity could be confused with "nature mysticism." John of the Cross's Christian mysticism, he thinks, is only remotely similar to listening to a Beethoven symphony or to an experience of rapture before a beautiful sunset. As we will see in chapter six, John of the Cross's mysticism has to do with a relationship with a *personal* being. Once again, however, panentheism allows one to talk both about the real presence of the divine in nature *and* about a personal divine being who is not identical to any particular natural object. But even Frost has to admit that, after first gaining knowledge of self, knowledge of creatures is the next requirement for John of the Cross in his search for God.[10]

Kavanaugh supplements the efforts of Brenan to emphasize the importance of nature in John of the Cross's personal life. He notices the interpenetration of the natural and the liturgical seasons in John of the Cross; his experience of reading the Bible by the sea in Lisbon; his favorite, silent grotto at Segovia, which was hollowed out of rock and which overlooked a great stretch of landscape; his exhortations to the friars to get out into the open air, for too much time in the monastery makes one want to leave it; and his preference for the country (for example, El Calvario) as opposed to the city (for example, Baeza). Hence, Kavanaugh is not surprised that for John of the Cross the beauty of creatures is due to some "trace" of divinity in them. My hope is that my panentheistic interpretation of John of the Cross provides a more adequate interpretation of these sanjuanistic traces than that offered by either traditional systematic theology or by pantheism.[11]

As I have noted above, the union between God and creatures always (*siempre*) exists in that God preserves (*conservándole*) nature by a sustaining divine presence. But in addition there is a transformative union that must be achieved. If God's presence in all were lost, annihilation would occur; but there is the added presence of spiritual affection. If one strips the soul of dissimilarities from divinity, God's natural presence will be supplemented, he promises, by a transformative presence. Although we do not have the same nature as God (in that we are not capable of cosmic influence or receptivity), we are *somewhat* identical to (*mismo*) God, just as a window in a sense *is* the ray of the sun by participation (*participación*). John of the Cross goes so far as to claim that to become one with God by participant transformation (*transformación participante*) makes the soul appear to be God (A, II, 5; S, 11, 3). (Note both "appear" and "to be.") His is indeed a strong defense of divine immanence.

The omnipresence of divinity is often kept a secret, however, by virtue of the fact that we can only become aware of transformative union as individuals, as solitary sparrows (Ps. 101:8). This difficulty can be overcome because each individual can drink in as much from the fountain of God's universal love as the individual can hold (A, II, 14, 21; S, 14, 24), and this because personal contact with God can occur anywhere, he thinks. Prayer is not annexed to any particular temple or mountain (A, III, 39). Strange as it sounds, particular apertures into God are ubiquitous. Nonetheless, as with most nature lovers John of the Cross is cognizant of the sense of place in which he dwells:

> There are three different kinds of places, I find, by which God *usually* moves the will. The first includes those sites which have pleasant variations in the arrangement of the land and the trees, and provide solitary quietude, all of which naturally awakens devotion. . . . The second kind of place in which God moves the will to devotion is more particular. It includes those localities, whether wildernesses (*desiertos*) or not, in which God usually grants some very delightful spiritual favors to particular individuals. . . . The third kind of place comprises those in which God chooses to be invoked and worshipped. For example: Mount Sinai. . . Mount Horeb (A, III, 42—emphasis added).

Although he was cognizant of place, the word "usually" in the above quotation indicates the scepticism John of the Cross would have regarding localized (for example, Heideggarian) ontologies, a scepticism which is even more obvious in the following exhortation:

> When a person, therefore, prays in a beautiful site, he should
> endeavor to be interiorly with God and forget the place, as though
> he were not there at all. For when people wander about looking
> for delight and gratification from a particular site, they are in
> search, as we said, for sensory recreation and spiritual instability
> more than spiritual tranquility. The anchorites and other holy
> hermits, while in the loveliest and vastest wilderness, chose for
> themselves as small an area as possible, built narrow cells and
> caves, and enclosed themselves within. St. Benedict lived in one of
> these for three years, and St. Simon tied himself with a cord so as
> not to use up more space or go farther than the cord allowed him.
> There are many other examples of this kind of mortification of
> which we would never finish speaking. For those saints clearly
> understood that without extinguishing their appetite and covet-
> ousness for spiritual gratification and delight they would never
> become truly spiritual (A, III, 42).

Or again:

> When you pray enter into your secret chamber, and having closed
> the door, pray (Matt. 6:6); or if not in one's chamber, in the solitary
> wilderness, and at the best and most quiet time of the night, as
> He did (Luke 6:12—A, III, 44).

Beautiful places are only apparent ends in themselves; as parts of
the whole they should be appreciated as means, as notes within a
symphony of love (S, 14, 26).

John of the Cross's awareness of the togetherness of creatures
in the uni-verse was not a (Schelling-like) night in which all cows
were black in that he was also well aware of the countless variety
of animals and plants and the remarkable diversity of creation
(S, 4, 2). His overall view, however, is that each created thing has
some beauty in it, some trace (*rastro*) of God (S, 5, 1). The divine
trace that is in all things is the topic of the lines from "The Spiritual
Canticle" quoted at the beginning of this chapter. God *is* the mountains, for John of the Cross, but God is also much more than the
mountains; God *is* the wooded valleys, at least, but more than these.
And this is what we learn in transformative union (S, 14, 5).

It is no accident that when John of the Cross looks for a simile
for God, or for the soul's desire for God, he often reaches to nature:
our desire for God is like a hart's desire for water (Ps. 41:2); and
God is like a watered, enchanted, flowering garden in spring when
winter has passed; indeed, God is like a whole mountain of flowers

and balsam trees overflowing; there is a garland of various flowers in the soul from God; the soul is a turtledove in love; and so forth (D, II, 20; S, 22, 5; S, 22, 7; S, 24, 3; S, 24, 6; S, 25, 6; S, 30, 6; S, 34, 5). The question is, which theistic, conceptual scheme allows one to take these similes seriously without forcing one into pantheism? My response is that it is panentheism that allows one to make sense of the idea that God's love is diffused (*difunde*) through the world like the rays of the sun as well as the idea that God is sublime (L, 1, 15; L, 1, 26).

God deifies (*endiosando*) the soul by absorbing (*absorbe*) it into divinity (L, 1, 35). This absorbtion was ever on John of the Cross's mind, as Brenan emphasizes in his description of the hermitage up a hill at El Calvario, where, in spring, a wild landscape of *montes, valles,* and *riberas* came alive with broom, lavender, cistus, irises, jonquils, and bee orchids. In the midst of all this, John of the Cross would frequent the chapel among the elm trees and aromatic herbs, and then be compelled to preach about the beauties of creation. And every Saturday, when he set out for Beas, he hiked along the summit with its panoramic view of the mountains,[12] where he would be inspired to say something like the following regarding the soul:

> It seems to it that the entire universe is a sea of love in which it is engulfed, for, conscious of the living point or center of love within itself, it is unable to catch sight of the boundaries of this love (L, 2, 10).

Sublimity

In chapter one, I argued that John of the Cross's asceticism, his defense of the disciplined life, is a mean between an overly soft life of self-indulgence and an overly rigorous life where one thinks too little of oneself. In this section of chapter four, I would like to make an analogous claim regarding John of the Cross's view of God. He is careful to avoid a merely pretty view of God (as evidenced in the flowers and rippling streams) and a view of God as strictly terrible, a terrible God who is either removed from human concern or who frightens us *because of His* concern. Belief in divine immanence often tends toward the former; belief in divine transcendence toward the latter. John of the Cross's dipolar theism tries to *incorporate* both of these tendencies: God is sublime because God is *so* ubiquitously immanent. When *all* creatures are considered together (as before, when they are considered as parts of a uni-verse), they are constituents of a sublime symphony surpassing all particular melodies (S, 14, 25). At times John of the Cross exhibits the inter-penetration of the aesthetic value of prettiness or cuteness (as in the enjoyment of flowers), on the one hand, and powerful emotions like sublimity, on the other. For example, it is possible for John of the Cross to speak of sublime joy (*goza subidísimamente*) when viewing an event in nature, like a bird alighting on a branch (S, 16, 1; S, 34, 6).

At other times, especially in the dark night, John of the Cross does in fact speak of God as an immense, powerful voice who "sounds" in us when there is an awakening of God in the soul. Or better, there is a breathing in of God, to the extent that our knowl-edge will allow, an in-spiration which causes us to become aware of both the intimacy *and* grandeur of God. God is intimate because through this spiration the soul is delicately transformed into God: one breathes out in God and to God the very divine spiration that one had previously received. John of the Cross thinks of God as immense or grand because in the process of becoming deiform (*deiforme*) we realize that we are literally conspirators with *all* hu-man beings (L, 1, 17; L, 4, 2; L, 4, 4; L, 4, 10; L, 4, 16–17; S, 39, 3–4; S, 39, 8).

If one overconcentrates on God as immanent and particular, one will miss divine sublimity, that aspect of God which is, as Kavanaugh puts it, unknown or inadequately grasped and still to be spoken.[13] Traces of God in nature can, however, lead us to con-sider what John of the Cross calls a certain "I-don't-know-what" quality of God (S, 7, 9). One of the virtues of systematically demar-cating one's religious beliefs in philosophy of religion is that one develops a conceptual scheme whereby one can recognize a surpris-ing fact as such, one can be in a position to appreciate this "I-don't-know-what" quality. Those who do not systematize their beliefs are, presumably, prepared to have any event occur next with equal probability as any other. They cannot be surprised, hence they are likely to become victims of what John of the Cross abhors: tedium in religion (A, III, 22). John of the Cross's attitude here is close to Whitehead's: seek simplicity, then distrust it; think carefully about God, then be prepared to have an experience of divine sublimity, which alters one's thoughts.

For John of the Cross the weight of God's greatness is over-whelming (as in Job 23:6). Especially in the dark night the soul feels:

> ... as if it were swallowed by a beast and being digested in the dark belly, and it suffers an anguish comparable to Jonas's when in the belly of the whale (Jonas 2:1–3). It is fitting that the soul be in this sepulcher of dark death in order that it attain the spiritual resurrection for which it hopes. . . . When this purgative contemplation oppresses a man, he feels very vividly indeed the shadow of death, the sighs of death (D, II, 5–6).

Once again, the religious life for John of the Cross does not merely consist in, although it does include, smelling pretty flowers. It also includes:

> ... a painful disturbance involving many fears, imaginings, and struggles within a man. Due to the apprehension and feeling of his miseries, he suspects that he is lost, and that his blessings are gone forever. This sorrow and moaning of his spirit is so deep that it turns into vehement spiritual roars and clamoring (D, II, 9).

In response to the "roars" of this spiritual presence, the human being, in turn, may very well roar (D, II, 9). That is, if God is sublime, and if human beings can achieve union with God, then the human reception and savor of the divine is itself sublime (*subidamente*), as when the old man (*el hombre viejo*) dies to let the transformed individual live (D, II, 16).

In order to appreciate the pretty-beauty of a lotus pond, all one needs to do is walk a few steps to see the pond. But in order to appreciate the sublime-beauty of being confronted face-to-face with a wild animal (think of Blake's tiger), or of looking down a sheer rock face, or of experienceing the cold desolation of the arctic, one must prepare a great deal. And those who have experienced these examples of sublimity claim that the rigorous preparations were worth the effort. These examples should be kept in mind when we see John of the Cross talk of the sublime (*subido*); and we should remember, when we see his hundreds of uses of *subido* or its cognates, that the term literally means "strong" as well as "high." Consider John of the Cross's claim that:

> ... one does not receive this touch of so sublime an experience and love of God without having suffered many trials (D, II, 12).

As we have noted before, however, this sublime experience is simultaneously, and oxymoronically, delicate. John of the Cross offers no apologies in holding that there is no adequate means to signify (*significar*) so sublime (*subida*) an understanding *and* so delicate (*delicado*) a feeling as union (D, II, 17). John of the Cross's view of nature, I allege, is like his theism in being dipolar.

The tension in "delicate sublimity" can be relieved if one realizes that the reason why delicacy, wisdom, and charity are sublime in God is that these attributes in God admit of vast, universal application (S, prologue). God cares for all. To paraphrase Henry Thoreau, there are continents and seas in the religious world yet unexplored, and each person is an isthmus who makes accessible these unexplored regions. But mystical wisdom has the habit of:

> . . . hiding the soul within itself. Besides its usual effect, this mystical wisdom will occasionally so engulf a person in its secret abyss that he will have the keen awareness of being brought into a place far removed from every creature. He will accordingly feel that he has been led into a remarkably deep and vast wilderness, unattainable by any human creature, into an immense, unbounded desert, the more delightful, savorous, and loving, the deeper, vaster, and more solitary it is. . . . The lightning of God illumining the whole earth signifies the illumination this divine contemplation produces in the faculties of the soul; the shaking and trembling of the earth applies to the painful purgation it causes in the soul (D, II, 17).

Such powerful passages, however, can only be understood adequately when balanced against the experience (or better, when seen *along with* the experience) of the rising of the soul, the bride, to the level of sublime (in this case, *alto*) love of God (S, 1, 21).

Periodically, it seems, it is good not to stop to gather flowers in that some beauty is not pretty. At these times, we should not fear wild beasts or mountainous heights (S, 3, 10). Moses, for example, had more accurate glimpses (*visos*) of the sublime, of the height and beauty of the hidden divinity, than most because he had the courage to confront the void (*vacío*), the heavy darkness of God (S, 11, 5; S, 11, 7; S, 13, 1). Although the preparation for contemplation takes a long time, the soul's sublime experience of God as an awesome (*terrible*) power is intermittent and swift (S, 13, 8; S, 14, 4–5). John of the Cross compares this power to a raging river that besieges and inundates everything; it is a torrent which overflows in glory (Isa. 66:12). But because the sublime wisdom and knowledge of God overflows into the human intellect, it is somewhat misleading to refer to God as *omni*potent: human beings have some power, at least, to affect each other and to affect God. The empirical familiarity John of the Cross had with the spiritual lives of others prevented him from engaging in hasty generalization. In some, contemplation is always gentle, but tremblings and torrents are more likely, especially in the beginnings of divine illumination. Perhaps having Kierkegaard in mind, Kavanaugh cleverly translates *temor y temblor* as fear and trembling (S, 14, 18). These emotions constitute an awe-full experience similar to that described by St. John in the Apoc. (14:2) when he heard the "voice" of so many waters that they sounded like thunder (S, 14, 9; S, 14, 11–12; S, 14, 21).

Thus far we have seen John of the Cross speak of sublimity to refer to at least three things: (1) the immense, awesome aspect of God, (2) the tender, loving, wise aspect of God when conceived in its ubiquity, and (3) the effect these two varieties of sublimity produce in the human soul through transformative union. The effect of sublimity (3) alerts us to the sanjuanistic belief (S, 26, 10) that the divine drink deifies, elevates, and immerses one into God (*Esta divina bebida tanto endiosa y levanta al alma y la embebe en Dios*). The awesome aspect of God (1) alerts us to the belief that this drinking from the divine torrent (S, 26, 1) is a bit like taking a sip from a fire hydrant at full force. And the tender, loving, wise aspect of God in its ubiquity (2) alerts us to the fact that for John of the Cross even love, mercy, wisdom, and goodness can be experienced as sublime in that they are, in addition to being ever-present, among the immense (*inmensa*), deep things (*profundos*) of God (S, 14, 4; S, 20, 1; S, 32, 1; S, 32, 8; L, 2, 4).

God is compared by John of the Cross to a deep thicket into which one can always traverse further, nonetheless the wise person finds divine sublimity somewhat accessible (S, 36, 10; S, 37, 2). Or again, God is like a deep cavern or a recess in a mine whose terminus can never be reached, although one *can* know that one is in fact in a cavern or mine (S, 37, 3–4). That is, rational persons can express in an articulate way *that* God exists and they can give reasons to show why God is supremely dependable as well as receptive, and so forth. What articulate, rational discourse cannot do is state in precise terms, without the use of metaphor or analogy, what it is like to receive influence from *all* creatures and what it is like to harmonize all of the joys and sufferings of creatures. Sanjuanistic in-spiration, the spirit of God which breathes through the soul in a sublime way, is one means by which we can gain some understanding in this regard. In union there are interior exchanges between God and the soul that produce sublime delight (*subido deleite*), and in deifying union we are at least vicariously included into the mind (*mente*) of God (S, 17, 8; S, 26, 13; S, 30, 1).

In *Living Flame of Love* John of the Cross often refers to the sublime flashes of contemplative glory in the soul as flares. To be ignorant of these, perhaps because one is too busy to notice them or because one's sensibilities have not been trained to receive them, is a sign of little love. The soul who loves sublimely does so because of its response to a preexistent, sublime possession by (or better, inclusion in) God (L, 1, 1; L, 1, 3; L, 1, 6; L, 1, 28). These flares themselves are sublime, hence strange (*extrañas*), gifts to souls. They are strange because, whereas human beings as fragments should not be able to know what it would be like to be a cosmic individual, they do, in transformative union, help to bring to the fore such sublime knowledge (*noticia*). This knowledge includes the realization that death is best accompanied by a swan song in that our fragmentary earthly contributions will not be forgotten by the everlasting being-in-becoming. We can bear the sublimity of death by realizing that at each moment the suffering of love is like dying (S, 7, 4; S, 39, 13; L, prologue; L, 1, 30).

The sublimely delightful cautery that God produces in the soul, to be treated in detail in chapter six, is sometimes brought about by intellectual means (*forma intelectual*), hence the soul's intellectual journey to God can be sublime, for John of the Cross. In fact, the soul itself is sublime when it is considered that it is capable of divine union when recollected in itself. The soul is an abyss (*abismo*) in the sense that it is as vast as the desert, hence actually going to a desert is not a bad idea, according to John of the Cross (L, 2, 8–9; L, 2, 13; L, 3, 4; L, 3, 30: L, 3 56; L, 3, 64; L, 3, 71; M, letters, 28). Vast barren stretches of nature, like tundras or deserts, or the tremendous voice of roaring water, like the Niagara, as Frost notices,[14] are better able to put us in a position to appreciate the grandeur of God (L, 3, 78) than those parts of nature which we control, or at least which we try to control. Anthropocentrism, in general, and ecological rapacity, in particular, are bothersome for many reasons, not least of which, from the perspective of sanjuanistic mystical theology, is the fact that they prevent us from appreciating that there is something greater than humanity in the universe, that there is a God who delivers sublime unctions to us, a God who shades our souls with a presence cosmic in scope (L, 3, 41; L, 3, 45).

John of the Cross as Proto-Romantic

Thus far in this chapter, I have tried to understand John of the Cross's approach to nature through the concept of panentheism, a concept which, I allege, allows us to understand both the enormous number of passages where John of the Cross indicates divine immanence as well as the equally enormous number of passages where he indicates divine sublimity. Further, I have implied that John of the Cross's panentheism makes a great deal of sense in that its alternatives are in different ways defective. Systematic theology has traditionally failed to adequately explain *how* a strictly *super*natural, timeless, unmoved, being can be a divine person who is related to the natural, temporal world; nor has it explained how a divine being can be all-loving if such a being is only externally related to natural creatures and could just as well do without them. And pantheism altogether fails to account for God as a person. If pantheism refers to the belief that God is in all aspects inseparable from the sum or system of dependent things or effects, then pantheism denies that there is *any* externality of concrete existence to the essence of deity. The trick is to make sense of both the divine attributes of ubiquity (as in omniscience, omnibenevolence, and the universal scope of divine influence), on the one hand, and a distinct divine personality (who does this knowing, caring, and influencing), on the other. John of the Cross's God is, if anything, a person. It is the inability of traditional systematic theology and pantheism to offer a consistent theoretical defense of a God who is anything even remotely like a human person that creates the problem of the God of "the philosophers." But philosophers and systematic theologians need not be as inconsistent on the issue of divine personality as traditional thinkers have been.

In this section of the chapter, I would like to suggest that, although John of the Cross would not have used these particular designations, he was not only a panentheist but also a romantic. In defense of this latter claim, it is worthwhile to consider the thought of one of the great romanticism scholars, Thomas McFarland. "Romanticism" is one of those words thrown around loosely by almost everyone who has some facility with the English language. Sometimes it is synonymous with Hollywood films, at other times with unbridled hopes or emotions. McFarland's more precise use of the term refers to a "phenomenology of the fragment."[15] At every turn it seems that human existence is fragmentary. Our perception only gives us a limited grasp of reality. How limited a grasp we have is the topic for epistemologists. Right now I am viewing a bookcase whose back I cannot see; David Hume made much of this. And, as McFarland notes, the books in my bookcase are fragments of intellectual history; even the best libraries are fragments. Romanticism, like religion, consists in how one reacts to the diasparactive character of human existence (from the Greek *diasparaktos,* to be torn to pieces). The romantic theist (think of John of the Cross's poems titled "Romances") exhibits two features. He (1) longs for reticulative wholeness (2) in the midst of the diasparactive shards of life.

John of the Cross's life was a romantic one in the sense that he had an intense longing for wholeness because, like a field of ice, his life was broken into fragments which were "wracked grotesquely out of their plane."[16] From chapter two, we can recall some of the salient features of this life: the death of his father, his homelessness as a child, his persecution by the Calced and then by the Discalced, his illness then early death, and so forth. But John of the Cross never lost sight of the fact that these splinters came from a vast quarry. Nor did he ever pity himself in that he was well aware of the fact that incompleteness, fragmentation, and ruin were not idiosyncratic to his life, but are central features of human existence itself. Peter Brown's description of Augustine as a romantic could apply just as well (or even better, given the intense living flames of love in his thought and given the longing he had for God as an organic head to the mystical body of the world) to John of the Cross:

> If to be a "Romantic" means to be a man acutely aware of being caught in an existence that denies him the fullness for which he craves, to feel that he is defined by his tension towards something else, by his capacity for faith, for hope, for longing, to think of himself as a wanderer seeking a country that is always distant, but made ever-present to him by the quality of the love that "groans" for it, then Augustine has imperceptibly become a "Romantic."[17]

It is ironic that the Catholic church was, in John of the Cross's day if not in Augustine's, a diasparactive mess when it is considered that the word "catholic" literally means universal or "through the whole."

A sense of longing permeates the thought of John of the Cross and of the greatest romantics. This longing often appears in romanticism as a fascination for distant countries or times, as in Samuel Taylor Coleridge's *Kubla Khan,* or as in John of the Cross's fantasy poems, including "The Spiritual Canticle." An inner sanctuary is also a logical outcome of such longing. This sanctuary is a function of the desire to make it less likely that there be inner ruin even if it is assured that there be outer ruin in one's life. It is here that the oft-noted distinction between classicism and romanticism should be noted, with John of the Cross exhibiting many of the tendencies of the latter. The classical ideal was found in the alleged perfection of human nature and in the wholeness of human institutions. The Carmelite's interior castle is the locus for longing, for melancholy if not self-pity, and is an indication of the belief that human wholeness can only be achieved by union with an other being who is truly a whole. As we have seen above, fragmentariness can easily be a feature of supposed wholes like nations. A spiritual person like John of the Cross is attractive to us today largely because his imperfect striving for union with a real whole strikes us, in an age far more characterized by diasparactive confusion than John of the Cross's, as more authentic than flawless striving for a pseudo-whole.

It needs to be emphasized that from the diasparactive character of human existence John of the Cross did not infer pessimism or cynicism. To banish imperfection is to banish expression; to bemoan our fragmentariness is dangerously close to giving up on the only instrument we have to achieve union with God.[18] As with most romantics, John of the Cross sees nature as an organic whole, and as with many romantics, he symbolizes God as the head of this whole. As McFarland puts the point:

> . . . organism and symbolism address themselves to the same problem: they both are endeavors to adjudicate the relationship of parts to wholes. They are, moreover, concerns in which, although the wholes are accorded theoretical honor, the experienced reality is that of parts. In truth, the very word symbol, in its Greek derivation, implies a putting together of something torn apart. . . . The symbol is a diasparact. . . . In every symbol the mind proceeds from the contemplation of a fragment of reality to the apprehension but not the comprehension. . . of a larger entity.[19]

John of the Cross's (and Teresa of Avila's) fascination with water in particular as a symbol for divine presence, with the ocean as a symbol for infinity, and with a stream as a symbol for process, makes it possible to read the following prose from William Wordsworth in sanjuanistic terms:

> Never did a Child stand by the side of a running Stream, pondering within himself what power was the feeder of the perpetual current, from what never-wearied sources the body of water was supplied, but he must have been inevitably propelled to follow

this question by another: "towards what abyss is it in progress?
what receptacle can contain the mighty influx?" and the spirit of
the answer must have been, though the word might be Sea or
Ocean, accompanied perhaps with an image gathered from a Map,
or from the real object in Nature—these might have been the
letter, but the *spirit* of the answer must have been *as* inevitably, a
receptacle without bounds or dimensions, nothing less than infinity.[20]

And it should be noticed that the close connection between a vast,
cosmic wholeness and sublimity, a connection found often in John
of the Cross, reached a crescendo in the romantic writers of the
nineteenth century. Or derivatively, the sublime is symbolized in
John of the Cross through very large fragments, such as mountains.[21]

Imagination is one logical response to diasparactive limitation,
but the construction of false wholes constitutes another response.
Books feign completeness, but any book, including this one, is a
fragment. This is a diasparactive study of John of the Cross's fragmented life and thought, but both of these diasparacts are parts of
a reticulative intent. McFarland asks the following key questions;
he also implicitly answers them:

> . . . how can a fragment be identified as a fragment unless
> there is also the conception of a whole from which it is broken off?
> On the other hand, if wholes exist, either in conception, or, as
> seems the case, in actual experience, how can it be maintained
> that our perception of reality is in fact fragmented?[22]

This contraction and expansion of vision, both of which are needed
in the religious life, can be understood better if three sorts of wholes
are distinguished: (1) nominal wholes (like John of the Cross's works
or books about John of the Cross's works), and (2) organic wholes
(like John of the Cross himself or the author of the present book)
are, when contrasted with (3) The Great Whole (God), diasparacts.
Hence no harm is done by analyzing John of the Cross's works,
liberating them by literally breaking them up. As McFarland has
it, regarding the art of criticism:

> It is a diasparactive process: a tearing apart of a cultural configu-
> ration. Every critic in some sense murders to dissect; his armed
> vision, like Goethe's microscope, gains greater understanding at
> the cost of less naturalness. Every critic to some extent peeps and
> botanizes on the grave of richer emotion. And yet without this

rendering of an entity into its components, no criticism is
possible.... The philosopher finds combination only through
dissolution.... A tearing up of and tearing about in torn up things.
It is thereby both an examination of and an exemplar for the
primacy of diasparactive forms.[23]

Throughout this book, however, I have taken great pains to
support the productive/disruptive philosophical and theological categories I have used with evidence from John of the Cross's texts. In
this case, can there be any doubt that John of the Cross was aware
of the diasparactive character of human existence? He notices
(D, II, 11) that many people wander about cities howling and sighing
because they are not filled with love (Ps. 58:7, 15–16); they suffer a
(spiritual) hunger like the dogs. Yet, in the midst of the dark, the
soul feels the presence of someone; it is conscious within itself of
the lack of an immense (*gran*) and incomparable good (D, II, 13).
John of the Cross looks like a pessimist, even like a nihilist, if one
only notices his claim that *life is short* and that all comes to an end
and fails like falling water (2 Kings 14:14), but John of the Cross
takes literally the biblical notion (Luke 14:11; Matt. 23:12) that
God exalts those who are humbled (S, 1, 1; S, 34, 1). The caverns of
feeling suffer profoundly when they lack God, he thinks, but the
reason why these caverns are so deep in the first place is that they
are naturally fit to receive a deep object (L, 3, 18; L, 3, 22). (Here
John of the Cross has God inside of humanity, but this is not so
much a reversal of panentheism as an unintended consequence of
John of the Cross's tendency to view the relationship between God
and the soul in terms of sexual union.)

As before, the fragmentary character of human existence is
mirrored in writing, and in writing about God in particular, and
most particularly in John of the Cross's writings about God. The
nuns at Granada, pestered by Diego Evangelista, burned a whole
sack of John of the Cross's letters and writings.[24] And several of his
extant letters are fragments because they were cut up so as to be
placed in reliquaries.[25] Even more significant, however, is the
diasparactive character of John of the Cross's major works. Consider
Brenan's remark:

The *Ascent of Mount Carmel* and the *Dark Night of the Soul*
in reality make up one book. In the *Living Flame of Love* (I, 25) San
Juan brackets them together under the title of *The Dark Night of
the Ascent of Mount Carmel*.... The *Ascent,* which is divided up

into three books, describes their (the senses and the spirit) active purgation, whereas the *Dark Night,* which is divided into two books, describes their passive purgation. Both are written in the form of commentaries on his poem *En una noche oscura,* but the *Ascent* does not get beyond the exposition of the last line of the second stanza, while the *Dark Night* stops suddenly one line further on. Thus the six stanzas of the poem which describe the illuminative stage and the state of union receive no commentary at all.[26]

Why were these works not finished? Did John of the Cross not have time to finish them? Or were his completed versions of these works lost after his death? The former is a real alternative. John of the Cross informs us that because of a lack of time (and, in some instances, a lack of paper!) his writings had to be concise (although he complains about the shortness of the letters he receives). He had so much to do in life that when he had a chance to write he did so in haste. At other times he could not write letters because he was in an out-of-the-way place like Segovia (M, counsels, 1; M, letters, 4, 10, 20). And even with respect to the writings he did complete, John of the Cross felt the need to leave additional reminders to his followers so they would not get confused; he had to emphasize to his followers the need to ruminate on his sayings like sheep.[27]

Like many romantics, John of the Cross mythically locates (A, III, 26) a state of *human* wholeness "in the beginning":

> In the state of innocence all that our first parents saw, spoke of, and ate in the garden of paradise served them for more abundant delight in contemplation, since the sensory part of their souls was truly subjected and ordered to reason (*razón*).

And like the romantics, John of the Cross indicates that springtime recapitulates this state of *inocencia* for us; as does dawn; and as do the virtues which are acquired in youth, the period which John of the Cross refers to as life's cool morning (S, 30, 3–4).

However, John of the Cross's usual level-headedness is evident here. His point is not to deny the fall, "when" human nature was corrupted (see "The Spiritual Canticle," 1-12), a denial which would also constitute a rejection of the disparactive character of human existence, wherein one is tempted to weep for fear that one has been forgotten ("More Stanzas," 2). Rather, his point seems to be that divine hope springs eternal ("Song of the Soul," 1–2), as the cliché has it, even in the midst of fragmentation; he believes that this "in the beginning" innocence is recoverable at any moment *because* it is eternal ("Romance 1," 1–2). Creation is *always* the body of Christ ("Romance 4," 14), as is alleged in panentheism. Union with God, which is the goal of mystical theology, is the sweetest spring of all. There is always fragmentation, but there is always this opportunity for union with God. The footprints of the religious seeker are the traces of a soul seeking the prior path trod by God; the religious seeker can always detect the fragrance of God's prior presence (S, 25, 3–4; S, 39, 8). A nightingale's song makes a difference to God (even the fall of a sparrow makes a difference to God), but a human being's search for God is of much greater importance, of such importance that only an omnibenevolent being is worthy of such a search (S, 39, 9; M, sayings, 32).

It should now be obvious that John of the Cross's response to the fragmentary character of human existence, and to the fragmentary character of events in nature, was not to justify an exploitation of nature. Both human beings and other natural fragments are included within Nature as an integral whole, that is, within the life of God. As Frost quaintly puts the point, one will not be at peace as long as one wants to pluck a flower rather than to admire it.[28] John of the Cross's panentheism, linked with a type of aestheticism, will remain unintelligible to those who only notice how human achievement is ruined. But, as Wordsworth noticed at Tintern Abbey and in "Intimations of Immortality," even the contemplation of ruins and of failure can be edifying in that when human constructions fall nature continues to grow in the cracks. Further, human achievement can never be totally lost if there is a God: what having been, must ever be. For example, today in Israel at Wadi Es Siah lie the ruins of the original Carmelite community, ruins which are neither totally secluded, as in a deep valley, nor high on a mountain overlooking all surrounding them. Rather, these instructive ruins exhibit a balance in that they are enclosed enough to remind one that God is one's focus in a sanjuanistic life, yet open enough to the nearby Mediterranean that one can appreciate God's presence in the world at large.[29]

CHAPTER 5

Language

Do not send me
No quieras enviarme
Any more messengers,
De hoy más ya mensajero,
They cannot tell me what I must hear. . . .
Que no saben decirme lo que quiero. . . .
Silent music,
La música callada,
Sounding solitude.
La soledad sonora.

St. John of the Cross, "The Spiritual Canticle"

May the tongue I speak with
Con mi paladar se junte
Cling to my palate
La lengua con que hablaba
If I forget you
Si de ti yo me olvidare
In this land where I am. . . .
En la tierra do moraba. . . .
Babylon.
Babilonia.

St. John of the Cross, "By the Waters of Babylon"

Orality and Literacy

Thus far in this book I have used language, and I have quoted the language of others, in the attempts to understand John of the

Cross and to use John of the Cross to help us today to understand mystical theology. It has been my hope that solitude and *praxis,* as well as the importance of gender issues in religion and a concern for nature, have been served well in my efforts. The present chapter is an attempt to analyze the instrument through which we, along with John of the Cross, can talk about God and the religious life. The first step in such an analysis will be an elaboration of the distinction between oral and literate uses of language, a distinction which will be helpful in understanding both John of the Cross, in particular, and religious discourse, in general. Most are now familiar with Marshall McLuhan's famous dictum that "the medium is the message."[1] Simply put, he suggests that the form of any medium, as well as its content, determines what is being communicated. In this section of the chapter, I suggest that McLuhan's dictum is a helpful one in understanding John of the Cross.

My thesis centers around the notion of a sensorium, by which I mean the entire external sensory apparatus of a human being. What is little noticed is the way in which the sensorium is organized. It can justifiably be said that there have only been two organizing principles to the sensorium in Western religion: the oral-aural mode of organization and the visual mode of organization. Furthermore, there has been a major shift in that sensorium, an ignorance of which causes many problems in religion.

The history of the West started in an oral-aural culture. The medium of speech-hearing dominated the other senses. In preliterate society truth was found in the word, that is, in the spoken word of myth. Cultural memory was preserved in the mnemonic devices incorporated into epic poetry, making it possible for the Homeric bards to have "memorized" all of the *Iliad* and *Odyssey.* These bards were not just poets or performers, but also encyclopaedists preserving expertise in ruling, sailing, religion, war, agriculture, ad infinitum. The hypnotic effect of the bard's medium led to a formulaic approach to knowledge that precluded analyticity. Just as we know the length of the months through the saying "Thirty days hath September. . ." the preliterate person preserved all of his knowledge about the world in this fashion. *To the extent that* John of the Cross's poetry commits him to orality he also exhibits these qualities of orality.

After thousands of years of oral-aural culture, a significant shift in the sensorium occurred, a shift which itself took centuries to accomplish. The written word gave prominence to vision in that the word was no longer primarily spoken-heard, but seen on the spatial continuum of a page. Literacy was not just an aid in the recording of information. It also caused a revolutionary shift in the sensorium and in religious consciousness, as we will see in the case of John of the Cross. The key figures in this transition were Homer and Plato. Although Homer's myths were written down, it is surprising how few people ever read them. It was the bard with his mesmerizing power who kept these stories alive for so many centuries.

Plato's critique of Homer must be seen in this light. In a thesis-antithesis relationship, Plato's forms were polar opposites to the oral-aural life-world. Spoken words are events in time; specifically, present time. Their transitoriness contrasts with the forms, which are outside of time; not heard, but "seen" by the mind's eye. The Greek word *idea* itself means the look of a thing. It was only an escape from the constant recitation of the mythic stories that allowed theology and philosophy to be born in the light of a new day for the West. But the transition from orality to literacy was not complete in Plato, nor is it in John of the Cross. Plato's great teacher, Socrates, left nothing of his philosophy in writing. This is a state of affairs that is incomprehensible from the perspective of a literate culture, but is one that makes sense against the oral background of ancient Greece. Plato did write, but calculatingly in the dialogue style to preserve the cast of dialectic, which is basically an oral medium. His distrust of writing if often exhibited, for example in the *Phaedrus* (274) when he suggests that writing is merely useful for recall, not for wisdom, and in the *Seventh Letter* (344), where he suggests that no knowledge worth having can be communicated in writing. It is helpful to consider Plato here because, as we will see, John of the Cross has a similar reverence for, yet scepticism of, intellect and language.

This shift in the sensorium continued throughout the Middle Ages. There is a famous scene in the *Confessions* (Book VI) where Augustine saw Ambrose reading without speaking, without even moving his lips. Augustine was amazed! Two conclusions can be reached: that by the fifth century A.D. literacy had worked its way into culture *and* that this literacy was rare. The oral media of rhetoric and dialectic still held sway. Even as late as the high Middle Ages orality concomitantly reigned with literacy. As in ancient Greece, students read very little. Just as it is difficult to imagine Aristotelian peripatetics reading as they walked (although we can imagine them talking), it is also difficult to imagine students reading much in the medieval universities, contrary to the bookish reputation of the scholastics, because of the paucity of written works. Disputation was the order of the day, and it was only after disputation that anyone would (or perhaps could) consider writing. Notice the reversal at work here from the perspective of a more complete literacy. Cicero delivered his oration first and *then* wrote his words down, sometimes years after the speech. Thomas Aquinas disputed first (as with Cicero, without written notes) *then* wrote the *Summa Theologiae* in a style only understandable against the background of a residual orality: objections first, position, replies to objections.

The triumph of literacy (sight over sound) initiated by Plato was never consummated until just after John of the Cross around the time of Descartes. His logic was not the art of discourse of earlier ages, which demanded a communal setting, but the art of meditation; that is, isolated and individual meditation. What is important is that this triumph was largely due to the medium of print, as opposed to the handwritten texts of the Greeks and medievals. Descartes was perhaps the first truly great philosopher after Gutenberg. The commitment of sound to space initiated with the alphabet and intensified by the movable type altered humanity's attitude toward itself and the world. Both were curiously silent.

The separation from the source of oral spontaneity makes possible the life-giving potential of alienation. Reading and writing allow one to keep life at arm's length. Integral to oral culture is the live interaction between speaker and audience. But reading and writing are usually done (and best done) in the absence of others. Without direct audience pressure it is possible for solitude, irony, and subtlety to triumph over *mimesis*. Since persons communicate with each other largely through voice, the silencing of words portends withdrawal into oneself. Think here of John of the Cross with his ever-present Bible in hand, not for the purposes of preaching, but for meditative purposes.

It is my hope that the patient reader can see why this brief history of the transition from orality to literacy is helpful when considering John of the Cross. He, like Plato and the medievals and Descartes, straddles both orality and literacy, but he leans more toward the post-Gutenberg Cartesians than any of the medievals *largely because* of the structural changes in the media in which religious discourse was engaged. It is also worthwhile noting that both sanjuanistic *soledad* and Cartesian meditation are largely due to the Jesuit educations that John of the Cross and Descartes received, educations where the private workings of imagination were emphasized.

That John of the Cross saw value in orality can be seen when he supports the Pauline dictum (Rom. 10:17) that *hearing* is believing (A, II, 27; A, III, 31; S, 14, 15), a dictum which made a great deal of sense in the first century when it is considered that most of Paul's hearers would have been illiterate. Nor should it escape our notice that Jesus was, like Socrates, an oral teacher who only wrote, as far as the biblical evidence suggests, in the sand. This makes it clear why he spoke in parables and through repetitive mnemonic devices (for example, blessed are the poor in spirit for they shall receive the kingdom of God, and so on). John of the Cross characteristically, however, takes Paul's dictum to refer not to physical hearing, but to the soul's "hearing," which is, he thinks, allied to the intellect's "vision." Likewise, Brenan alerts us to how moved John of the Cross was by the popular love songs he heard from his brother, Francisco; but John of the Cross took them in a religious sense.[2]

John of the Cross also notices that in the biblical account of the Creation, it is when God *said* "Let there be light" (*fiat lux*) that light came into being (L, 3, 71; also his poem on creation, "Romance, 4"). But in general John of the Cross is sceptical of orality in that it seems to be the locus for many useless things. He finds that people work hard at flattery and ostentatious utterances (S, 28, 7), hence it should not surprise us that he personally disliked unnecessary conversation.[3]

We know that when John of the Cross preached he did so with lucidity and conviction,[4] but preaching was a provocative good that could easily be abused. Preaching is only worthwhile if the good it produces is spiritual rather than vocal, if its beauty lies not in exterior eloquence but in interior benefit. Reminding us of claims made in chapter two on *praxis,* John of the Cross emphasizes that more important than eloquence (although this is somewhat important) for a preacher is practicing what one preaches.

> No matter how lofty the doctrine preached, or polished the rhetoric, or sublime the style in which the preaching is clothed, the profit does not ordinarily increase because of these means in themselves. . . . The better the life of the preacher the more abundant the fruit, no matter how lowly his style, poor his rhetoric, and plain his doctrine. For the living spirit enkindles fire. But when this spirit is wanting, the gain is small, however sublime the style and doctrine, and well-chosen words are more moving and productive of effect when accompanied by this good spirit, yet, without it, even though delightful and pleasing to the senses and

> the intellect, the sermon imparts little or no devotion to the
> will. . . . The sermon merely delights the sense of hearing, like a
> musical concert of sounding bells. . . . It is of little significance that
> one kind of music is more pleasing to me than another. . . . Although
> the preacher may speak remarkable truths, these will soon be
> forgotten since they do not enkindle the will. . . Accidents of the
> sermon. . . . Indeed, neither is the Apostle's intention nor mine to
> condemn good style, and rhetoric, and effective delivery. . . . Elegant
> style and delivery lifts up and restores even those things that
> have fallen into ruin, just as poor presentation spoils what is good
> and destroys (A, III, 45).

John of the Cross's scepticism regarding orality, however, is
not utter disdain. He was, after all, a poet, and a poem is, like a
dialogue, a written work that has its roots in orality, in the *sound* of
words. Poems are meant to be recited aloud. Brenan alerts us to
the great burst of poetic composition John of the Cross had while in
prison in 1578, a burst which continued for a few years afterwards,
but with diminished force. Immediately after his escape, he recited
these poems to the nuns at Beas who *then* wrote them down. Only
parts of these poems were written down in prison when a jailer
slipped writing implements to him under cover. I will argue, however,
that these poems, written in contemplative prayer (*en oración*), owe
more to the *soledad* ushered in with literacy than they do to the
chatty world of the marketplace.[5]

The three great lyric poems of John of the Cross (*Cantico, Noche
Oscura,* and *Llama*) have established him as one of the greatest
Spanish poets. It is through literacy that we must trace the flow of
poetic words, a flow which leads us to the source of John of the
Cross's wisdom, to what he believed to be the literal in-spiration
which "dictated" to him. Brenan notes the following regarding the
influences on John of the Cross's poetry:

> There is the popular element of the song books and of rural life;
> the influence, prosodic and pastoral, of Garcilaso de la Vega and of
> Renaissance Italy; the erotic and oriental layer of the *Song of Songs,*
> and lastly his personal experiences.[6]

These sources of John of the Cross's poetry are real enough, but
one should also notice the directness of John of the Cross's language,
his lack of ornamentation:

> The *Cantico* starts out with a cry of longing and anguish, but
> almost at once this changes to an air-borne feeling of lightness,

clarity, exhilaration, speed of movement. There is a sense of travel and adventure: mountains, rivers, valleys, dawns, breezes, "strange islands" come and go; lions, antelopes, birds, flowers are seen and left behind. . . . Yet the voluptuousness that blows in from the East is tempered by an astonishing delicacy. This poetry is virginal. . . . The distinctness and precision of the language. As each verbal note is struck, another follows without blurring or overlap. The words are clear, clean, almost transparent, yet sufficiently full for their purpose. . . . Adjectives. . . are rare. . . . It is this, of course, that gives his poems their lightness and speed of movement. . . . There is a density and complexity of allusion in these poems that prove the absurdity of supposing that San Juan de la Cruz was merely an "inspired" poet who wrote his poems in ecstasies. A long period of preparation, both conscious and unconscious, preceded their composition.[7]

Brenan's last remakrs correctly alert us to the fact that John of the Cross's inspiration should not be taken to mean that he did not have to *think* long and hard about what it was that he wanted to say. John of the Cross's poetry is due, as the romantics have it, to powerful emotions, but these are powerful emotions recollected in tranquility. Or again, consider how careful John of the Cross was in his poetry when he is compared to other poets who also dealt with biblical or romantic themes. Regarding "The Spiritual Canticle," Brenan suggests the following to anyone wanting to read the poem:

> . . . before beginning to read it to make oneself familiar with the *Song of Songs*. . . . One senses its presence everywhere even when one cannot recall the precise allusion. So far as I know there is nothing else quite like this in literature. Milton's poetry is saturated with classical and biblical reminiscences, yet these are brought in mainly as learned references to confirm the fact that he is writing at the end of a long and complex tradition. Eliot's quotations in *The Waste Land* are there to provide a contrast between the sordid present and the lost world of beauty and significance that lies in the past. San Juan's poem on the other hand rises out of another and distinct poetic plane. . . . Yet in doing so its tone has largely been totally changed and sublimated. The *Song of Songs* is a sensual poem dealing with sexual love, whereas in the *Cantico* everything is pure and delicate, most of all the acts of the lovers. . . . For few if any of the words in San Juan's poetry are adventitious or ornamental.[8]

The centrality of poetry in John of the Cross's writings is indicated when he tells us that his stanzas contain all of his doctrine

(A, theme). But along with the nuns at Beas, who were staggered by the depth of John of the Cross's poetry, we feel the need for these stanzas to be explicated, hence we should be grateful for John of the Cross's extensive prose works.[9] Given the economy of sanjuanistic expression and given his desire for solitude, it should not surprise us that these prose commentaries, although extensive, are not nearly as varied or as long as the works of Augustine or Thomas Aquinas. Further, all of John of the Cross's major works were written in the last fourteen years of his life, from the time he was thirty-six until he was forty-nine, hence there is not much to be gained by treating them chronologically; John of the Cross starts writing as a mature thinker.[10]

Later in this chapter, I will treat the issue of whether John of the Cross views language purely as a means to achieve union with God (or to achieve an understanding of that union), or if language should be savored as an end in itself. He gives evidence for both. The careful placement of words in his poetry leads one to believe that the words are to be savored. *If* there are uses of language that are to be valued in themselves, quite apart from the religious effects they bring, they are more likely to be found in John of the Cross's poetry than in his prose. He frequently exhibits an "Aw shucks!" embarassment regarding his prose, with what he considers to be its unpolished style (A, II, 14). Prose is to poetry as a sketch is to a painting, he thinks (S, 12, 6). The predominantly utilitarian approach he often has in his prose work becomes evident in the following:

> . . . even if it were presented with greater accuracy and polish, only a few would find profit in it, because we are not writing on pleasing and delightful themes addressed to the kind of spiritual people who like to approach God along sweet and satisfying paths (A, prologue, 8).

At other times, John of the Cross is kinder to himself, and rightfully so. There is nothing wrong with teaching through a simple prose style which lacks affectation (M, censure). Nor is there anything wrong with writing after one has used one's time in silence well, and as long as one is committed to working through in a practical way the consequences of what one has written. The object of John of the Cross's admonition is the person who is *quick* to write, for he is also likely to be slow to turn to God (M, letters, 7). In subsequent sections of this chapter, however, we will see that there are some things that no writing, poetic or prosaic, unreflective or contemplative, can accomplish. A preliminary example is the inability anyone has of putting to paper *exactly* how it feels to be lonely (M, letters, 10).

The sort of preparation for writing that John of the Cross has in mind largely consists in reading the Bible carefully and repeatedly. John of the Cross himself did his own translations of Scripture from Latin into Spanish, especially the *Song of Songs*. In fact, he paid much more attention to the Bible, it seems, than to other poets.[11] The type of biblical scholarship with which John of the Cross would have been familiar is described by Thompson:

> . . . he has inherited a tradition of exegesis with which today's historical, critical scholarship is almost entirely out of sympathy. It was not until the eighteenth century that the old tradition began to break down; until then, the generally accepted view was that the Bible could be interpreted in different, mutually complementary ways. First came literal or historical exegesis, then the moral sense, the allegorical and finally the analogical or mystical. . . . The analogical and mystical allowed for great imaginative scope in explaining the meaning. . . San Juan does make some use of the literal way, but he has inherited the accepted view that hidden under Scriptural figures lay many clues to the spiritual life which he, either following previous exegetes or using his own insight, was able to uncover.[12]

It is worth reiterating that when one is trying to appropriate the properly spiritual sense of scripture several interpretations are possible even if relativism is defective. Thompson's legitimate insights should be held in check by the equally legitimate insight (or better, invective) of Frost, that modern commentaries on Scripture are surprisingly too literal:

> Anyone who can free himself from the merely literal and so often dreary and commonplace—where not also destructive—character of most modern commentaries upon Holy Scripture, will find here something of that richness which was ever the food and delight of Christian souls, until so many were led astray by the wiles of the devil, who, as Aldous Huxley has so aptly said, began by quoting Scripture, and when that failed, used the Higher Criticism to prove that it had no more value than the *Pickwick Papers*.[13]

John of the Cross uses the following simile to describe his view of legitimate discourse about Scripture: those with poor sight see little in a painting, whereas those with acuity and discipline see so much that there always remains more to be seen in a classic painting (A, II, 5). Religious classics, like the Bible or John of the Cross's own writings, are analogously polysemic, not in the sense that any interpretation is legitimate, but in the sense that an abundance of meaning in religious classics allows a plurality of readings. To claim that several legitimate readings of a classic are possible is not to claim that there are no illegitimate readings. In order to preserve the normative role of religious classics, one need not make the dogmatic claim that only one reading of a text is possible; one only needs to hold that one can have false readings caused by any one of a number of distortions: anachronism, logical inconsistency, the fallacy of accent, and so forth. It is possible to defend a theory of interpretation that allows for both a plurality of readings of a classic and a normative role for the classic in spite of this plurality. Karl Popper has made a similar claim regarding science: several tenable hypotheses for a given state of affairs can be tolerated without abandoning the belief that some hypotheses are untenable, indeed are false.[14]

Language: Literal, Symbolic, and Interpretive

John of the Cross's concentration on the Bible, his use of it as a source, and the fact that he was both a poet and a mystic might lead one to assume that for him all religious discourse was symbolic. The purpose of this section of the chapter is to indicate that this is not entirely true, even if it is largely so, in that there are several layers of religious discourse in John of the Cross that should be distinguished.[15] These layers will be mapped on to distinctions already made in this book regarding dipolar theism. In the next sections of the chapter, I will support the claims made in this section with numerous examples from John of the Cross's writings.

First, regarding the abstract features of God, John of the Cross speaks literally. If one grants the distinction between divine existence and divine actuality, between the fact *that* God exists as opposed to *how* God exists, then it is clear in John of the Cross *that* God's existence is necessary and *that* God cares for all. We have no literal grasp, however, of what *exactly* it is like to exist forever, nor regarding *how* a single being can care for all others.[16] Regarding the *mode* of God's existence, we must resort to analogy (for example, the claim that divine feeling is like human feeling, but without its defects) or symbol (for example, the claim that God feels as a parent). For simplicity's sake, I will refer to both analogical and symbolic uses of religious discourse as symbolic.

Discourse about the necessary existence of deity is literal because it does not need to take account of the differences between one non-divine thing and another (they are all contingent) and because necessary existence can be defined without remainder as the inconceivability of the nonexistence of God. Divine love, however, cannot be talked about literally in that there is no way to state precisely and without remainder the *qualitative* differences between human and divine love. A human being appreciates qualities of this or that person, but God (as *omni*benevolent) cannot not regard the weals or woes of any sentient being. The issue is not resolved by resorting *simpliciter* to negative theology. It is comparatively easy to utter the claim that divine parental love is "nothing like" the love of a human parent, but it is not so easy to defend this claim with consistency. That is, divine symbolism depends on some sort of prior understanding of human attributes or occupations (like love or parenting). Otherwise one runs the risk of an overly zealous journey down the *via negativa:*

> An all too negative theology made God the great emptiness, and an all too negative anthropology made the creatures also empty. I suggest that nothing is only nothing, that the divine attributes are positive, and the creatures' qualities are between these and nothing.[17]

The claim to know God in some sense or fashion is not the same as the claim to know all that God knows; to claim to know *that* God feels all is not to claim to know in any detail what such an awareness would be like. It can be stated literally that God knows all of the United States presidents, but, as Hartshorne asks:

> How, concretely, does God evaluate President Kennedy, in relation to all other men, living and dead, and to all other things, present and past? No combination of human sentences could sensibly pretend to answer this question. Here there is silence. . . . Concreteness is the mystery; the abstract, essential, and necessary we can grasp, and our theoretical intelligence is thus most at home in pure mathematics, dealing with essences and necessities. Theologians seem slow to learn the lesson from this.[18]

It is precisely this concreteness that John of the Cross longs for; it is this intimacy that sanjuanistic union with the divine alleges to give, albeit in a symbolic way, at best, or in an ineffable way, at worst. In either case, John of the Cross in effect confirms Hartshorne's point.

It is here that the continuity between John of the Cross's romantic view of nature and his largely symbolic use of language can be seen. A symbol is, as McFarland reminds us, a comprehensible, diasparactive perception of something less comprehensible but larger. Coleridge puts the point this way regarding a symbol, which is characterized:

> ... above all by the translucence of the Eternal through and in the Temporal. It always partakes of the Reality which it renders intelligible; and while it enunciates the whole, abides itself as a living part in that Unity, of which it is the representative.[19]

McFarland brilliantly draws the connection between symbols, in general, and the necessity of faith, in particular, a connection which will operate like a high-powered searchlight in the illumination of John of the Cross's texts in the next section of this chapter:

> When, for example, I drive a motorcar along a road at night, what I actually perceive in my headlights is a white line and a sign indicating a curve to the right; what I infer from that is that the road is actually going to continue and will indeed turn to the right. But my perception as such is fragmentary—a piecemeal breaking; I act from faith in the symbolic implications of that fragment... as Carlyle says, "It is in and through *Symbols* that man, consciously or unconsciously, lives, works, and has his being. . . ." Were my faith in such symbolic extensions and organic continuations to be in vain, life would be madness, if it could be lived at all. We would all be like the boy in Stevenson's novel, sent up a broken staircase supposedly to a bedroom, to discover by a flash of lightning that an abyss looms before us. Without faith, in other words, diasparactive awareness would be horror. . . . Faith is the necessary complement of the diasparactive perception of reality; it is, as the Bible says, "the evidence of things not seen."[20]

For all of their help, however, symbols can hinder union if their symbolic value is not appreciated and if they are taken in a crude literalness; that is, if they are taken as ends in themselves.[21]

In contrast to some contemporary, rather popular, theories of interpretation fostered by the deconstructionists, there is no isolated world within words for John of the Cross. Rather, for him words are Platonized and used for an ulterior purpose. Words act in John of the Cross as mediators between humanity and God, as instruments used in the discovery of God. And the words used by scholars of John of the Cross should be informed by this discovery. Nietzsche's dictum (which functions normatively for deconstructionists), "There are no facts, only interpretations," is a canard when applied to John of the Cross, who so earnestly states what he believes to be the truth about ourselves and our relationship with God. In this book I have used what Susan Sontag calls "the old style of interpretation," prominent in which is a "piety towards the troublesome text."[22] John of the Cross's text is indeed troublesome, but every intelligent reader agrees that the goal of John of the Cross's mystical theology is union with God. That is, there are some recalcitrant facts about his writings that are just not open to interpretation.

I admit that any interpreter, even one who does not erase or rewrite the text, alters is. My reader's job is to determine if I have, and the degree to which I have, done an injustice to John of the Cross by my alteration. My own sense is that I am "reading off a sense that is already there."[23] That is, there is some legitimacy to what in the introduction I have called the "author-centered approach" in interpretation. But the interpreter should not try to end discourse about an author with a totalitarian-like *braggadocio* that seems to say that "This is what John of the Cross is *really* about." My purpose is the exact opposite: to complicate discourse about John of the Cross, or better, to enrich it by calling attention to aspects of his thought largely ignored in previous treatments of him, even the best ones.

Equally defective as deconstructionist criticism is what Sontag calls "the modern style of interpretation," a position which is defective because of its "open aggressiveness" toward the text, its attempt to get "behind" the text "to find a sub-text which is the true one." (She seems to have certain Freudian, Marxist, and structuralist critics in mind.) My thesis, however, is that we need not get "behind" John of the Cross's works to see that he has a great deal to say about solitude and action, gender and nature, and, of course, mysticism. We need only to read carefully the texts themselves. According to Sontag, today is a time:

> ... when the project of interpretation is largely reactionary, stifling. Like the fumes of the automobile and of heavy industry which befoul the urban atmosphere, the effusion of interpretations of art today poisons our sensibilities. ... Interpretation is the revenge of the intellect upon art.[24]

But I have tried to show that John of the Cross truly is a breath of fresh air; he is a thinker *worthy* of our consideration.

Sontag also (rightfully) bemoans the fact that recent interpretation "tames the work of art. Interpretation makes art manageable, conformable."[25] But I prefer to leave John of the Cross wild, outside of contemporary society's and contemporary academe's neatly tended gardens, in whose bookstores there is no place for John of the Cross or for the other great religious mystics. And if there were such a place, it would be among the occult "sciences" which John of the Cross detested.

What leads many interpreters of John of the Cross astray is the depth of his depressions and the height of his elevation. To assume that the two are mutually exclusive is to fail to consider that they may be the result of looking in opposite directions from one consistent position. Language is the incarnation of thought and is developed from this position. One four-term analogy is to be rejected and another adopted if we are to understand John of the Cross's view of language. The misleading analogy suggests that:

expression: meaning : : garb: body

More helpful is this:

expression: meaning : : body: soul

Words do not merely mirror reality. They reach beneath the transient reality, or grasp above it, to *touch* the enduring reality, to embody it. Symbols and metaphors and analogies do not describe facts but evoke a sense; they evoke a meaning. John of the Cross was astute enough to realize that philosophy and theology are not types of *techne* which encode data; they *need* similes and metaphors and the like. Like amphibians we emerge from our aqueous caves in search of the sun; like lightning God shines the way.

What is not often noticed in some deconstructionist treatments of great writers is that if "literary anarchy" were the case not only could we not (nor could John of the Cross) state the truth with any degree of certainty, but we could not even objectively state what was false. Falsification with assurance (for example, my scratching my head is *not* the cause of the earth rotating on its axis) presupposes that the state of affairs in question is in conflict with some stable reality that acts as a standard. (On deconstructionist grounds we could say only that it does not *seem* that my scratching my head causes the earth to rotate.) John of the Cross was quite definite about what he rejected; even his symbols make this obvious. He indicates his foundationalism in what he refutes as much as in what he defends.

The very notion of a linguistic symbol betrays *some* sort of ontological distinction between the familiar world and that less familiar world that is symbolized, where the latter does not *seem* to be there (the Greek *me on*) to be directly experienced in the familiar world. John of the Cross's genius at least partially consists in taking this less familiar world seriously without falling into surrealism, whereby the world of experienced reality is abandoned altogether. The "meontic" variety of religious language in John of the Cross honors this world, even in its minutiae, while transcending it through a participation (the Greek *methexis*), albeit vicariously through words, in the divine reality. Like the unfolding of a carpenter's rule, a cantilevering of meaning, John of the Cross's words receive their meaning in the act of extension; the meaning of John of the Cross's words is marked on the rule itself to the extent that we get closer to God through them. Yet meontic activity is also a consummatory "shimmering" in its own right, a shimmering which alleviates the diasparactive burden of sanjuanistic fragmentation.

Knowledge of God and Language

Obviously many of the statements made in the previous section of the chapter need support. In this and the remaining sections of the chapter, I will try to treat in detail John of the Cross's texts so as to support the above views. It should first be noted that John of the Cross's concern for language is bound up with his concern for intellect, for saying what one knows. Hence we must return to the strengths and weaknesses of intellect as John of the Cross sees them.

Because of the initial distance between creatures and God (A, I, 5), human beings must use all available means to achieve union with God, including intellect, but not the intellect that seeks to dominate or which is led around by the nose by the senses. Rather, it is a cleansed intellect, and one that is aware of its own limitations, an intellect which is instrumental in achieving union, an intellect whose search for wisdom is compatible with subtle ideas and lofty spiritual concepts (*sutiles y levantadas noticias y conceptos*). Hence, as before, the attempt to gain natural knowledge through sensation can cause advantage and harm (*provecho y daño*) to the soul, depending on exactly how and why such an attempt occurs (A, II, 9–10). John of the Cross's mystical theology has a favorable attitude overall toward intellect largely because in contemplation the natural good of intellectual knowledge is perfected (A, II, 8). John of the Cross is very much interested in improving descriptions of God, even if complete descriptions are beyond our grasp (S, 38, 8).

Knowledge of God is greater to the extent that it is interior, hence natural knowledge gained through sensation is improved if it is supplemented by the "internal senses" of imagination and phantasy, upon which meditation depends (A, II, 12). It must be admitted that imagination is like sensation in that it is not, *strictly speaking,* proportionate to God. But the limitations of imagination help to define the region within which it is helpful. The thought of Roland Barthes can be used here to locate John of the Cross between two extremes. At one end lies Ignatius of Loyola, who takes language very seriously in the effort to provide images to spiritual seekers who are without them, to frame through language, for example, the details of Jesus at supper with his disciples. Indeed, Barthes refers to the "imperialism" of the linguistically constructed image in Ignatius, of the "totalitarian economy" of such images, and of Ignatius's search for a theophany that is really a semiophany. At the other end of the spectrum lies the quietists, who *completely* relinquish images, whether linguistically evoked or not, and who set up a region of experience *completely* discontinuous with language and imagery, a region which is *completely* ineffable. John of the Cross, as Barthes insightfully notices, lies between these two extremes, such that if one emphasizes only the discontinuity between union and articulation, and if one overemphasizes John of the Cross's notion of ineffability (thought about and *described*) by John of the Cross!) he begins to look like a quietist. It is understandable why some interpreters lean in this direction, for by saying that language meant little or nothing to John of the Cross, they hope to exalt the interior longing for God in John of the Cross, which is alleged to be trans-linguistic. But if these interpreters are correct, why does John of the Cross take great pains to speak in such a way as to have us imagine in detail Christ crucified? Likewise, an injustice is done to John of the Cross's mystical theology if he is turned into a logocentric, categorizing systematic theologian.[26] The trick, as before, is to do justice to the complexities of John of the Cross's thought.

John of the Cross is quite clear that our knowledge of God should be remembered as often as possible (A, III, 14), and rational creatures can indeed have vivid knowledge (*vivo conoce*) of God; its vividness indicating cooperation between intellect and imagination. This knowledge is gained both through one's own consideration of God and through a (dialectical) consideration of what others have said (S, 7, 6). That is, knowledge of God is likely, he thinks, if one no longer wants worldly rhetoric, that dry eloquence which feigns true wisdom, and if one directs one's attention to a better (*mejor*) *expression* of God's attributes (L, 3, 14; M, sayings, prologue). In the previous chapter, I claimed that one of the benefits of taking reason seriously in religion, and of explicitly articulating one's rational commitments, is that one is in a better position to notice the surprising religious fact; without such explicit commitments one is in no position to distinguish the surprising fact from the banal one. Consider John of the Cross's own words in this regard:

> Those who understand God more, understand more distinctly the infinitude which remains to be understood; whereas those who see less of Him do not realize so clearly what remains to be seen. . . . The soul experiencing this is aware that what she has so sublimely experienced remains beyond her understanding, she calls it "I-don't-know-what." Since it is not understandable, it is indescribable. . . . Stammering, a trait we notice in children's speech, means that one is unsuccessful in saying and explaining what one *has to say* (S, 7, 7–10—emphasis added).

The limitations of intellect in the religious life only become apparent when intellect is pushed too far. Fideists are fond of saying that one can only go so far in religion with reason, without themselves finding out *how* far. John of the Cross realizes that reason has its limitations because nothing, strictly speaking, *equals* God, and therefore not even the efforts of the most rational human being can fully comprehend God (A, I, 5). Or more precisely, no creature is identical to God's being or God's inner essence even if there *is* union with God's becoming-in-a-context-of-relations. It is the former that is impregnable to rational analysis, and it is the former that we proceed to by way of unknowing (*no entendiendo*); with respect to the latter, reason *is* useful (A, II, 8). Not even imaginative visions are proportionate to, or proximate to, God's *inner* life, to God's being (A, II, 16). It is only easy to understand God's being if we talk uncritically about God in terms of distinctions, like that between genus and species (A, III, 12). As we will see in a moment, in *some* sense it is fair to say that our natural abilities to think and to use language are insufficient to achieve union with God (even if they are necessary) in that at some point contemplative silence must enter into the picture for such union to occur, a condition in which we are removed from the contradiction of tongues so that we can be interiorly absorbed into God (D, II, 14, 16).

John of the Cross is not so much worried that we will think too much in the spiritual life, as that we will think inappropriately. His greatest fear seems to be that we will think that we can obtain "supernatural knowledge" through the senses, and because it comes through the senses we think that we are acting rationally by believing in such "knowledge." John of the Cross is adamant that God's communication to a human being is interior and spiritual and that we should flee from and distrust "voices" from God. Believing in such communications, he thinks, breeds error, presumption, and vanity (*error y presunción y vanidad*). One who purports to receive "supernatural communications" through the natural senses, according to John of the Cross, usually develops a "fine opinion of himself" that is not deserved. Hence, for this reason alone, such communications should not be accepted as reliable. Further, if the whole point to the spiritual life is to develop an interior life so as to be aware of one's diasparactive fragmentation as well as one's inclusion within the divine whole, then such a project is thwarted if one develops a fetish for, and a possessiveness with respect to, these "communications." One can easily start to put stock in these voices or visions or trances to the point where it is difficult to return to reason or to faith. John of the Cross's poetic way of putting the point is to suggest that these "communications," if taken seriously, are as difficult to eliminate as the beast of the Apocalypse (A, II, 11).

Another sort of "communication" that receives criticism from John of the Cross is evidence from God through dreams. Even if God does communicate to us in dreams, there is no assurance that we will understand God any better than we do while awake. The literal interpretation of dreams, like the literal interpretation of the Bible, is, according to John of the Cross, the outer rind (presumably, to be spit out). For example, when God promised Jacob to lead him out of Egypt, Jacob failed to understand that this promise referred to his offspring, hence for Jacob to take solace for himself from the dream is an exemplification of the consistent sanjuanistic belief that the "animal man" can only think literally (that is, in this instance, crudely). Alluding to 2 Cor. 3:6, John of the Cross affirms the belief that the letter kills, but the spirit gives life (A, II, 19).

To trust in voices and the like is to suggest that there is not enough food for thought and meditation, and not enough prompting from God, found in Jesus: neither *logos* nor *Logos,* nor both together, are deemed sufficient. Quoting Matt. 17:5, John of the Cross thinks it appropriate that God was pleased with the Son (A, II, 22; also "Romance, 8"). Even if the Word is hidden in each soul, those who seek for It will, he thinks, find; and Jesus as an ethical teacher is readily available to all (S, 1, 6). Those who flock to the sites of supposed miracles or who champion this or that vision no doubt think that they are doing religion a favor, but actually they are unwitting partners in the process of religious decay. The sanjuanistic response to such decay, evident already in John of the Cross's day, is to redeem language, to remake it into the sort of instrument which facilitates union with God: The Word is immensely subtle and delicate (*El Verbo es inmensamente sutil y delicado*—L, 2, 19; also see "First Romance"), as opposed to garish and histrionic.

In short, for John of the Cross miracles should occasion little joy because they do not unite the soul with God as well as love does. Using Paul and Matthew for his purposes, John of the Cross puts the point as follows:

> If I speak with the tongues of men and of angels and have not charity, I am become as the sounding metal or bell. And if I should have prophecy and know the mysteries and all knowledge, and if I should have all faith so as to move mountains, and have not charity, I am nothing" (1 Cor. 13:1–2). . . . "Lord, did we not prophesy in your name and work many miracles?" He will answer: "Depart from Me, workers of iniquity" (Matt. 7:22–23; A, III, 30).

Even if one receives communications from God through the natural senses (and we are told that John of the Cross himself had a few visions, although he makes nothing of them), these are not to be confused with union. Rare experiences are more remarkable than they are credible (S, 1, 4; L, 1, 15). Thoreau, whose quiet religiosity is in many ways similar to John of the Cross's, catches well John of the Cross's sense when he says regarding a hardworking man named John Farmer, who was asked:

> Why do you stay here and live this mean moiling life, when a glorious existence is possible for you? Those same stars twinkle

over other fields than these. But how to come out of this condition and actually migrate thither? All that he could think of was to practise some new austerity, to let his mind descend into his body and redeem it, and treat himself with ever increasing respect.[27]

It is precisely such "respect" that devotees of visions and trances lack.

It might be asked at this point what sort of communication from the divine to the human can legitimately occur for John of the Cross. Two sorts of response are possible. First, as we have seen, John of the Cross believes that "God speaks" through Jesus (*logos*), such that, in a way, God becomes mute (*mudo*) for those who do not engage in an appropriate reading of Scripture (A, II, 22). The second sort of response presupposes an understanding of three sorts of divine locution, the first two of which John of the Cross rejects: (1) Some of these locutions are successive, wherein the hearer "hears" precise words from God strung together; John of the Cross thinks that these words are often false and that usually nothing whatsoever has really happened when such locutions are alleged to occur. Although it is *possible* that these locutions be part of discursive meditation, it is more than likely, *if* they occur, that they encourage vainglory, hence they are not nothing but "worse than nothing." (2) The other rejected sort of locution is formal, where one word is "heard" without a succession. *If* such a locution occurs, John of the Cross urges, one should resign oneself to its occurrence and then ignore it (A, II, 29).

(3) The third sort of divine locution, and the second sort of legitimate communication from God in addition to that which comes from appropriate reading of Scripture, is what John of the Cross calls "substantial" or "vital" locution, which one should receive quietly and with dignity. Here we do not use our ears but our hearts; these divine words paradoxically require silence to be heard, a paradox to be treated in the next chapter (A, III, 3). Here I would like to emphasize that for John of the Cross appropriate communication with God requires a symbiosis of Aaron's eloquence and Moses' stammering; one without the other is defective (A, II, 22). The tranquility of the spiritual person would be disturbed by such "supernatural" phenomena such as "voices" as well as by natural phenomena such as memories, the latter of which lead to an unsettled (*alterada*) soul (A, III, 5–6). Or more precisely, in order to "hear" God, one needs detachment from memories, except perhaps the habitual remembrance of God from previous experiences of union (A, III, 15; D, I, 12–13; D, II, 8).

It must be admitted that John of the Cross did, in fact, believe that people had experiences of God in which sensory evidence was the medium for the experience, but he believed that such experiences were rare. Further, like William James, he believed that it is not the mere having of such experiences that is important, but their efficacy. And according to John of the Cross, the efficacy of raptures and the like is minimal because if these experiences occur it is only at the beginning of a truly spiritual life (D, II, 1), in that a person with a firm interior life does not need a parade of extraordinary experiences to have a relationship with God. Hence, the issue which is of immediate interest to many when they consider mystical theology, that of determining criteria for discerning true supernatural experiences from false ones, is not crucial for John of the Cross, although he is aware of the dangers of egregiously false discernment, as when magicians or soothsayers are taken seriously (A, III, 31).

Those who have achieved some measure of spiritual perfection do receive communications from God, but they are the sorts of tranquil and loving communications mentioned in chapter one, those that are characterized by a silent music and sounding solitude (*callada música y soledad sonora*) which melts the soul (S, 13, 6; S, 24, 6; L, 1, 17). For John of the Cross it is the *solitary* bird who sings sweetly in the contemplation of its spouse (M, maxims, 42), a contemplation to be treated in much more detail in the final chapter on mysticism.

Means and Ends

The seriousness of language in John of the Cross becomes apparent when he criticizes spiritual directors who create something of a Tower of Babel by failing to understand the importance of religious language (A, prologue, 4). The issue I am concerned with in this section of the chapter is the problem of how one can pay careful attention to language and hence value it for its own sake, on the one hand, and simultaneously see language as a means to union with God, on the other. A preliminary example of how an entity can be both a means and an end is provided by food, which is conducive to bodily health, but is also, one hopes, tasty in its own right. To concentrate solely on the instrumental value of food is to aesthetically diminish life in a significant way, whereas concentrating solely on the taste of food as an end in itself, say by only eating sweets, is physiologically unsound. An analogous situation exists with respect to language. By concentrating solely on language as a religious tool we aesthetically diminish life, say by failing to appreciate John of the Cross's poetry; but by overconcentrating on the pleasing surface of his poetry we miss the substance of his work.

Kavanaugh points out the obvious distinction between art and entertainment, where the latter refers to an overconcentration on the words or images in themselves with no ulterior purpose.[28] He catches well here the spirit of John of the Cross. John of the Cross is clear that there is nothing wrong with religious art (a redundancy in John of the Cross) *as long as* it helps one to advance spiritually (A, III, 15). That is, "the good soul should. . . be. . . cautious in the use of good things." Words and images are good things largely because they are motivating means toward religious improvement, hence it is crucial, according to John of the Cross, to distinguish the accidental from the spiritually substantial in a work of art (A, III, 37). If one remains fixed on the pleasantness of words used in spiritual exercises, there is a tendency to do the exercises only for the sake of their satisfaction, for example, there have been many performances, no doubt, of Bach's Mass in B Minor where little religious value was accrued to either the musicians or audience. To be detained by the satisfaction of religious means, John of the Cross thinks, shows not a highly refined aesthetic sensitivity, but the faulty working of one's will (M, precautions, 17; M, letters, 12).

The instrumental/intrinsic value found in language applies as well in John of the Cross to other human constructions like statues and paintings. These are valuable for several reasons: if done well (that is, if they have intrinsic value as works of art), they awaken us from religious lukewarmness and they remind us, however inadequately, that God is a person, which is no insignificant point. But the devout person, John of the Cross thinks, does not need many of these works of art to derive their benefit, nor does he need to rejoice in their ornamentation with jewelry, and so forth, a practice which John of the Cross views as an abomination. A statue's instrumentality (*medio*) should always be made compatible with a religious believer's simple and pure (*pureza*) heart (A, III, 35–36). Likewise, there is no need for extravagance in religious ceremonies, even if there is a need for religious ceremony, as we saw in chapter two. A strong attachment to ceremony is, for John of the Cross, unsufferable (*insufrible*), especially because such an attachment is but half a step away from superstition. The more one trusts ceremonies, he thinks, the less trust one has in God. That is, ceremonies and prayers should be engaged in mindfully, hence if one finds oneself saying mindless prayers, he thinks, one can better occupy oneself with *praxis* until ready to pray in a purer frame of mind (A, III, 43–44).

Language, works of art, beautiful natural settings, pilgrimages, church architecture, et al., can be good things. For example, a beautiful church (as opposed to an ugly one) can obviously facilitate meditation, but if one becomes too attached to stained glass one might not be able to meditate anywhere but in church, hence John of the Cross urges a minimalist approach whereby one should meditate where meditation is hindered least. For this reason churches can be beautiful, but they should not be too comfortable; religious pilgrimages should not turn into Club Med vacations; and although the workmanship (*hechura*) of a statue should be acknowledged, it should not be taken in itself as a divine gesture (A, III, 36, 39, 41).

Frost understands John of the Cross's view well:

> St. John. . . has some very plain things to say about the use of sacred images, and makes severe strictures upon various pious practices almost in the tone of a non-Catholic. It might almost be said that he is at one with the latter in regarding Catholicism as a dangerous religion, for the reason that it does make an appeal to the aesthetic and emotional side to human nature. But he knows, as the non-Catholic does not, that its danger derives precisely from the fact that it is such a good thing, since it is the best not the worst things which are most dangerous to man. . . . A practicing Christian may listen to music, look at pictures, read novels, take an interest in all kinds of "non-religious" things, play games, etc., so far as and as long as none of this begins to infringe upon his love and service of God.[29]

Frost is correct in alerting us to the fact that it is not always the most exquisite art that moves us religiously. We are told that John of the Cross himself carved simple religious figures out of wood and that he had paintings done for the cloister. His own drawing of Christ crucified, which served as a model for the famous painting by Salvador Dali, serves as an example of simple, albeit religiously powerful, art. The desire for grand works of art, for baroque ornamentation, is analogous to the desire to found religion on grand or ornate religious experiences, like vision or voices. Frost is again helpful regarding:

> . . . those various physical phenomena of rapture, trances and
> the like which, regarded by some as evident signs of high sanctity,
> are but the consequence of the inability of the frail body to bear
> the increasingly strong spiritual communications made to the soul,
> and which, as the sensible part grows purer, flow from the soul
> into the senses, sometimes causing bodily sufferings. . . . there are
> numerous instances of saints who have prayed that God would
> lessen such communications because of the effects they caused in
> the body.[30]

Here Frost not only properly locates the status of divine signs
manifested in a physical way, he also offers a clue as to how such
signs (as in the stigmata) can be seen as compatible with a natural-
istic view of the world.

Grand art that feigns religious fervor (as in Wagnerian opera)
is also dangerous because it is barely distinguishable from the
symbolism of mass movements in modern culture. However, Frost
would discourage us from the inference that religious festivals or
other public expressions of religiosity should be abandoned, as has
come to be the case in northern Europe and throughout most of the
English speaking world. Festivals are not necessarily primitive and
do not necessarily predispose one to an uncritical approach to religion. For example, Frost emphasizes the sanjuanistic approach to
miracles in these terms:

> . . . the Christian will always do best in following the example
> of St. Louis who, being told that a miracle was taking place at
> Mass, refused to go and witness it, saying that no miracle was
> needed to assure him of the truth.[31]

The point deserves repeating if only because of a pervasive misun-
derstanding of mystical theology, concerning which John of the
Cross can act as an antidote. The highest degrees of the spiritual
life do *not* include the following:

> . . . ecstasies, locutions, visions, and other extraordinary
> phenomena. . . . These things are "extraordinary," gratuitous graces
> which have nothing essentially to do with the higher stages of the
> Christian life.[32]

If one understands the function of language in John of the Cross
one can better understand ecstasies and the like. Such experiences
are best judged by the effects they bring on subsequent thought

and behavior and are not to be savored primarily for their own sake.[33]

Language per se, as opposed to other human art forms or other religious instruments, can easily degenerate into the habitual imperfection of trifling conversation, an imperfection which often appears in the guise of loquacity or eloquence (A, I, 11). When human language or image making is engaged in for the purpose of recreation it is in effect turned into an end in itself, an object whose purpose is to please the self rather than God (A, III, 24). Because of these and other passages in John of the Cross, it must be admitted that, although language is valuable both as an instrument and intrinsically, it is the former sort of value which has the upper hand in John of the Cross. But as we have seen in other passages, and in the fact that John of the Cross is such a deliberate poet, he is willing at times to pull his vision up short to view his instrument approvingly, as when someone who is looking through a window calls his attention to the cut glass in the window itself. Consider John of the Cross's criticisms of writers or artists who are either unskilled or who show little respect for the seriousness of their calling. The integrity of their craft is compromised when they desire personal profit (*intereses*) or a festival for themselves rather than giving themselves over, as it were, to their medium. Especially at the beginning of one's artistic career one should be gratified by the sensual delights of one's medium (A, III, 38–39). But even later on one should be bothered, say, by a fine painting or poem which is "painted over" by a hack (L, 3, 42).

The most obvious intrinsic good is love; only love is commensurate with love. That is, everything other than love is subservient to it (S, 9, 7). Hence, a poetry lover can treat language as an intrinsic good *to the extent that* language can be loved. The danger is that this love of language or connoisseurship would degenerate into a possessiveness of heart rather than grow into a legitimate concern for craft, based on a pure motivation where one seeks no superfluous rewards for one's labors (D, I, 3; S, 29, 11). For example, vocal ceremonies performed well (as in a nuanced rendition of a familiar Biblical passage) are *in themselves* good, as well as good instrumentally, just as the human soul is good *in itself* even as it contributes to God (A, III, 44; S, 33, 7).

I would like to conclude this section of the chapter by noting some passages in John of the Cross (also see A, III, 45, treated above in section 1 of this chapter) where he treats instrumental and intrinsic value *together*. For example:

> I should like to offer a norm for discerning when this gratification of the senses is beneficial and when not. Whenever a person, upon hearing music or other things, seeing agreeable objects, smelling sweet fragrance, or feeling the delight of certain tastes and delicate touches, immediately at the first movement directs his thought and the affection of his will to God, receiving more satisfaction in the thought of God than in the sensible object that caused it, and finds no gratification in the senses save for this motive, it is sign that he is profitting by the senses and that the sensory part is a help to the spirit (A, III, 24).

At first glance it may seem that John of the Cross is here talking only of instrumental good, but notice that he thinks it important to tell us that the objects he has in mind are "agreeable," that the fragrances are "sweet," that the tastes give "delight," and that the touches be "delicate." In *Ascent of Mount Carmel* (A, III, 27) he makes it explicit, as does Plato in Book One of the *Republic,* that the greatest goods are neither instrumental goods alone (as in bad tasting medicine which nonetheless cures disease), nor intrinsic goods alone (as in a beautiful shade of red all by itself), but both together. The greatest goods are desirable "because of what they are in themselves (love, tranquility, peace, right use of reason). . . because of the good effected through their instrumentality." Of course *the* greatest good is God, hence one should praise God both for the goods one has received from God and because of God's intrinsic properties. It is a defective type of religion (actually, it is a crude, utilitarian calculus) that encourages us to have more regard for God's blessings than for the divine nature itself (L, 3, 84; M, maxims, 59). In order to avoid this defect one is well-served, according to John of the Cross, by preparing oneself to appreciate God's intrinsic goodness by learning to appreciate why lesser intrinsic goods, like poems, are worthy of our attention.

God as Ineffable

At several points in this book, we have noted divine dipolarity in John of the Cross. We have noticed it with respect to divine permanence in the midst of change, in traditionally male as well as traditionally female predicates, in God as sublime as well as God as delicate, in God as transcendent as well as God as immanent, in *how* God exists in contrast to the fact *that* God exists, and so forth.

Human rationality and language seem to apply more easily to the latter element in each of these contrasts (not contradictories!), hence in many important respects reasonable language can be used to describe God. (That is, in many important respects God is "effable.") But with respect to the issue of *how* God can be so immense in time and space and care so as to exert causal influence over *all* of reality, we largely remain speechless. In this section of the chapter, I will consider the sense in which, and the extent to which, God is ineffable in John of the Cross. We should keep in mind, however, that John of the Cross never turns himself into a Tertullianite or a fideist or a quietist. God often seems secret and dark to us, he thinks, to such an extent that we often have to be quietly aware of God before we can eventually try to come up with language for some particular aspect of the divine (D, II, 17), just as anthropologists have difficulty describing some cultural artifact with which they are initially unfamiliar.

All such efforts at description of contemplation involve "translations" that are jagged, translations which arrive at attenuated versions of the initial experiences. And translations from Spanish into English involve attenuation of meaning, even in Kavanaugh's excellent rendition. But not all is lost in efforts at translation. The Spanish *simpatico,* for example, cannot be rendered exactly in English, but "sympathy" is much closer to a synonym than "corkscrew." Once again, the fact that we can easily notice egregious errors in translation indicates that all is not lost, and much is gained, in a good translation, especially if it is compared to other translations.[34] Further, commentators like myself who "translate" John of the Cross's thoughts into contemporary terms obviously bring about attenuation of meaning, but we also, when taken collectively and taken at our best, make it possible for living religious seekers and living scholars to *find* meaning in John of the Cross, especially if our efforts are used to keep each other honest.[35] The key is to avoid egregious errors at translation, then to avoid the next most obvious set of errors, and so on, so that one can asymptotically approach one's goal. But it is because of these edges mentioned above, which always remain somewhat jagged, especially those which occur when we try to "translate" contemplative experience into any language, that one can legitimately claim that God is ineffable and that all efforts at interpretation are diasparactive.

The problem is that particular terms used to describe God fail to catch the immensity, ubiquity, and depth of the divine; general terms offer a bit more success, but they, too, fail in that they miss the personal relationship between a loving human being and God because they tend of necessity to turn God into an abstraction (A, II, 26). Thus, as we have noted, there always remains a sublime, still to be spoken, "I-don't-know-*what*" aspect of God. Pessimism is avoided by virtue of the sublime traces in the world that human beings *can* apprehend; there is, in fact, an "I-do-know-*that*" aspect of God. Because God's immensity surpasses understanding, John of the Cross often uses the term *balbucir* (to stammer) to refer to our childlike (not childish) efforts at saying inadequately *what must be said* (emphasis added). My point is that the inadequacy of religious language (that is, God's ineffability) is at best half the story.[36] Only the experience of death, not God, is altogether beyond our stammering. In fact, it is precisely when transformation occurs to the soul that this "I-don't-know-what" asserts itself (S, 7, 5; S, 7, 9; S, 39, 1). John of the Cross relies on Job 4:2 in the asking of the following rhetorical question: who can keep back the word he has conceived without saying it?

Our knowledge, even at its best, is remote with respect to God's own being (which John of the Cross likens to a hidden jewel), as opposed to God's becoming-in-a-context-of-relations-with-others. But this situation is not hopeless. When two lovers are removed from each other, they can still communicate in a bastardized or vicarious way through letters (S, 2, 1; S, 6, 5). It is true that God does not reveal himself as he is in himself (or as the biblical language has it, no one can see God's face—Exod. 33:20); however, in contemplation, as we have seen, one can be transformed because of a mute, divine, spiration (S, 11, 3; S, 11, 5; S, 26, 4; S, 39, 2; S, 39, 12). John of the Cross consistently defends the dictum that we should never speak more than is necessary, and it is not necessary to try to describe in detail divine sublimity. God, he thinks, will understand silent love, just as God will understand calm speech when there is sufficient warrant for it (L, 2, 21; M, maxims, 3, 53; M, letters, 7, 11).

Thompson is correct in asserting that although there is much talk about ineffability in John of the Cross, there is no evidence in John of the Cross to support the claim that mystical experience is self-authenticating.[37] Rather, ineffability must be brought within the larger context of the religious life as a whole, many of whose elements can be meticulously articulated. And Frost correctly alerts us to the fact that, although John of the Cross's ideas were "lived" before they were written, they were in fact written down so as to provide a skeleton for a religious life that would otherwise be a formless blob. Further, John of the Cross's thoughts on ineffability must be reconciled with his view that one's approach to God should never result in quietism, but should always include efficacious action: *"Obras, que no palabras"* (with *palabras* here standing for language in general, including sounding solitude).[38]

The "end" of a human being, for John of the Cross, is not a full stop, but a perfected ability to respond to God. In this attempt to perfect oneself, one needs to rely on religious classics, like those of John of the Cross, whose reading is never finished. These classics are like God in that something always remains to be said about them. And in the religious life one can use these classics as dark mirrors to see God.[39] To the extent that these mirrors are dark, God is ineffable; to the extent that they are indeed mirrors one can continue to talk about what one sees in them.

CHAPTER 6

M y s t i c i s m

18. There He gave me His breast;
   18. *Allí me dió su pecho,*
There He taught me a sweet and living knowledge;
   Allí me enseñó ciencia muy sabrosa,
And I gave myself to Him,
   Y yo le di de hecho
Keeping nothing back;
   A mí, sin dejar cosa,
There I promised to be His bride.
   Allí le prometí de ser su esposa.

        St. John of the Cross, "The Spiritual Canticle"

2. That perfect knowledge
   2. *De paz y de piedad*
Was of peace and holiness
   Era la ciencia perfecta,
Held at no remove
   En profunda soledad,
In profound solitude.
   Entendida (vía recta).

      St. John of the Cross, "Stanzas Concerning an Ecstasy"

Love turns all to one sweetness
   Todo lo hace de un sabor,
Transforming the soul in itself.
   Y al alma trasforma en sí.

St. John of the Cross, "Commentary Applied to Spiritual Things"

Forgetfulness of creation,
  Olvido de lo criado,
Remembrance of the Creator,
  Memoria del Criador,
Attention to what is within,
  Atención a lo interior
And to be loving the Beloved.
  Y estarse amando al Amado.

St. John of the Cross, "The Sum of Perfection"

From Meditation to Contemplation

In this chapter, I hope to make explicit what mysticism is in John of the Cross, a topic which has remained implicit thus far. Further, the sort of receptivity presupposed by mystical experience will be treated, a receptivity which, in turn, presupposes an embodied knower who has the mystical experience. The quality of sanjuanistic mystical experience will also be discussed. This will be a discussion that will rely on comparisons and contrasts with Eastern mysticism, and which will build on the other chapters of this book, including the recent discussion of ineffability in John of the Cross.

Frost can get us started in our analysis of John of the Cross's mysticism when he makes the following, quite accurate remarks:

St. John makes the whole of the prayer life consist of two main activities, meditation and contemplation, each of which has its own degrees of progress and intensity, although it is with those of the latter with which he is most concerned. The passage from one to the other is one of the most serious import in the spiritual life. . . . The crisis is common to all souls who are persevering in Christian practice, and ignorance of its nature or of how to act when it comes about is largely responsible for the fact that so many souls who have made progress sooner or later come to a halt, and settle down into mediocrity, remain in a troubled and disturbed state, or fall away altogether. The cause of this crisis lies in the fact that the first stage of the spiritual life, which consists in the conquest of the passions, the formation of good habits, the walking in the ordinary way of Christian practice, is but the first stage, the preparatory school of the spiritual life. . . . But sooner or later, to the surprise and consternation of the soul, the very opposite happens, that which was imagined to

be an open road apparently ends in a *cul-de-sac*. . . . The first im-
pulse of the soul is to look for the cause of all this within
itself. . . . There may then follow the temptation to ask whether
the cause does not lie in religion itself, whether the whole thing is
not a delusion. . . his main purpose is to lead souls through and
beyond the crucial point at which, if progress is to be made, meditation must give way to contemplation. This is, perhaps, the most
serious crisis in the spiritual life since "in such seasons it is a
difficult and troubling thing for a soul to understand itself or to
find anyone who understands it.[1]

This section of the chapter is concerned with precisely the problem
of how and when to move away from one's former manner of
progress. The problem is difficult if only because it is not necessarily
time for contemplation if meditation fails, but also because some
fear that they are "doing nothing" in contemplative silence. And
this night of spirit, in contrast to the night of sense discussed in
chapter one, can last for several years.[2]

There is nothing to be gained by leaving discursive meditation
too soon, and much to be lost, in that if one is not adequately
prepared for contemplation one will be forced to return to meditation
to (re)think the major issues and symbols and emotions of the
spiritual life. Then again, it is also possible that one would, like
Hamlet, dwell too much in discursive and pensive meditation. There
are no error free algorithms for determining when to pass on to
contemplation, like the rules for long division which, if followed,
always give the correct answer. Nonetheless there are heuristic
devices that point one in the right direction. For example, when
climbing a mountain it is generally true that one should make the
next step on ground higher than the previous one. If one is forced
to decrease elevation one should always be on the alert to get back
to higher ground. Likewise, a sanjuanistic heuristic to make the
transition to contemplation consists in the suggestion that the release from meditation (even if one retains the habit of meditation,
a habit which can be tapped if necessary) should occur when there
appears to be neither savor nor benefit in discursive speech or
thought, as well as in the suggestion that loving quietude should
not be confused with melancholy (A, II, 13).

Kavanaugh is correct that mystical experience is "mystical"
because it is hidden, and it is hidden because it excludes discursive
meditation.[3] But this should not be taken to mean that when one
passes from meditation to contemplation one permanently crosses

a divide that precludes return. John of the Cross is quite clear that the *habit* of contemplation builds on the *habit* of meditation. Even the most spiritually advanced person periodically needs to return to meditation (A, II, 15), just as Larry Bird periodically needs to practice free throws when his more difficult three-point shots fail. That is, meditation is a necessary but not sufficient condition for union. The road to spiritual perfection is gradual in John of the Cross, starting with ascetical discipline, intellectual rigor, and discursive meditation. But just as gradually we need to be weaned from discursive meditation as a baby's diet is changed when he or she starts to eat solid food. Or better, the gradual progress in the spiritual life has as its aim not so much perfection of self, which sounds too self-centered for John of the Cross, but union with God, especially the "transforming" union indicated by the present participle. The words *unir, transformar, igualar,* and *juntar* (to join) or their cognates are used well over a thousand times in John of the Cross; synonyms for "perfection" are far less frequent and are always used in conjunction with *unir,* and so forth. (And we should remember from chapter four that union in John of the Cross also refers to solidarity with creation.) One of the difficulties in moving to contemplative union too quickly is that by failing to meditatively discipline oneself one is more easily amenable to "visions":

> . . . a person frees himself from the task and danger of discerning the true visions from the false ones. . . . Such an effort is profitless, a waste of time, a hindrance to the soul, an occasion of. . . spiritual stagnancy, since the individual is not then employed with the more important things and disencumbered of the trifles of particular apprehensions (A, II, 17).

That is, by opening oneself up to visions and the like one is feeding the soul morsels when more substantial food is needed (also see A, II, 24; A, II, 27; A, III, 8).

Meditation and a life of virtue prepare the way for contemplation, but some are so excessively diligent in traveling down the meditative road that they miss the exit to contemplation, which lies on a less traveled and more leisurely road (D, I, 8–10). The transition from the lowly communion of meditation to the higher communion of contemplation can be understood only if one realizes that a second night or purgation, that of the spirit, is needed to supplement the ascetical night of the senses described in chapter one. John of the Cross puts the matter this way:

> The difference between the two purgations is like the difference between pulling up roots and cutting off a branch, or rubbing out a fresh stain and an old, deeply embedded one. As we said, the purgation of the senses is only the gate. . . . This sensitive purgation, as we also explained, serves more for the accommodation of the senses to the spirit than for the union of the spirit with God (D, II, 2; also see D, II, 3).

The desolation of the night, which can initially be painful to the intellect, yields to transforming divine touches wherein one achieves/ receives an inner communion (*comunicación*) with God (D, II, 7, 9, 23).

The perfected habit of knowledge in contemplation, as opposed to the loss of that knowledge, is a part of that transition which occurs when one loses all that is not God. Union and companionship and an elevated intellect replace meditation in solitude; or more accurately, they signal a perfected solitude which, once purified, no longer suffers in the dark night. (The darkness is disconcerting largely because we are not used to it.) But in order to receive divine influence in contemplation one must be prepared to receive such influence, just as the proper flask is needed to receive superior liqueur (S, 26, 16; S, 29, 11; S, 35, 1; L, 2, 24–25). Hence at this point I will move directly to the activity of receptivity.

Receptivity

As was noted in chapter one, it is simplistic to say that meditation is active whereas contemplation is passive, but it must be admitted that there is at least some degree of truth in this caricature. More precise would be the claims that all meditative activity includes some passivity, say the sort of passivity required in reading, and that one must actively work to put oneself in a contemplative position where one can be receptive to divine (take your pick) inflow, infusion, manifestation, illumination, illustration, and so forth, but without the aid of the senses.[4] To take a few examples from sensation itself of active passivity, consider once again the concentration needed to hear another person's argument, or the attentiveness needed to appreciate the counterpoint in a difficult symphony. One cannot just drag a child to a Poulenc opera and automatically expect the child to really hear the work.[5]

Contemplation, or, if one prefers, mystical experience, does not require, could not require, the abandonment of all activity; it requires the abandonment of multiple activities or the sorts of activities which are not conducive to union. Regarding multiple activities Frost uses the following simile:

> One cart horse can, we will suppose, draw a heavy load along a level road but is totally unable to do so up a steep hill. The carter yokes another horse to the wagon and now the hill is surmounted. The point to notice is that the addition of the second horse does not make the task easier for the first.[6]

Therefore, one should be careful in determining which hills are worth climbing. Especially in the early stages of the spiritual life a great deal of activity is needed. But even later on one should do everything *appropriate* to achieve union. This appropriateness includes a concentrated activity whose purpose is receptivity; what is constituted is what Frost calls a melange of activity and passivity:[7]

> The maximum of the positive, grace-aided activity of the soul is not directed to bringing about an empty inactivity, but the fullest activity of which it is capable, that in which the whole being harmonized and united in one act of desiring love is capable. . . . The active and passive states do not simply succeed one to another, the former being left entirely before the latter is entered upon, but that the passive state is one in which the activity of the operation of God gradually coincides with the activity of the soul. . . . So the understanding of the soul is now the understanding of God. . . activity is child's play in comparison with this passivity of the soul which, far from being a "doing nothing," is, in reality, the highest activity possible to us. . . as Rupert Brooke said, to "busy our hearts with quietude," against the ultimately destructive forces of speed and noise to oppose those of deliberation and silence. . . . It may be said, then, that contemplation is both acquired and infused, but not that acquired contemplation differs in kind from infused contemplation. . . the whole tenor and progress of the spiritual life, which is never one of sharply separated sections but of an ebbing and flowing rhythmic activity determined by the growth of charity within the soul and the intensity of its work as purifying, illuminating, or uniting at any moment. Thus each stage may, and commonly does possess characteristics which when dealt with separately for the sake of logical and theological clarity of analysis, may convey an impression of successiveness.[8]

Entering on the road to union means leaving one's own road; it means leaving one's self far off (*saliendo de sí*) so as to live *in* God, as described in chapter four above. The more one concentrates on self, the less on God, and an exclusive concern for intellect fails to take us to God's being (A, II, 4). Although even language based on contemplative, mystical experience cannot adequately express God's being (pace chapter five), the divine influence received in contemplation does allow us to speak more accurately about God's being than we could without such influence. The overall point I am trying to make here in this section of the chapter is that one needs to work hard (sometimes with intellect) to receive such influence, just as one needs to actively clean a smudgy window to receive sunlight through it (A, II, 5). As we will see, John of the Cross refers to divine infusion as a ray of darkness because of *the peculiar sort of ineffability it brings.*[9] But the following metaphor may help: in order to reach the religious heights of union we need intellect and discursive meditation as rungs on a ladder, but then we need to spring off of the highest rung, thereby kicking the ladder away so as to vault ourselves over the wall that separates us from God. This leaves us, to say the least, in a precarious position, a position which leads some to desire the sweet earth at the base of the ladder. But it is also a position where we must *receive* help from God if we are to land safely. John of the Cross puts the point this way:

> . . . a man, who wants to arrive at union with the Supreme Repose and Good in this life, must climb all the steps, which are considerations, forms, and concepts, and leave them behind (A, II, 12).

It is more usual, however, for John of the Cross to refer to union in terms of the active amelioration of impediments, comparable to veils; or in terms of God rushing in *when room is made for* divinity. There is no void (*vacío*) in nature, he thinks, such that God is more than willing to eliminate any supposed vacuum. Hence the pacification of the soul (*pacificar el alma*), that is the preparation of the soul for God, is no small accomplishment (A, II, 15):

> As a window is unable to hinder the ray of sunlight shining upon it and is disposed through its cleanness to be illumined passively without active effort, so too, however much a person wants to reject these visions, he cannot but receive the influences and communications of those figures (A, II, 16; also see S, 10, 6).

John of the Cross is well aware of the fact that by emphasizing our active attempts at passivity we might puff ourselves up into thinking that *we* are responsible for contemplation. Therefore, he thinks it important to emphasize that we be passive (*pasiva*) or negative (*negativamente*) with respect to God, the latter signifying the fact that contemplation is always on God's terms, not ours (A, III, 13). In short:

> *God must place* the soul in this. . . state. Nevertheless, an individual must insofar as possible prepare himself (A, III, 2—emphasis added).

Further, when John of the Cross claims that receptivity with respect to God is compatible with service rendered (*servido*) to others, we should realize once again that there is no incompatibility between mystical experience, on the one hand, and the emphasis on *praxis* discussed in chapter two, on the other (A, III, 32). In fact, contemplative purgation produces nakedness or poverty of spirit (D, II, 4). (And this is precisely the poverty of spirit which is conducive to the sort of *praxis* needed in capitalist culture.) The infused contemplation or the inflow of God found in the second dark night produces a very useful peace of soul not to be confused with anaesthesia (D, II, 5, 9).

It should now be clear that for John of the Cross a human being can receive knowledge through his creaturely senses or from God, and that knowledge from God can: (1) be mediated through the senses, as in visions; but (2) is more likely received, and more productively received, in a spiritual way. The whole purpose of this chapter, and of this section of the chapter in particular, is to come to an understanding of this receptivity. John of the Cross's emphasis on the (literal) passion of love, rather than on an exercise of will, should alert us to the fact that it is in the nature of love (and illumination) to bring about unity. Relying on the ancient dictum that like knows like, John of the Cross is not surprised that if one searches for God out of love, and if God is searching for this person even more due to a much greater love, then the two should get together (D, II, 13).[10]

Because the activity of the senses must be suspended, or at least diminished, in order to allow our powers of passivity to be accentuated, it makes sense for John of the Cross to say that God is the doer of all in contemplation; God brings the soul into himself (L, 1, 9; L, 3, 10; L, 3, 36; L, 3, 44). By way of contrast, the constant activity of the senses prevents inner solitude because this is an inappropriate sort of activity in the spiritual life, just as hammering away at the horseshoe rather than at the nail is a wasted activity if one's goal is to shoe a horse (L, 3, 45).

> If a person should, then, desire to act on his own through an attitude different from the passive loving attention we mentioned... he would utterly hinder the goods God communicates... to him in the loving knowledge... a person, if he wants to receive it, should be very annihilated in his natural operations, unhampered, idle, quiet, peaceful, and serene, according to the mode of God.... A person should not bear attachment to anything, neither to the practice of meditation, nor to any savor, whether sensory or spiritual, nor to any other apprehensions (L, 3, 34).

Even in contemplation God is not shown or felt completely, but to love God in God (that is, to be receptive to God in God) provides us with the only sure way we have as human beings to escape ignorance regarding our place in the overall scheme of things (S, 13, 10; L, 3, 70; L, 3, 82).

The following quotations from John of the Cross make clear the importance of the activity of passivity in his thought:

> Not everyone capable of hewing the wood knows how to carve the statue, nor does everyone able to carve know how to perfect and polish the work, nor do all who know how to polish know how to paint it, nor do all who can paint it know how to put the finishing touches on it and bring the work to completion.... If you are only a hewer, which lies in guiding the soul to contempt of the world and to mortification of its appetites, or a good carver, which consists in introducing it to holy meditations, and know no more, how can you lead this soul to the ultimate perfection of delicate painting, which no longer requires hewing or carving or even relievo work, but the work that God must do in it? (L, 3, 57–58).

Note that the art of *applying* paint to canvas is more "active" than the "passive" affair of carving, where one peels away so as to reveal the wood which is *already there*. Or again, regarding the cooperative effort of union:

> Being in the shadow of God through this... transformation, it performs in this measure in God and through God what He through Himself does in it (L, 3, 78).

But by emphasizing the preeminent effort of God in contemplative union, John of the Cross is not trying to diminish the rigor of the life of virtue, which remains an integral part of the spiritual life *as a whole:*

> Let them reflect how necessary it is to be enemies of self and to walk to perfection by the path of holy rigor. . . . There are three signs of inner recollection: first, a lack of satisfaction in passing things; second, a liking for solitude and silence and an attentiveness (*acudir*) to all (M, maxims, 6, 40).

Continental philosophers like Charles Scott and Edith Stein (not surprisingly in the case of the latter, who was a Carmelite nun herself) are helpful in pointing out that human receptivity may be somewhat diminished in our world due to the loss of the Greek middle voice. That is, there is something crude in assuming that "I showed X to Y" and "Y showed X to me" exhaust the ways in which we can talk about action and passion. The Greek *phainesthai,* the middle voice of *phaino,* refers to "what shows itself." But even this rendering is inaccurate in that reflexive formations that must use "self" and must use pronouns like "what" or "it" fail to capture "the occurrence of self-showing" or the coming to light without nominal action found in the middle voice. Without the middle voice we are always tempted to look for a permanent subject, a material lump, who causes the showing. John of the Cross's point, if I understand him correctly, is that the inner life of God, God's being (as opposed to God's relational character) is elusive, as I have tried to show in previous chapters. Therefore, one should not expect the experience of God to occur in the same way that one experiences a blow to the head. Rather, God is manifested spiritually in the divine "showings" found in contemplation and in the letting-be of God. Although Spanish also lacks the middle voice, John of the Cross often makes it clear that in contemplation there is a "deifying" of the soul when the soul allows God to enter.[11]

A Type of Knowledge

Because contemplation consists in a type of receptivity, it should not surprise us to find that it is also, for John of the Cross, a type of knowledge. If one distinguishes two different types of knowledge, with one sort cognitive and discursive and the other consisting in spiritual (ap)prehensions, then it is obvious that mystical experience is not knowledge in the former sense, as Zwi Werblowsky notes.[12] Rather:

> Mystical consciousness is a type of apprehension which is different from our usual rational or empirical modes of thought, but which is nevertheless to be regarded as a very real type of "knowledge". . . . it is just such a form of knowledge which St. John refers to as "unknowing". . . . it does not involve annihilation of the soul's faculties.[13]

That is, in Green's terms, "mystical consciousness" consists in the reception of a ray of intense light, hence a ray of darkness (*rayo de tiniebla*), which, as in Plato's myth of the sun, makes everything else intelligible even if this ray itself blinds us. John of the Cross refers to contemplative union, or what is commonly called "mystical experience," as a state of unknowing because in such experience there is a:

> . . . state of understanding all but thinking about no specific item of knowledge; perceiving all but conceiving of nothing particular. . . . The spiritual knowledge now communicated to the mystic is not confined to any particular matter of reason, imagination or sense-perception. . . . To know nothing, then, as St. John says, is to know all, i.e. to empty oneself of all particular ideas and images is to apprehend all things seen in their true light, through that principle which is their ground or basis.[14]

It is my hope that this detachment (*desasimiento*) from particulars so as to know all should be more understandable because of our consideration of panentheism in chapter four above.

Green is helpful regarding the normal, cognitive faculty of knowing in relation to mystical knowing in John of the Cross:

> This process of the emptying of the faculties does not, however, mean that we restrict them from operation altogether; on the contrary, it is necessary that they should continue to operate if we are to fulfill the Divine Will in everyday life. What is important is to remain detached from the faculties and the communications received through them. . . they perform their functions *more* perfectly for our being detached from them. . . . The emptying of the self is only one half of a process, of which the complementary half is far from being annihilistic or negative, for it consists in receiv-

ing God in the depths of the soul. . . . By knowing the inward
principle at the basis of all, we come to understand the outer
world in a truer and deeper way.[15]

It is precisely this mystical knowing gained in contemplation, this
knowledge in unknowing (*saber no sabiendo*—"Stanzas Concerning
an Ecstasy"), that enables us to say, with no small dose of irony,
that John of the Cross was dying to live. The "dying" part of this
desire to live John of the Cross sometimes refers to as an abyss
(*abismo*), but this is an abyss which is instrumental rather than
consummatory.

Leo Spitzer, like Green, emphasizes the often noted connection
between mystical knowledge and biblical knowing, the latter of
which he refers to as a "Jewish sensibility."[16] It is no accident, he
thinks, that John of the Cross wrote one of his greatest poems as
an extension of the Jewish *Song of Songs,* nor that John of the Cross
embodied the Bible in that he had memorized vast chunks of it. We
should remember here that Spain had just recently been the greatest center of Jewish culture, and that even without direct contact
with Jews, John of the Cross could have indirectly been influenced
by the Jewish tradition of biblical knowing. And, as we noticed in
chapter two, Teresa of Avila herself had Jewish roots, with her
literacy making her an object of interest to the Inquisition precisely
because such a skill would have been identified in a woman as a
Jewish trait. This idea of using literacy to bring about a knowledge
through *contact* with others or with God is evidenced in John of the
Cross's "Sayings of Light and Love," which are the result of intimate
conversations he had with others. And his incompleted works of
analysis (A as well as D) are understandable because analysis itself
(that is, breaking up into parts) is never ending in contrast to the
experience of reticulation and completeness in mystical or biblical
knowing.

In our culture, where physical exchange often acts as a symbol
of, or a substitute for, intimacy, we may be ill-prepared to appreciate
John of the Cross's use of cautery or healing burns as metaphors
for contemplative union. As a poet John of the Cross was a sensual-
ist who described the intimate, sometimes painful, knowledge a
spiritual lover has for God. Today "being burned" refers to robbery,
but John of the Cross sees fire as the perfect metaphor for a purifying agent to burn off the dampness and impurities of the soul, such
that eventually the fire is not external to the wood; the wood itself
catches fire, just as the soul *becomes part of* God.

Spitzer's point is that the action of "The Spiritual Canticle" is conceived in bodily terms, at least it is so conceived until the last stanza when the normal activity of the soul ceases (*ceso todo*). Or better, John of the Cross writes of union through the use of bodily terms like "pain" so as to eventually lead us to understand the achievement of a self-forgetfulness free from pain:

> The decision of the soul is, indeed, a *venture* into the unknown, an *adventure,* not in the trivial sense of today (a capricious interruption of everyday life), but in the sense in which is has been said that in the Middle Ages all of life was an adventure: man's venturesome quest for the *advent* of the divine.[17]

Contemplative knowing recapitulates the late Greek commonplace that *steresis* (privation) leads to *hexis* (contact), to a "theopathic" state that alternately gives the mystic piercing pain and sublime sweetness. Spitzer says the following regarding "The Dark Night":

> Lethean self-forgetfulness is achieved in our poem by a combination of two devices: we are offered a picture of bodily relaxation, leading to psychic extinction (*recliné mi rostro, dejéme*), together with an acoustic effect of lulling incantation, produced by the monotonous repetitions of sounds. As for the first, *el rostro recliné,* "I let my face fall," suggests clearly the physical; *dejéme,* "I abandoned myself," perhaps a blend of the physical and the spiritual; while, of course, *dejando mi cuidado,* "leaving my sorrow forgotten. . . ," describes purely a state of the soul. The psycho-physical and the active-inactive aspect of the mystic experience could not be better expressed than by this ambivalent *dejar. . .* unlike such a German mystic as Jacob Bohme, who resorts to new coinages in the attempt to express the inexpressible, adding the mystery of words to the mysterious experience, our poet. . . is content with the stock of words already given by the language and, even here, limits himself to a restricted number. At the same time, however, he multiplies, by repetition, variation, and syntactical disposition, the density of the web of semantic interrelations, resuscitating the memories (memories of the soul in the flesh) that are latent in popular terms. Thus, although the poem contains only familiar Spanish words which can be understood by the Spaniards of today as well as they were in the sixteenth century. . . these words have become endowed with a mystical depth.[18]

Part of John of the Cross's genius consists in doing as good a job as can be done in talking about mystical experience without making such talk itself "mystical" in the pejorative sense of the term.

It should now be clear that mystical experience for John of the Cross does *not* consist in the supposed journeys outside of the body found in the occult "sciences," disciplines which, in *our* culture, are often confused with Christian mysticism. First, as Spitzer notes above, John of the Cross is quite content to use ordinary Spanish in his descriptions of contemplation. And second, as Thompson notices, when one speaks loosely in a sanjuanistic vein about losing one's identity in Christ it would perhaps be more precise to speak of one's identity not so much being "lost" as *transformed* in Christ. In pan*en*theism, the creature is *in* God, such that the creature is at least metaphysically distinct from the creator.[19] That is, all of the world's great religions, including the pantheistic ones, have their mystics, but this designation is not terribly informative given the wide variety of mysticisms. Thompson notes that:

> William James states that "no account of the universe in its total-
> ity can be final which leaves these other forms of consciousness
> quite disregarded." It is not confined to Christianity; indeed, it
> has been much less influential in Western Christian thought than
> in the Christian East or the non-Christian Orient. Islam, Bud-
> dhism, Hinduism, Judaism and the many brands of Animism all
> have their mystics, and so did the dead religions of Egypt, Greece
> and Rome. . . to call him (John of the Cross) a mystic is no more
> than to describe Beethoven as a composer. Today, mysticism is
> associated with a whole range of things with which it has little to
> do: it is used almost synonymously for anything mysterious or
> supernatural, including miracles, astrology, and the whole realm
> of the occult. Not only would San Juan have failed to recognize
> them as such, he would have condemned them as cheap and dan-
> gerous substitutes leading men towards the demonic, not the
> divine.[20]

John of the Cross's mysticism, his account of contemplative union, is very much characterized by his desire for knowledge in the sense of personal contact, by his desire for loving intimacy with God.

James himself proposes four marks in *The Varieties of Religious Experience* by which we can label a religious experience as mystical, two of which I have treated already: such experiences are, *in a way,* ineffable and they require a certain passivity or receptivity in that they are given by God. Third, and this is the point I am trying to emphasize in this section of the chapter, they have a noetic quality; though they appear as states of feeling, mystical experiences communicate to the receiver (intimate, "biblical") knowledge of God. Finally, such experiences are transient. To use John of the Cross's language, not only in the spiritual betrothal but also in the spiritual marriage contemplation eventually gives way to meditation, and to the practical demands of day-to-day living, including the life of virtue. There is *something* permanent in the spiritual marriage (the habit of contemplation or the very real possibility for contemplation at any time), but this "something" is not contemplation itself. None of these four criteria (all of which can be found in John of the Cross) suggest that the mystic has an alternative to the life of virtue or that he possesses a *techne* with which he can discover by secret means that which can only be discovered through intellect. Nor does John of the Cross ever ignore Scripture, as Karl Barth at several points in *Church Dogmatics* implies that he should. John of the Cross does look within himself, but what he finds there is God; hence John of the Cross's concern for interiority in no way leads to selfishness or solipsism. James is helpful in responding to Barth's concerns. Even if mystical states are authoritative over the individuals to whom they come, there is no authority that emanates from them which should make it a duty for those who stand outside of them to accept these states uncritically, although John of the Cross does try to coax us to *experience* mystical knowing.[21] John of the Cross is quite explicit that we should put out of our minds any "information" received in contemplation regarding how we can meddle in the religious lives of others.

The habitual transformation of the soul in God (that is, what John of the Cross means by habitual union with God or by the spiritual marriage) constitutes a sweet knowledge (*la ciencia sabrosa*) whereby the transformed soul is *intimately* transformed in love (S, 24, 4; S, 26, 4; S, 26, 11; S, 26, 14; S, 27, 5–6; S, 37, 6; S, 38, 1; S, 38, 3). This intimacy can be expressed in many ways, sometimes through the metaphor of an interior spring or river, and at other times, as we have seen, through a log which catches fire. In any event, the intimacy of the mystic's relationship with God, a relationship wherein the soul is "dead to itself" and alive in God, would, if taken pantheistically as opposed to panentheistically, mean the annihilation of the self. But John of the Cross is clear that even when absorbed in God one still stands on his own two feet (L, prologue, 3; L, 1, 1; L, 2, 34; L, 3, 36). For example, the following quotation can be given either a pantheistic interpretation or a panentheistic one, with the latter having the advantage of preserv-

ing a sense of divine transcendence. The quotation also indicates
the cooperative effort of intellect and will (that is, love) in the
acquisition of mystical knowing:

> . . . the ultimate reason for everything is love (which is seated
> in the will), whose property is to give and not to receive, whereas
> the property of intellect (which is the subject of essential glory)
> lies in receiving and not in giving, the soul in the inebriation of
> love does not put first the glory she will receive from God, but
> rather puts first the surrender of herself to Him through true
> love, without concern for her own profit (S, 38, 5).

God as Ubiquitous

As was seen in chapter four, it makes a great deal of
(panentheistic) sense to say that, for John of the Cross, God is both
immanent and transcendent. Regarding the former, John of the
Cross realized (especially because he was a poet) that wherever
experience is most vivid and clear, observation reveals that it has
(divine) feeling, not an insentient something, as its datum. Or to
use his language, there are divine traces throughout the world. In
some ways, the mysticism of John of the Cross consists in becoming
conscious of this fact, as opposed to what happens in our animal-
like selves, which remain semiconscious or ignorant of these traces.
That is, John of the Cross reminds one of what is always there; but
what is always there is not cheapened by its ubiquity if it is relatively
rare that one notices it.[22] To contemplate is, in a certain sense, to
oxymoronically get a rare glimpse of that which is always there;
this is a type of vision for which we need to prepare ourselves, just
as a climber needs to gradually get used to breathing the air at
great heights.[23] Or better, as Brenan puts the point:

> Just as a beam of light, when concentrated to form a laser, ac-
> quires an extraordinary power of penetration, so the mind is able
> to attain a preternatural intensity of vision when concentrated on
> one object, God.[24]

When we see a ray of sunlight through a window, we begin to
notice the particles of dust that were always there, and the smudges
on the window that had previously escaped our notice. Initially,

however, the sunlight may have been so bright that we would have been tempted to pull the shade, thereby preventing our awareness of the dust or smudges (A, II, 14; D, II, 8; S, 26, 17). For John of the Cross, intellectual and especially spiritual vision is far more clear and delicate than corporeal vision. Unfortunately, our spiritual sight does not usually come in the form of a long lasting gaze. Rather, it is like a lightning flash which, for an instant, makes divinity quite apparent to us, only to leave us in partial darkness; but not in complete darkness because quietude, gladness, and a loving inclination toward God remain (A, II, 24; A, III, 13). The "secret wisdom" of contemplation is not secret in a Gnostic sense so much as it is largely secret from *ourselves*. We receive *noticias* from God but we do not usually notice them, a lack of attention which can easily breed a distorted understanding of, and a discontent with, the spiritual life.

To understand John of the Cross's mysticism, one must come to terms with his belief in a theology that is literally incarnational, and this because God is diffused throughout nature, as we have seen. The spiritually advanced person attends to events happening in their presence (*presentes*); that is, he attends to the present qua present, which is no easy task, as Augustine among others has noticed. Initially one may not perceive the divine inflow because, as before, such influence often comes in terms of a pure light or ray of darkness (which are rough equivalents). Relying on Plato and Aristotle, John of the Cross notes that:

> ... the clearer and more obvious divine things are in themselves, the darker and more hidden they are to the soul naturally.... The brighter the light, the more the owl is blinded; and the more one looks at the brilliant sun, the more the sun darkens the faculty of sight, deprives it and overwhelms it in its weakness (D, II, 5).

Yet we need the light not only for contemplation to succeed, but also to realize in the first place that we are in the dark (L, 1, 22; A, II, 26; D, I, 11).

The remarkable presence (*la grande presencia*) of God, because it is ubiquitous (say through divine omniscience and omnibenevolence), means that the soul does not really receive anything new in contemplation, but it does receive something in an explicit way which is usually implicit (S, 12, 5; S, 20, 12). "Only at intervals is one aware of these feelings (of divine inflow) in all their intensity.

Sometimes this experience is so vivid. . . " (D, II, 6). During these Wordsworthian "spots of time" even one's faults (one's smudges), which had previously escaped notice, are lighted up to see, but this causes joy because when the contemplative experience is over one is in a position to know how to further purify oneself and how to reinforce the habit of contemplation (D, II, 10):

> If a person at the time of these darknesses observes closely, he will see clearly how little the appetites and faculties are distracted with useless and harmful things (D, II, 16).

It is quite possible to have habitual virtues (like that of preparing oneself for contemplation), which one enjoys intermittently rather than continually, such that even for the spiritually advanced person there is always a danger that he will become lost in himself (S, 24, 6; S, 29, 10). Therefore, one must at various points make efforts to reactivate the activity of passivity whereby one can feel:

> . . . love-stirring breezes. . . a "whistling," because just as the whistling of the breeze pierces deeply into the hearing organ, so this most subtle and delicate knowledge penetrates with wonderful savoriness into the innermost part of the substance of the soul, and the delight is greater than all others (S, 14, 14).

Note that God's touches, God's divinized (*endiosa*) "breezes," are gentle; they are not compared to gale-force winds. Even a thin veil can prevent us from seeing or feeling divine influence; but if the veil-like impediment is removed, we can once again be transformed in divine beauty (S, 36, 8; L, 1, 32; L, 2, 3; L, 2, 17).

Johannes Bendick draws a helpful analogy between twentieth-century physics and sanjuanistic mysticism regarding how the ubiquitous features of the world can be the least obvious to us when we are engaged in our so-called natural and everyday perception.[25] A long effort is required to make contact with subatomic particles or even with atoms, cells, or molecules. Likewise, John of the Cross promises that anyone who detaches himself in the proper way, who prepares himself properly through discursive meditation, and who appropriately engages in the activity of passivity, cannot fail but to receive divine touches in contemplation. That is, John of the Cross would not necessarily agree with the commonly held view that scientific claims are independently testable by others whereas the claims of the mystic are not. Both theoretical physics

and mysticism are difficult to understand because each is equally
far removed from everyday experience, and both involve (esoteric)
experiences which are, in principle, capable of being corroborated
by others. This is a bold claim on John of the Cross's part (treated
in previous chapters) that those who are properly prepared for
contemplation *cannot fail* but to receive contemplative solace! Hence
Bendick thinks it more a wonder that John of the Cross's writings
survived *at all* than the fact that they survived in their present
diasparactive condition. Bendick also notices John of the Cross's
boldness with respect to his concept of *amor,* which Bendick thinks
"has nothing to do with feeling. It is entirely compatible with his
'intellectualism.' " (Bendick exaggerates here, but there is nonetheless something to be said for his claim.) And finally there is boldness
with respect to John of the Cross's theology of nature, concerning
which Bendick says the following:

> Besides and after St. Francis it may be that no other great Chris-
> tian has turned so positively to the world and experienced its
> beauty as did John of the Cross, though it must not be forgotten
> that they (creatures) first passed through God.[26]

God can be discovered in nature, Bendick thinks, if we pay attention
to John of the Cross's "*la música callada / la soledad sonora,*" concerning which he prefers a translation by Felix Braun: "Music is no
longer heard / But solitude will resound."[27]

One of the problems involved in contemporary individuals coming to terms with mysticism is that the designation "mystic" is
used to refer to two theoretically distinct persons: (1) the one who
has had immediate experience of God; or (2) the one who insists
that God is ineffable or who says that God can only be characterized
in paradoxical, or, at least seemingly, contradictory ways. The two
designations seem quite distinct in that we can imagine them
predicated of individuals separately, even if some individual mystics
are deserving of being called "mystics" in both senses of the term.
However, it is the first sense that is primary in John of the Cross's
thought because ineffability has a carefully demarcated role to play
in his thought, as we have seen in chapter five.

Concerning the first sense of the term "mystic," Charles
Hartshorne had made some important observations.[28] It would be
odd, he thinks, if an ubiquitous being-in-becoming could only be
known or affirmed indirectly. But if direct contact with God requires true solitude, we can understand why many would think

that no direct contact with God is possible. Regarding the rarity of true solitude, Hartshorne says the following: "Infants and subhuman animals do little introspecting, and the rest of us are more like them in this than we usually admit."[29] If solitude occurs, however, one in solitude can learn that the most readily detectable data are those that are sometimes present, sometimes not, like redness or pain. What is always given tends to escape notice. Consider the claim, made by many, not to experience spatial extension in sounds (although they experience it in colors), despite the fact that spatiality is given in all experiences, even auditory or religious ones. Or consider the fact that human feeling is largely "feeling of feeling," because we can feel as individuals only because our cells can feel at a primitive level. In localized pain we become aware of what we could always be aware of: that we are composed of tiny, albeit living, loci of feeling whose cell walls can be damaged and agitated.

Now we know that the extended cosmos is a society of sentient creatures whose influences upon one another conform largely to the patterns traced by physics. Theists influenced by John of the Cross are likely to call this society "God," a personal being who imposes limits upon mutual conflict and disorder in the natural world. That is, the pervasive unity of the spatial world is, somehow, an aspect of divine unity; we do not merely infer space in that we are directly and always in contact with it, as the contemplative realizes when he becomes aware of himself as a part of the mystical body of Christ:

> ... the difference between mystics and others (is) a relative not an absolute one. The mystic is one who is aware of experiencing what we all do experience, whether aware of the fact or not. In mystics unconscious intuition, in the sense in which infants and the lower animals are unconscious, that is, without introspective judgments, becomes also conscious.[30]

The language of Whitehead may help here. Most human beings "prehend" God in the sense that they *grasp* implicitly meaning in the world. That is, they *feel* as an inchoate object of experience that they are parts of a meaningful whole, that there is a concrete fact of relatedness between themselves and the personal force at work in the cosmos. But the subjective form this prehension takes in the mystic is that of an explicit, conscious "apprehension." In effect, the prehension/apprehension distinction is analogous to the Leibnizian distinction between perception/apperception, with the mystic exhibiting an acuity with respect to the latter element in these pairs which the rest of us possess only potentially. This acuity, however, is not aggressive, as Wordsworth (who, along with Leibniz, influenced Whitehead) noticed: ". . . I deem that there are Powers/ Which of themselves our minds impress;/ That we can feed this mind of ours/ In a wise passiveness." We fail to feed our minds this wise passiveness largely because "The world is too much with us; late and soon,/ Getting and spending, we lay waste our powers."

John of the Cross and the East

Although God is ubiquitous, a fact which John of the Cross appreciates more than most, it nonetheless remains true that one's privileged access to the divine lies through one's self. Anthony Haglof has written an excellent article where the identification of the center of the soul with God is compared to Eastern religion, specifically to Hinduism and Buddhism. In this final section of the chapter, indeed of the whole book, I would like to rely on Haglof and others to determine the similarities and differences between John of the Cross's mysticism and that of certain Buddhist monks. Throughout this book I have tried to use as many apertures as possible to pry open John of the Cross's thought, while simultaneously respecting the integrity of that thought. I will try to do the same here with respect to the relationship between John of the Cross and a most fecund source for contemporary interest in mysticism.

To make the panentheistic claim that we are in God, that we are parts of God, is not to literally claim that God can be broken up or parcelled out:

> Where any of it is, there is all of it, the life of God in its entirety. . . . As the soul, entering more deeply into itself, approaches its center, the boundary distinction between itself and God becomes more and more tenuous, for the soul is discarding all the egoistic accoutrements which hinder the realization of its true life in God.[31]

Those who fall short of contemplative union with God often use symbols that mythically project into the future the entire life of God which is now present, however obscured this life is by our superficial selves. These symbols include heaven, the coming of the kingdom, parousia, and so forth. The fall (again, mythically projected into the remote past) is a symbol, according to Haglof, for the need one has to grow back into God, a growth which first requires the realization that one is alienated from God (who is the True Self, as many Hindu mystics would put the point). As the soul approaches union (or better, re-union, as in the Hindu *samadhi*) with God, the distinction between itself and God becomes more and more tenuous as it discards its egoistic accoutrements.

Haglof traces the parallel lines along which Buddhist mystics and John of the Cross travel, a tracing which points out certain tendencies in John of the Cross not necessarily found in other Christian mystics, even if John of the Cross himself is thoroughly Christian in his outlook. Two points are emphasized. First, the Buddhist notion of *anatta* (no-self) includes the belief that the soul is not a substantial, fixed unity but a process of readjustment and integration:[32]

> . . . my private, hard-core, separate personality is more fragile than I ordinarily admit. . . . To think that there is any permanent and unchanging substance which is my own private property is pride and arrogance but, even worse, an illusion. If such a static substance of my own did or could in fact exist it would have no possibility of change. . . forever just as it is. . . ordinarily each of us has a solid self-concept of precisely who we are and what differentiates us from other people. But. . . it is composed of entirely relative, fortuitous and transitory factors, e.g., who my parents were, what my education has been, where I have been, the people I have encountered and their influence on me, etc. These and other factors have gone into the construction of my present self-concept, but it is quite conceivable that they could have been different, in which case "my" self-concept would be different. . . "the real me," my self or soul, will be different. . . . Buddha does not conclude from this, however, as many of his Western interpreters have believed, that there is therefore ultimately just nothing, no stability to be found anywhere.[33]

This principle of stability in Buddhism is not called "God" and is not personified as it is in John of the Cross. But:

> . . . this reference by the Buddha to that which is unborn, unbecome, unmade and uncompounded is totally commensurate with the Scholastic concept of God as completely simple, absolute, eternal being. This is one significant piece of evidence that Buddhism is concerned with the same religious realities as Christianity.[34]

Note that Haglof refers here to God's being, which is, as we saw in chapter three, only one pole of God's dipolar nature. Haglof's overall point here is that:

> When John of the Cross says that virtue does not consist in experience or good works, but in the desire to be forgotten and held in contempt, he is saying essentially that the primary obstacle to a genuinely spiritual self is this over-refined and over-regarded sense of a stable self.[35]

And second, in addition to *anatta* the Buddhists have as a key notion *dukkha* (suffering or malaise):

> Once we have become aware of ourselves as separate and apparently independent beings we simultaneously feel a certain inadequacy. . . we automatically desire any number of things which will fulfill us or remedy this inadequacy. . . . It is for this reason that John of the Cross spends the entire first book of the *Ascent* explaining how desires are the root of evil.[36]

The Buddhist (and, to some extent, Hindu) way of putting the point is to suggest that it is necessary to extinguish desire in order to attain *nirvana,* the most integrated state of existence. Failing this we can expect *dukkha* to continue, which is thoroughly consistent with a sanjuanistic view of the world:

> *Dukkha.* . . . It does not refer to the extremes of suffering or grief, but rather to a general malaise or uneasiness. . . . It is what one poet called the "sad, still music of humanity," . . . a myopic view of the world which fails to take account of its ultimately unsatisfying and transitory nature. . . *dukkha* does not just mean that all life is suffering. . . . What it means is that life as the vast majority of the human race lives it is accompanied by the disappointment and frustration which result from attempting the impossible: fulfillment from things, events, people, the realm of phenomena (called by the Buddhists *samsara*).[37]

Given *dukkha,* it is understandable that religious seekers turn to intellectual concepts which can, in turn, perpetuate our dissatisfaction *if* they make God into a changeless, lifeless abstraction, although it is not necessary that intellect develop a fetish for changelessness. In fact, as I have tried to show through John of the Cross's texts, God can more consistently be conceived as a living person in process, to whose life we find ourselves contributing. Haglof links this process conception of God with the famous story in Exodus regarding God as YHWH:

> In Hebrew the "name" is not a noun but a verb form. . . literally meaning "I AM BEING" or "I AM EXISTING," with emphasis on the continuousness or the dynamism of the act of being or existing. . . . "All right, tell them that I AM BEING sent you."[38]

When one realizes that one can let one's self go and not lose anything in the process, indeed one gains all, according to John of the Cross, one is released into union with its fullness of detail and vivacity. Neither Buddhist nor sanjuanistic negativity are pathological in the sense of encouraging one to think too little of oneself. Rather, one gains all through the *vía negativa;* one gains a vaster self, which John of the Cross calls "God."

John of the Cross and the Buddhist mystics are also alike in being opposed to the "birds of appetite" in religion, as Thomas Merton refers to them. Those who look to gain something for *themselves* from mysticism are like buzzards encircling carrion flesh. "This hovering, this circling, this descending, this celebration of victory, are not what is meant by the Study of Zen,"[39] nor are these what is meant by John of the Cross's mysticism. The scavengers who are looking for visions or for histrionic display or for *self*-fulfillment in mystical experience will find that John of the Cross is not their kind of prey because he is interested in the *living* inflow from God received in contemplative solitude. Contemplative experience is, like virtue, its own reward, hence the birds of appetite in search of carrion flesh pass it by.

If Buddhist mysticism entails, as Frost alleges, that one go through life with one's eyes closed, and *if* it entails pantheism, then John of the Cross's mysticism is not at all like that of the Buddhist monks. Frost also worries that we would confuse John of the Cross with Eastern religion by claiming that *we* initiate contemplation by putting ourselves in a condition of passivity. Frost is correct in noting that it is God who ultimately makes it possible for one to enter contemplation.[40] But the point to this section of the chapter is not to reduce John of the Cross to Buddhist insights, which would be an impossible task given the direct and personal experience of God in John of the Cross. Rather, I am trying to use Buddhist notions as searchlights to illuminate features of John of the Cross's mysticism that might not otherwise be noted. For example, the dissolution of the self in Eastern mysticism is close (critics like Frost would say dangerously close) to John of the Cross's view, but John of the Cross prefers to use words like the transformation, absorption, participation, or inclusion of the self in God, thereby making it more accurate to call him a panentheist than a (Hindu) pantheist because these terms (transformation, etc.) do not imply *complete* loss of identity. When John of the Cross compares the soul to "burned away dew," however, his similarities to Eastern thought become more prominent, because this metaphor does in fact imply dissolution.[41] John of the Cross's stronger sense of "self" than Buddhism's or Hinduism's is evidenced in the fact that whereas Eastern religion aims at the cessation of all desire, John of the Cross only aims at the cessation of all desire that is not directed to God.[42] That is, loving affectivity is *central* to John of the Cross.

Whereas Frost emphasizes the distance between John of the Cross and Eastern mysticism, Teilhard de Chardin thinks that John of the Cross is *too* Eastern. A consideration of his criticisms will allow us to see why a coming to terms with the relationship between John of the Cross and Eastern thought is crucial for an understanding of the former.[43] Teilhard distinguishes between two spiritual roads. The road of the East tends toward spiritual unification, that is, toward a return to the basis underlying phenomenal appearances. A return to this basis, which is more real than the appearances, requires a direct suppression of the multiple contingencies of the world, including the contingencies regarding the self. The danger posed by this road, according to Teilhard, is that there is a tendency to relax the cosmic effort, to release the tension among individuals such that the outcome of contingent relationships among individuals is seen to be of little consequence. The second road, that of the West, can lead to union only if one takes to their limits the dispersed elements around us. A spirit of tension characterizes this road in that the separate demands and conflicts and dialectical tensions among individuals are here taken seriously.

Because John of the Cross's concern was cosmic, as opposed to anthropocentric (as in chapter four above), he wins Teilhard's approval. But because the virtues of both of these roads have been inadequately synthesized, "spiritual progress" has been halted. We need, he thinks, a strong notion of individuality and of concern for contingent particulars in order to produce a powerful version of *modern* mysticism. Christianity has always been driven *in the di-*

rection of unification and synthesis, but the "centrifying character" of the movement (whereby centers of activity like cells or like individual human beings are taken seriously) has not been adequately defined. Teilhard's thesis is that John of the Cross was carried along by the general movement of Christianity in the sublimation of creatures in their convergence in God. That is, John of the Cross has been carried along by Christianity's Eastern tendency (Palestine is in Asia, after all) to denigrate science.

There is nothing to be gained by claiming that Teilhard misunderstood John of the Cross. In fact, there is much to be learned by taking his criticisms seriously. Throughout this book I have tried to disassociate John of the Cross from quietism and from the charges that he was naive in practical affairs or that he denigrated nature. Nonetheless Teilhard is instructive regarding how much more vigilant defenders of mysticism must be in the contemporary era. We now know that political indifference can actually play into the hands of tyrants; mystics can no longer, if they ever could, treat the political details of culture as disposable epiphenomena on the ("Eastern") road to permanent reality. So also it is no longer enough, as Teilhard implies, to merely be a nature-lover without also being a nature-understander. The current ecological crisis, if nothing else, should force us to take seriously the degree of centeredness in cells and nonhuman animals, and so forth, because not to notice nascent subjectivity in nonhuman nature is, in effect, to allow nature to be commodified and exploited as never before. To adequately respond to Teilhard's criticisms, it is not enough to establish that John of the Cross was not a quietist or that he avoided naiveté. It is also necessary to insist that a responsible twentieth-century mysticism of a sanjuanistic variety must be familiar with the ("Western") road along which lie several acute problems that cannot be ignored by any spiritual seeker worth his salt.

If it is true that Teilhard serves a useful function for scholars of John of the Cross, it is equally true that admirers of John of the Cross can provide a service for those traveling along the Western road. It is typical of those in the West (including most in Japan, etc.) to hope that with their technological prowess they can solve all problems, a type of *hybris* which causes a great number of problems in its own right. Some even try to infiltrate *techne* into the spiritual life, but the technique of prayer (say by mechanically going through a routine of *lectio divina*-detachment-discursive meditation, etc., or by engaging in Eastern relaxation techniques) is only helpful as a means to the end of union with God. There must be a truly theological moment for prayer to reach its *telos,* a contemplative moment when one "sees" God because one is first seen.[44]

John of the Cross realizes that if the writings of mystical theologians are not read properly they will appear to be irrational (S, prologue). The surest sign, he thinks, of the sanity of mystical theology (his description here reminds one *somewhat* of Buddhist or Epicurean repose) is that:

> . . . a person likes to remain alone in loving awareness of God, without particular considerations, in interior peace and quiet and repose, and without the acts and exercises (at least discursive, those in which one progresses from point to point) of the intellect, memory and will; and that he prefers to remain only in the general, loving awareness and knowledge we mentioned, without any particular knowledge or understanding (A, II, 13).

The belief that mystical theology is irrational, by way of contrast, is fostered by the aforementioned birds of appetite who want wide-screen visions, whose "source lies in a failure to walk wholly on the road of nakedness" (*desnudez*—A, II, 18). Or again, once one admits that there is a theological moment in sanjuanistic contemplation, and once one notices that *desire* for God is central to John of the Cross, one can nonetheless see a Buddhist (or Thoreauvian) economy and simplicity in his thought:

> I consider the desire for knowledge of things through supernatural means far worse than a desire for spiritual gratifications in the sensitive part of the soul. I fail to see how a person who tries to get knowledge in this supernatural way—as well as the one who commands this or gives consent—can help but sin, at least venially, no matter how excellent his motives or advanced in perfection he may be. There is no necessity for any of this kind of knowledge, since a person can get sufficient guidance from natural reason, and the law and doctrine of the Gospel. There is no difficulty or necessity unsolvable or irremediable by these means, which are very pleasing to God and profitable to souls. . . we accept only what is in harmony with reason and the Gospel law (A, II, 21; also see A, II, 22).

Ecstatic experiences, if they occur, do not help in the effort to love God as much as "the least act of living faith and hope made in the emptiness and renunciation (*vacío y renunciación*) of all things"

(A, III, 8). And it seems clear that John of the Cross realized that his "Buddhism" would offend those who become indignant when their exotic experiences are not taken seriously.

Of course John of the Cross never came into contact with Buddhists, but St. Paul served him just as well (D, II, 8): *Nihil habentes, et omnia possidentes* (2 Cor. 6:10—in having nothing, one possesses all things). Because the positive sense of "having nothing" (or better, of having no-thing) is crucial for John of the Cross, one's spirituality is most likely to come to a halt or to regress *if* one fails to understand the dark night, or better, the dark night*s* (of sense and spirit, respectively):

> Although this night darkens the spirit, it does so to give light. . . this happy night. . . humbles a person and reveals his miseries, it does so only to exalt him; and even though it impoverishes and empties him of all possessions and natural affection, it does so only that he may reach out divinely to the enjoyment of all earthly and heavenly things, with a general freedom of spirit in them all (D, II, 9).

It is toward the *end* of the dark night, perhaps, that the meaning of sanjuanistic optimism begins to dawn on the religious seeker, as in the following poem:

> To reach satisfaction in all
> desire its possession in nothing.
> To come to possess all
> desire the possession of nothing.
> To arrive at being all
> desire to be nothing. . . .
> And when you come to the possession of the all
> you must possess it without wanting anything. . . .
> For in coveting nothing,
> nothing raises it up
> and nothing weighs it down,
> because it is in the center of its humility.
> When it covets something
> in this very desire it is wearied (A, I, 13).

Those who are sceptical regarding the claims of the mystic are closer to the truth than they know when they say with a sneer that mystical theology is "ethereal." John of the Cross in a peculiar and quite ironic way agrees that the flames of mystical love yield enkindled air (L, 3, 9), and that "contemplation is active while the soul is in idleness and unconcern. It is like air that escapes when one tries to grasp it in one's hand" (D, I, 9).

Summary

As the subtitle to this book indicates, I have tried to offer a contemporary appreciation of Saint John of the Cross. In general this appreciation has consisted in using various tools in contemporary philosophy and theology to understand features of John of the Cross either ignored or underemphasized in previous treatments of him as well as in using John of the Cross to critique several features of contemporary thought and contemporary society. I also hope that I have made several particular contributions to scholarship on John of the Cross.

In the first two chapters, I have shown that solitude (which is not to be confused with loneliness or with atomic individualism) is not at odds with liberation or with *praxis* or with freedom, but actually enhances these phenomena. This enhancement, I have argued, occurs as a result of a moderate asceticism for which one need not apologize, and is also a result of a more complex relationship between activity and passivity than is usually considered by scholars of John of the Cross. Further, the particular configuration of John of the Cross's asceticism consists in a unity-in-variety that is anything but superficial, although the dark nights in his thought are not at all morbid. Human beings are, he thinks, strange islands, but John of the Cross's thought can nonetheless be used today in an instructive ideology critique, just as it was used in his own day in the effort at Carmelite reform, in that he was, in addition to being a saint, also a spiritual soldier and a sage who fought for, and thought about, real riches and real freedom.

Chapters three and four have shown that John of the Cross's criticisms of systematic theology from his own perspective in mystical theology prefigure in several important ways the contemporary criticisms of systematic theology by process thinkers. His dipolar theism makes room for what have traditionally been conceived as feminine predicates to be attributed to God, and it also makes room for a Christian variety of nature theism that is not a type of pantheism. That is, John of the Cross's instructiveness regarding male bias in religion and regarding the connection between much systematic theology and ecological rapacity has previously been under-played by interpreters. His opposition to a dualistic view of the human person and to cosmological dualism makes it possible to call him a panentheist, a designation which, however inadequate, is nonetheless a better designation for him than "traditional theist" or "pantheist." And, as we have seen, his panentheism consists in a romantic balance between prettiness and sublimity (albeit with a tendency toward the latter), a romantic balance between divine immanence and transcendence, and a romantic desire for reticulative wholeness in the midst of the diasparactive shards of human exist-ence. Further, John of the Cross shows a greater balance between rationality and love, I think, than previous commentators have been willing to admit.

Divine dipolarity has many versions in John of the Cross: in divine permanence in the midst of change, in traditionally male as well as traditionally female predicates, in God as sublime as well as God as immanent, and in *how* God exists in contrast to the fact *that* God exists. In chapter five, I emphasized how human rational-ity and language seem to apply more easily to the latter element in each of these contrasts. Hence, in many important respects, reason-able language can be used to describe God. But, in order to under-stand this language, distinctions must be made between oral and literate uses of language, and among literal, symbolic, and inter-pretive uses of language. Further, language for John of the Cross is both a means and an end (primarily the former), but in some respects God is ineffable. Ineffability is a feature of John of the Cross's thought that must be carefully demarcated, however, so as not to commit the familiar mistake of overemphasizing its significance. Mysticism consists, as was seen in chapter six, in the move from (language-centered) meditation to contemplation, in the development of a refined sort of receptivity or knowledge of the ubiquitous pres-ence of God in the world, a type of receptivity which shows certain similarities to, and differences from, Eastern sensibilities. It has been my hope that sanjuanistice uses of language and sanjuanistic receptivity can be more adequately understood as a consequence of my analyses. The steps I have taken toward an understanding of John of the Cross, and toward an appropriation of him for the purposes of present philosophizing and theologizing, may be few in number, but when dealing with the enormous issues treated in John of the Cross (with both the issues and his treatment of them sublime in their own right), taking a few short steps in a positive direction may be going a long way.

Notes

Introduction

1. See Bede Frost, *Saint John of the Cross* (New York: Harper and Brothers, 1937), pp. 42, 323; Gerald Brenan, *St. John of the Cross: His Life and Poetry* (Cambridge: Cambridge University Press, 1973), p. 122.

Chapter 1

1. I have relied to a great extent here in the beginning of chapter one on Merton's "Notes for a Philosophy of Solitude," in *Disputed Questions* (New York: New American Library, 1965), pp. 139–160.

2. Ibid., p. 140.

3. Ibid., p. 151.

4. Ibid., p. 153.

5. The edition I will use throughout this book is *Vida y Obras de San Juan de la Cruz,* ed. by Crisogeno de Jesus (Madrid: Biblioteca de Autores Cristianos, 1955). Other Spanish editions include *Biblioteca Autores Españoles,* vol. 1 (Madrid, 1948) and *Obras de San Juan de la Cruz, Doctor de la Iglesia,* ed. by Silverio de Santa Teresa, 5 vols. (Burgos, 1929–1931). The latter is especially helpful regarding the two versions of *The Spiritual Canticle.* Unless otherwise noted, I will use the Kieran Kavanaugh and Otilio Rodriguez translation in English, *The Collected Works of St. John of the Cross* (Washington, D.C.: Institute of Carmelite Studies, 1973). To a lesser extent I have relied on E. Allison Peers, 3 vols., *The Complete Works of Saint John of the Cross* (Westminster, Maryland: Newman Press, 1949). When citing A and D, the roman numeral after the abbreviation refers to a

book number, and arabic numerals refer to chapter numbers. When citing S and L, the first number after the abbreviation refers to a stanza number, and the second number refers to a section number.

6. See William James, *The Varieties of Religious Experience* (Cambridge: Harvard University Press, 1985), "Religion and Neurology."

7. Henry David Thoreau, *Walden* (New York: New American Library, 1960), pp. 61, 70.

8. Porphyry, *De abstinentia,* I, 31. Also see my "Eating and Spiritual Exercises: Food for Thought from Saint Ignatius and Nikos Kazantzakis," *Christianity and Literature* 34 (Summer, 1983), pp. 25–32.

9. E. R. Dodds, *Pagan and Christian in an Age of Anxiety* (Cambridge: Cambridge University Press, 1965), pp. 28–36, 42, 60–66.

10. See Charles Hartshorne, *Creative Synthesis and Philosophic Method* (LaSalle, Ill.: Open Court, 1970), p. 311.

11. Nikos Kazantzakis, *Zorba the Greek,* trans. by Carl Wildman (New York: Simon and Schuster, 1962).

12. Brenan, *St. John of the Cross,* pp. 85, 133–135.

13. James, *The Varieties...,* pp. 304, 306, 413. James ia also ambivalent regarding St. Teresa of Avila. At times James indicates that St. Teresa of Avila was a typical "shrew" in that her outward expressions were more energetic than the receptive feelings that prompted them, and at other times he regards her as the "expert of experts" regarding the conditions of mystical experience. See my "Was St. Teresa a Shrew?," *The Downside Review 109 (1991), pp. 35-43.* Also see Rudolph Bell, *Holy Anorexia* (Chicago: University of Chicago Press, 1985), pp. xi, 18. Bell, on the one hand, suspects that Teresa of Avila was anorexic, and, on the other hand, leaves this issue to others with more expertise, but not without implying that belief in her anorexia can be based on the fact that she induced vomiting so as to not fear rejecting the host. Bell conveniently offers no textual citation for this implication.

14. Frost, *Saint John of the Cross,* pp. 29, 64, 142, 188, 198.

15. F. Brice, *Journey in the Night* (New York: Pustet, 1945), pp. 31–32, 41–42, 45, 90; E. Allison Peers, *Spanish Mysticism* (London: Methuen, 1924), pp. 109–111.

16. Deirdre Green, "St. John of the Cross and Mystical 'Unknowing,' " *Religious Studies* 22 (1986), pp. 29–40. Also see Pierre Gageac, *Saint Jean de la Croix* (Paris: Gabalda, 1958).

17. Kieran Kavanaugh, "Introduction," in *The Collected Works of St. John of the Cross,* pp. 44, 46, 48, 52, 56, 62–64.

18. Frost, *Saint John of the Cross,* pp. 153–154, 159, 167, 169, 180, 183, 191–192, 194, 202, 233, 237, 254, 349, 364, 399–405. Frost also alerts us to the "night of faith," which constitutes a transition from the night of sense to that of spirit. These three nights are John of the Cross's devices meant to fit into the three ways of traditional mysticism. The purgative way embraces the nights of sense and faith; the illuminative and unitive ways embrace the night of spirit. See S, theme. Although Frost's treatment of the three nights is instructive, it will not satisfy all. In fact, there does not seem to be any one way of demarcating the sanjuanistic nights or of demarcating activity and passivity in these nights that will please all. For example, contrast Frost with Gustavo Gutierrez's equally careful and textually based demarcation of the three nights. Gutierrez, a liberation theologian whose work more properly should be considered in chapter two, rightly alerts us to the fact that John of the Cross's concrete form of following Jesus is connected with the great historical movements of his age. These movements made it difficult to enter the first night, where one departs from material possessions, a departure that John of the Cross describes as a battle. The second night, a venture of faith, is somewhat dark to the intellect. But thanks to faith, journeying in the night is nonetheless secure. Gutierrez emphasizes that this night is the one in greatest solitude, but this solitude has very little to do with individualism. The third night, for Gutierrez, a night that is symbolized by the period just before the dawn, refers to an initial state of union with God possible in "this life." *This* darkness is not at all like midnight. See Gustavo Gutierrez, *We Drink from Our Own Wells* (Maryknoll, New York: Orbis, 1984), pp. 27, 83–87, 110, 129, 158, 162.

19. John of the Cross obviously knew nothing of Leibniz. But St. Thomas Aquinas anticipates Leibniz in many ways regarding mirror imaging, and it may well be that John of the Cross was influenced by Thomas in this area. For Thomas, human beings aspire to be (angelic) polished mirrors, *tabula depicta.* It is not often noticed that Paul's famous line about seeing God through a glass, but darkly, refers not to colored glass but to a cloudy looking glass, a mirror (*aisoptron*). See my "Rorty and Mirror Images in St. Thomas," *Method* 4 (Oct., 1986), pp. 108–114.

20. At L, 3, 43 Kavanaugh-Rodriguez translate (misleadingly, I think) *solitaria* as "lonely." Allison Peers does the same. I prefer "solitariness" because "lonely" in English has an inescapable pejorative sense. *Ocio santo* translated by Kavanaugh-Rodriguez at L, 3, 53 as "holy idleness" is a much better effort at avoiding English words with pejorative connotations, as in "laziness."

Chapter 2

1. See Kavanaugh's introduction to *The Collected Works* for a good place to start regarding John of the Cross's life.

2. See Brenan, *St. John of the Cross,* pp. 5–7, 9; Frost, pp. 3, 6; M. Cristiani, *Saint Jean de la Croix* (Paris: Editions France Empire, 1960); and Luis Prado, *San Juan de la Cruz* (Madrid: Compañia Bibliografica Española, 1963).

3. Kavanaugh, *The Collected Works,* p. 19.

4. Brenan, *St. John of the Cross,* pp. 10–11.

5. See Efrén de la Madre de Dios, *Tiempo y Vida de Santa Teresa* (Madrid: Biblioteca de Autores Cristianos, 1968). Also see Brenan, *St. John of the Cross,* pp. 9, 93, 95.

6. Frost, *Saint John of the Cross,* pp. 20–21.

7. Brenan, *St. John of the Cross,* pp. 14–15, 18.

8. The recent furor over the establishment of a *cloistered* Carmelite convent at Auschwitz, and the previous tenacity of the Nazis to hunt down Edith Stein in such a convent, indicate that contemporary culture is not yet totally indifferent to the contemplative life even if it egregiously misunderstands that life.

9. To say that John of the Cross's diet was austere is not to say that he did not take eating seriously. For example, if one took away all of Jesus's teachings while eating there would not be too much left. See Martinus Cawley, "Vegetarianism, Abstinence and Meatless Cuisine," *American Benedictine Review* 38 (September, 1987).

10. See the excellent chapters in Brenan on John of the Cross's stays at El Calvario, Baeza, Granada, and Segovia, especially pp. 60–62. Regarding the Discalced reform and the lack of reform among the Calced, it would perhaps be more accurate to say that the Calced were reformed by the Council of Trent and the Discalced were reformed in a more rigorous way by Philip II.

11. Ibid., pp. 63, 65–66, 70, 83. Also see Kavanaugh, *The Collected Works,* p. 29.

12. Frost, *Saint John of the Cross,* p. 143.

13. Lucien-Marie Florent, "Spiritual Direction According to St. John of the Cross," *Carmelite Studies* 1 (1980), p. 19.

14. Camillus-Paul D'Souza, "Poverty and Prayer in St. John of the Cross," *Carmelite Studies* 1 (1980), p. 206.

15. Brice, *Journey,* p. 34.

16. Green, "St. John..." p. 34.

17. See Colin Thompson, *The Poet and the Mystic: A Study of the Cantico Espiritual of San Juan de la Cruz* (Oxford: Oxford University Press, 1977), p. 169.

18. Frost, *Saint John of the Cross,* pp. 7, 199.

19. Brenan, *St. John of the Cross,* pp. 3, 68, 72, 74.

20. Ibid., p. 71.

21. In this first part of this section of the chapter, I have relied heavily on Thomas Merton, "The Primitive Carmelite Ideal," in *Disputed Questions* (New York: New American Library, 1965). It would perhaps be more accurate to say that culture—from *cultus* or worship—is a fruit of contemplation than it is of (unthinking) activity.

22. Ibid., p. 180.

23. Ibid., pp. 192–193.

24. See Fernand Braudel, *The Mediterranean and the Mediterranean World in the Age of Philip II* (New York: Harper and Row, 1975), pp. 35, 799, 956. Braudel points out that John of the Cross's dark night had an Islamic predecessor in Ibn Abbad. The issue of the sources for John of the Cross's wisdom is treated well in Jose Nieto, *Mystic, Rebel, Saint: A Study of St. John of the Cross* (Geneva: Droz, 1979). Nieto isolates at least five theories regarding the most significant influences on John of the Cross: (a) Baruzi leans to the view that John of the Cross developed his views independent of influence; (b) Alonso thinks John of the Cross transformed profane themes into religious ones; (c) Baralt emphasizes Islamic influence on John of the Cross—in fact there is some evidence that his mother may have had Morrish roots; (d) another theory emphasizes a Germanic approach in John of the Cross, say through the influence of Meister Eckhardt; and (e) some see in John of the Cross the influence of older Spanish or Latin cources.

25. Brenan, *St. John of the Cross,* p. 8.

26. See Thompson, *The Poet,* p. 169.

27. Ibid., p. 170.

28. Brenan, *St. John of the Cross,* p. 21.

29. Ibid., pp. 25, 96.

30. Ibid., pp. 77, 97–98.

31. Frost, *Saint John of the Cross,* p. 354.

32. See Brenan, *St. John of the Cross,* p. 98. Also see Kavanaugh, *The Collected Works,* p. 31.

33. Thompson, *The Poet,* p. 5.

34. Ibid., pp. 7, 9, 151, 168.

35. Ibid., pp. 151–152.

36. Ibid., pp. 152–153.

37. Frost, *Saint John of the Cross,* pp. 1–3, 6.

38. Ibid., p. 144. Jesus's command should not be forgotten here: Be perfect (*teleioi*—Matt. 5:48).

39. Ibid., pp. 160–161, 177, 190.

40. Ibid., p. 400. Also see Kavanaugh, *The Collected Works,* p. 575.

41. Frost, *Saint John of the Cross,* pp. 147–148.

42. Ibid., pp. 149–150.

43. Ibid., pp. 222, 285, 302, 316. Also see Kavanaugh, *The Collected Works,* p. 29.

44. See my "The Virtue of Boldness," *Spirituality Today* 37 (Fall, 1985), pp. 213–220.

45. Frost, *Saint John of the Cross,* pp. 54, 193, 256. For a more or less Marxist reading of John of the Cross see Manuel Ballestero, *Juan de la Cruz* (Barcelona: Ediciones Peninsula, 1977).

46. Brice, *Journey,* p. 3. Also see Kavanaugh, *The Collected Works,* p. 50.

47. See my "Adam Smith's *The Theory of Moral Sentiments* and Christianity," *American Benedictine Review* 34 (December, 1984), pp. 422–438; see "Benne and Novak on Capitalism," *Theology Today* XLI (April, 1984), pp. 61–65.

48. Alasdair MacIntyre, *Marxism: An Interpretation* (London: SCM Press, 1953), p. 122.

49. Karl Marx, *Die Frühschriften,* ed. by S. Landeshut (1953), p. 275.

50. Kenneth Leech, "Dark Night and Revolution: St. John of the Cross and Karl Marx," *The Modern Churchman* XXIX (1987), pp. 1–10.

51. Frost, *Saint John of the Cross,* pp. 14, 16–17, 58, 256.

52. Thoreau, *Walden,* p. 56.

53. Frost, *Saint John of the Cross,* pp. 13, 190, 395.

54. See Roland Barthes, *Sade, Fourier, Loyola* (New York: Hill and Wang, 1976).

55. Albert William Levi, *Philosophy as Social Expression* (Chicago: University of Chicago Press, 1974).

56. See Frost, *Saint John of the Cross,* p. 56.

57. Robert Neville, *Soldier, Sage, Saint* (New York: Fordham University Press, 1978).

58. Ibid., p. 27.

59. Ibid., p. 48.

60. Ibid.

61. Ibid., p. 71.

62. Ibid., p. 72.

63. Ibid., p. 121.

64. Ibid., p. 126.

65. Ibid., p. 129. Also see my "Back to Sainthood," *Philosophy Today* 33 (Spring, 1989), pp. 56–62; "Gandhi, Sainthood, and Nuclear Weapons," *Philosophy East and West* 33 (October, 1983), pp. 401–406; "Thoreau, Sainthood, and Vegetarianism," *American Transcendental Quarterly* 60 (June, 1986), pp. 25–36; and my review of John Ansbro, "Martin Luther King, Jr.: The Making of a Mind" in *Idealistic Studies* XIV (September, 1984), pp. 279–280.

66. Neville, *Soldier, Sage,* p. 127; also see p. 131.

67. Thompson, *The Poet,* p. 172.

Chapter 3

1. Caroline Walker Bynum, *Gender and Religion* (Boston: Beacon Press, 1986), pp. 257–288.

2. Jurgen Moltmann, *God in Creation* (San Francisco: Harper and Row, 1985), pp. 298–302. I have relied on Moltmann a great deal here in the first section of this chapter.

3. Gerda Lerner, *The Creation of Patriarchy* (Oxford: Oxford University Press, 1986), p. 178.

4. Constance Fitzgerald, "Impasse and Dark Night," in *Living With Apocalypse,* ed. by Tilden Edwards (San Francisco: Harper and Row, 1984), pp. 93–116.

5. See Charles Hartshorne, *Philosophers Speak of God* (Chicago: University of Chicago Press, 1953), p. 3. I am indebted to Hartshorne a great deal for details regarding dipolar theism.

6. Ibid., pp. 14–15.

7. Ibid., p. 24.

8. See Frost, *Saint John of the Cross,* p. 140.

9. See Leonard Eslick, "Plato as Dipolar Theist," *Process Studies* 12 (1982), pp. 243–251. Also see L, 4, 7 for more evidence of John of the Cross's dipolar theism:

...God always acts in this way...moving, governing, bestowing being, power, graces, and gifts upon all creatures, bearing them all in Himself by His power, presence, and substance. And the soul sees what God is in Himself and what He is in His creatures in only one view, just as one who is opening the door of a palace beholds in one act the eminence of the person who dwells inside together with what he is doing.

John of the Cross's concern for divine permanence in the midst of change is evident in the words "always," "being," "substance," and in his concern for what God is "in Himself." His concern for divine becoming is evident in the words "moving," "governing," "bestowing," "gifts," "presence," and in his concern for what God "is in His creatures." Further, the compatibility between these two concerns can be seen in the fact that John of the Cross thinks that these two poles can easily be grasped in a unifed glance.

10. Thompson, *The Poet,* p. 164.

11. Frost, *Saint John of the Cross,* pp. 179, 212.

12. See a letter of John of the Cross quoted in Kavanaugh, *The Collected Works,* p. 25.

13. See Monica Furlong, *Therese of Lisieux* (New York: Pantheon, 1987), pp. 2–4. In this chapter, I have assumed a familiarity with many of the issues discussed by contemporary feminists. See, for example, Sherry Ortner, "Is Female to Male as Nature Is to Culture?," in Rosaldo and Lamphere, editors, *Women, Culture, and Society* (Palo Alto: Stanford University Press, 1974); Nancy Holmstrom, "Do Women Have a Distinct Nature?," *The Philosophical Forum* XIV (Fall, 1982), pp. 25–42; and the American Philosophical Association's *Newsletter on Feminism and Philosophy.* Also see Mary Giles, ed., *The Feminist Mystic* (New York: Crossroad, 1982), where the contemporary feminist criticism of the spirit-body dichotomy is shown to

be an outgrowth of the mystic's desire to have a spirituality where anything less than *immediate encounter* with God is inadequate.

14. Ibid., pp. 9–10.

15. See P. E. More, *Christian Mysticism* (London: Society for Promoting Christian Knowledge, 1932), p. 62.

16. Thompson, *The Poet,* pp. 158–159.

17. Karl Barth, *Church Dogmatics* (Edinburgh: T. and T. Clark, 1939–1969), iv, 2, 284.

18. Thompson, *The Poet,* p. 159.

19. Ibid., pp. 160–161. Also on John of the Cross's view of the soul see Dom Philippe Chevallier, *Saint Jean de la Croix* (Paris: Aubier, 1958). On *eros* in John of the Cross see Eugene Maio, *The Imagery of Eros: A Study of the Influence of Neoplatonism on the Mystical Writings of St. John of the Cross* (thesis, UCLA, 1967).

20. Frost, *Saint John of the Cross,* pp. 118–119.

21. Ibid., pp. 115, 120, 122, 182.

22. Ibid., p. 220.

23. See Richard Swinburne, *Faith and Reason* (Oxford: Clarendon Press, 1981), pp. 104–111.

24. See Kavanaugh, *The Collected Works,* p. 52.

25. Frost, *Saint John of the Cross,* pp. 4, 33.

26. Ibid., pp. 51, 63.

27. Ibid., pp. 64, 81, 91, 94.

28. Ibid., p. 162. Also see pp. 113, 123–124, 131, 136, 161.

29. Ibid., pp. 211, 383.

30. Thompson, *The Poet,* pp. 15, 146.

31. Mary Daly, *Beyond God the Father* (Boston: Beacon Press, 1973), pp. 26, 34.

32. Kavanaugh, *The Collected Works,* pp. 395–396.

33. See Anders Nygren, *Agape and Eros,* trans. by Watson (New York: Harper and Row, 1969); Barth, iv, 2, 734–735.

34. See Paul Tillich, *Systematic Theology,* 3 volumes (Chicago: University of Chicago Press, 1951–1963).

35. See Thompson, *The Poet,* on this and other problems related to love, pp. 164–165.

36. Ibid., pp. 166–167.

37. See Kavanaugh, *The Collected Works,* p. 654. Or more accurately, John of the Cross's sayings were written for various individual nuns.

38. Ibid., p. 653.

39. Carolyn Walker Bynum, *Jesus as Mother* (Berkeley: University of California Press, 1982), pp. 170–265.

40. Frost, *Saint John of the Cross,* p. 304.

41. Sonya Quitslund, "Elements of a Feminist Spirituality in St. Teresa," *Carmelite Studies* 3 (1984), pp. 19–50. Also on the relationship between John of the Cross and St. Teresa of Avila see Trueman Dicken, *The Crucible of Love* (New York: Sheed and Ward, 1963). On St. Teresa of Avila herself, who is not the subject of my book, see Alison Weber, *Teresa of Avila and the Rhetoric of Femininity* (Princeton: Princeton University Press, 1990).

42. Ibid., p. 29.

43. Ibid., p. 41. Also see J. Ruth Aldrich, "Teresa, a Self-Actualized Woman," *Carmelite Studies* 2 (1982), p. 81.

44. See Brenan, *St. John of the Cross,* pp. 83, 110.

45. Ibid., pp. 119–120.

46. See Thompson, *The Poet,* pp. 102, 141.

47. In the remainder of this chapter, I will be relying on Charles Hartshorne, *Omnipotence and Other Theological Mistakes* (Albany: State University of New York Press, 1984), pp. 56–58.

48. Ibid., p. 58.

Chapter 4

1. Erazim Kohak, *The Embers and the Stars: A Philosophical Inquiry into the Moral Sense of Nature* (Chicago: University of Chicago Press, 1984), pp. 124–125. My use of the soul-body analogy in this section of the chapter relies to a great extent on the thought of Charles Hartshorne. It should also be noted that the cloistered life of Carmelite nuns, say, receives justification when the panentheistic, mystical body is understood. In that we are all parts of the cosmic body of Christ, those in the cloister function in a specialized way for the rest of us as the callused knees of the mystical body.

2. See Camille Campbell, "Creation-Centered Carmelites: Teresa and John," *Spiritual Life* 28 (1982), pp. 15–25; and Green, pp. 37–38, who thinks that John of the Cross's panentheism was influenced by the Jewish Kabbalah. Although I will emphasize John of the Cross's romanticism in this chapter, I will also try to avoid overemphasizing his romanticism. For example, the soul *is* trapped in the body, in a sense, as a result of "original sin," but the point is that original sin was not meant to be. That is, my commendation in this chapter of "creation-centered" theology is not meant to preclude the virtues of "redemption-centered" theology. As in chapter three, I am interested in balancing the legitimate claims of these two correlative poles.

3. Quitslund, "Elements of a Feminist," pp. 35–36, alerts us to the fact that this view of God as an all-inclusive organism, as a pregnant mother, in whom we live and move and have our being, goes back before St. Paul to Epimander. In fact, Plutarch suggests that *all* of the ancient philosophers, except the atomists and Aristotle, believed that the world was informed with an animal soul, a claim which, even if an exaggeration, nonetheless indicates the pervasiveness of this belief in ancient culture. See William Goodwin, ed., *Plutarch's Morals* (Boston: Little, Brown, and Co., 1870), vol. III, p. 133. Yet even in the highest union, when we know quite literally that we are in God, God is not revealed to us "as He (literally) is" (S, 11, 3).

4. Also see D'Souza, "Poverty and Prayer," p. 209, on the passage from Deut. 6:5 to the effect that we should contribute all to God.

5. Charles Hartshorne, *Wisdom as Moderation* (Albany: State University of New York Press, 1987), p. 91. Perhaps more accurate than the claim that we are fragments of a divine whole is the claim that we are fragmented fragments; that is, even in our fragmentary state we could do better jobs of managing our lives than we do.

6. Merton, "The Primitive Carmelite Ideal," p. 189. Although John of the Cross develops his own distinctive approach to nature, one cannot dismiss the influence of residual and oral Franciscan communities in Spain at the time. See Emilio Diaz, *Poesía y Mística de San Juan de la Cruz* (Madrid: 1959).

7. Lucien-Marie Florent, "Spiritual Direction According to St. John of the Cross," *Carmelite Studies* 1 (1980), p. 25.

8. Frost, *Saint John of the Cross,* p. 279. Also see pp. 86, 89–90, 97, 121, 279.

9. Brenan, *St. John of the Cross,* pp. 52–53, 75, 102, 108, 129, 132.

10. Frost, *Saint John of the Cross,* pp. 22, 37, 69, 215.

11. Kavanaugh, *The Collected Works,* pp. 30–32.

12. Brenan, *St. John of the Cross,* pp. 42, 44.

13. Kavanaugh, *The Collected Works,* p. 397. It should be noted that Kavanaugh's translation to the effect that God *is* the mountains is not entirely accurate, even if such translation has a commendable effect. Literally John of the Cross is saying "My Love, the mountains": *Mi Amado, las montañas.*

14. Frost, *Saint John of the Cross,* p. 379.

15. Thomas McFarland, *Romanticism and the Forms of Ruin* (Princeton: Princeton University Press, 1981), p. 3.

16. Ibid., p. 4.

17. Quoted in McFarland, *Romanticism,* p. 7. See Peter Brown's *Augustine of Hippo* (London: Faber, 1967), p. 156.

18. Again, see McFarland's excellent study, *Romanticism,* p. 24.

19. Ibid., pp. 26–27.

20. Quoted in McFarland, *Romanticism,* pp. 27–28.

21. Ibid., p. 29.

22. Ibid., p. 50.

23. Ibid., p. 55.

24. Kavanaugh, *The Collected Works,* p. 655.

25. Brenan, *St. John of the Cross,* p. 141.

26. Ibid., p. 138.

27. Kavanaugh, *The Collected Works,* pp. 653–654; see Brenan, *St. John of the Cross,* p. 140.

28. Frost, *Saint John of the Cross,* p. 188.

29. See Claudia Colville, "The Wadi Es Siah: Contemplative Aspects," *OCDS Bulletin* IX (1989), pp. 2–3.

Chapter 5

1. On the transition from orality to literacy see Marshall McLuhan, *The Gutenberg Galaxy* (Toronto: University of Toronto Press, 1962); Walter Ong, *The Presence of the Word* (New Haven: Yale University Press, 1967); and Eric Havelock, *Preface to Plato* (Cambridge: Harvard University Press, 1963). Ong is especially helpful regarding how literacy depends on orality; indeed in some types of literacy (as in John of the Cross's poems) one finds

a residual orality in that the written words are best appreciated when spoken aloud.

2. Brenan, *St. John of the Cross,* p. 52.

3. Ibid., p. 84.

4. Ibid., p. 45.

5. Ibid., pp. 101, 103–104. Also see George Tavard, *Poetry and Contemplation in St. John of the Cross* (Athens: Ohio University Press, 1988) for an effort to bridge studies of John of the Cross's poetry and studies of his theology.

6. Brenan, *St. John of the Cross,* p. 111.

7. Ibid., pp. 116–118.

8. Ibid., p. 123.

9. Kavanaugh, *The Collected Works,* p. 400. See an excellent article by Jorge Gracia, "Texts and Their Interpretation," *Review of Metaphysics* 43 (March, 1990), pp. 495–542, where the author makes helpful distinctions among mental, spoken, and written texts (especially helpful when John of the Cross's prison compositions are considered); conventional and natural texts (especially helpful when John of the Cross's nature poetry in considered); universal and individual texts (especially helpful when trying to decide on the truth of John of the Cross's claims); as well as distinctions among the author's intended text, the historical text that the historian has to consider, and the ideal text against which scholarly judgments are made. Further, in that John of the Cross's writings come down to us through various editors and translators, Gracia should be considered to distinguish among the historical author, "the pseudo-historical author," and "the composite author." Gracia also distinguishes among the various audiences for a text (especially helpful, say, in John of the Cross's desire to clarify certain issues for advanced religious seekers as opposed to beginners, etc.).

10. Kavanaugh, *The Collected Works,* p. 33.

11. Ibid., p. 37. And Brenan, *St. John of the Cross,* pp. 104, 110. Finally, see Damaso Alonso, *La Poesía de San Juan de la Cruz* (Madrid, 1942), 4th ed., on John of the Cross's literary influences.

12. Thompson, *The Poet,* pp. 15–16. Also see Jean Vilnet, *Bible et Mystique chez Saint Jean de la Croix* (Paris: Desclee de Brouwer, 1948).

13. Frost, *Saint John of the Cross,* p. 388; also p. 35.

14. On a religious classic see David Tracy, *The Analogical Imagination* (New York: Crossroad, 1981). Also see Luce Irigaray, "Divine Knowledge," in *Speculum of the Other Woman,* trans. by Gill (Ithaca: Cornell University

Press, 1985). If I understand Irigaray correctly, there is an analogy between the mystery of God the Father and the mystery of a text's meaning, hence both in religion and literature the "otherness" of God or of the text are primary. (If this is not what Irigaray is claiming she should have made her thesis clearer.) But, as I have indicated in this chapter, otherness is, at best, half the story regarding language about God. Once again, the fact that we notice egregious errors in religious language indicates to some extent, at least, a legitimate metaphysics of presence.

15. At the beginning of this section of the chapter I will be relying on Charles Hartshorne, *The Logic of Perfection* (LaSalle, Ill.: Open Court, 1962), pp. 133–147.

16. Frost largely agrees with Hartshorne regarding this distinction between God's existence as an abstraction and the concreteness of divine actuality, see pp. 80, 83, 85, 378.

17. Hartshorne, *The Logic of Perfection,* p. 147.

18. Ibid., p. 276. Also see pp. 152–159.

19. Quoted in McFarland, *Romanticism,* p. 31.

20. Ibid., pp. 43–44.

21. See Anthony Haglof, "Buddhism and the *Nada* of St. John of the Cross," *Carmelite Studies* 1 (1980), p. 195.

22. Susan Sontag, *Against Interpretation* (New York: Farrar, Straus, and Giroux, 1961), p. 5.

23. Ibid., p. 6.

24. Ibid., p. 7.

25. Ibid., p. 8.

26. Barthes, *Sade, Fourier, Loyola,* pp. 39, 50, 53, 66–68.

27. Thoreau, *Walden,* p. 151.

28. Kavanaugh, *The Collected Works,* p. 54.

29. Frost, *Saint John of the Cross,* pp. 174–175, 199. Also see p. 226.

30. Ibid., p. 358. Also see pp. 228, 230, 373.

31. Ibid., p. 320. Also see pp. 228, 235, 301–302.

32. Ibid., pp. 400–401.

33. See Thompson, *The Poet,* p. 155.

34. For example, compare Kavanaugh's generally literal translation with Antonio de Nicolas's, the latter being much more poetic if not as literal: *St. John of the Cross* (New York: Paragon House, 1989).

35. For some traditional Thomist interpretations of John of the Cross, or for interpretations that rely on twentieth-century continental thought, interpretations that differ from, but do not always contradict, my approach, see the following: Reginald Garrigou-Lagrange, *Christian Perfection and Contemplation According to St. Thomas Aquinas and St. John of the Cross*, trans. by Doyle (St. Louis: Herder, 1937); Edith Stein, *The Science of the Cross: A Study of John of the Cross*, trans. by Graef (Chicago: Regnery, 1960); Karol Wojtyla, *Faith According to Saint John of the Cross*, trans. by Aumann (San Francisco: Ignatius Press, 1981); and Denis Edward, "Experience of God and Explicit Faith: A Comparison of John of the Cross and Karl Rahner," *Thomist* 46 (1982), pp. 33–74.

36. See Brenan, *St. John of the Cross*, p. 111. Also see John of the Cross's poem, "Commentary Applied to Spiritual Things" on the "I-don't-know-what" (*Sino por un no se que*) aspect of God.

37. Thompson, *The Poet*, p. 170.

38. See Frost, *Saint John of the Cross*, pp. xii, 10, 16.

39. Ibid., pp. 24, 39, 50.

Chapter 6

1. Frost, *Saint John of the Cross*, pp. 259–261, 206–207.

2. Ibid., pp. 267, 347, 357.

3. Kavanaugh, *The Collected Works*, p. 394.

4. Ibid., p. 56.

5. See Frost, *Saint John of the Cross*, pp. xi–xii.

6. Ibid., p. 57.

7. Ibid., pp. 158, 275, 335.

8. Ibid., pp. 166, 262–263, 340, 352.

9. Peers, *Spanish Mysticism*, pp. 111–112.

10. Kavanaugh, *The Collected Works*, p. 569.

11. See Charles Scott, *The Language of Difference* (Atlantic Highlands, N.J.: Humanities Press, 1987), pp. vii, 67–68, 125–126, 136, 154, 165. However, it should be noted that Scott does not draw the same theological conclusions as Stein does from the middle voice.

12. See R. J. Zwi Werblowski, "On the Mystical Rejection of Mystical Illuminations," *Religious Studies* 1 (1965–1966).

13. Green, "St. John," p. 30.

14. Ibid., p. 32.

15. Ibid., pp. 33–34.

16. Leo Spitzer, *Essays on English and American Literature* (Princeton: Princeton University Press, 1969), pp. 153–171.

17. Ibid., p. 158.

18. Ibid., pp. 168–169.

19. See Thompson, *The Poet,* pp. 11–12.

20. Ibid., p. 147.

21. Ibid., pp. 148–150, 153.

22. See Hartshorne, *The Logic of Perfection,* pp. 127, 242, 286–287.

23. Frost, *Saint John of the Cross,* pp. 331, 348.

24. Brenan, *St. John of the Cross,* pp. 84–85.

25. Johannes Bendick, "God and World in John of the Cross," *Philosophy Today* 16 (1972), pp. 281–294.

26. Ibid., p. 290. On the connection between John of the Cross and Francis of Assisi, Bendick cites the work of several scholars (Baruzi, Milner, etc.) who think that John of the Cross explicitly had Francis in mind when he wrote about nature.

27. Ibid., p. 293.

28. See Charles Hartshorne, "Mysticism and Rationalistic Metaphysics," *Monist* 59 (1976), pp. 463–469. I have relied on this article by Hartshorne throughout the rest of this section of the chapter.

29. Ibid., p. 463.

30. Ibid., p. 467.

31. Haglof, "Buddhism," pp. 183–184.

32. See my *Hartshorne and the Metaphysics of Animal Rights* (Albany: State University of New York Press, 1988); "Gandhi, Sainthood, and Nuclear Weapons," *Philosophy East and West* 33 (October, 1983), pp. 401–406; and "Asymmetrical Relations, Identity, and Abortion," forthcoming.

33. Haglof, "Buddhism," pp. 186–187.

34. Ibid., p. 188.

35. Ibid., p. 189.

36. Ibid., p. 190.

37. Ibid., p. 191.

38. Ibid., p. 193.

39. See the "Author's Note" in Merton's *Zen and the Birds of Appetite* (New York: New Directions, 1968).

40. Frost, *Saint John of the Cross,* pp. 11, 37, 41, 162, 241, 338.

41. See Thompson, *The Poet,* pp. 162–163.

42. See Brice, *Journey,* p. 60.

43. See Teilhard de Chardin, *Activation of Energy,* trans. by Rene Hague (New York: Harcourt, Brace, Jovanovich, 1971), p. 225; and *Toward the Future,* trans. by Rene Hague (New York: Harcourt, Brace, Jovanovich, 1975), pp. 52, 194, 200–201, 211. Also see Francis Nemeck, *Teilhard de Chardin et Jean de la Croix* (Montreal: Bellarmin, 1975).

44. See Steven Payne, *John of the Cross and the Cognitive Value of Mysticism* (Boston: Kluwer, 1990), pp. 17, 149, regarding the ways in which John of the Cross disagreed with Thomas Aquinas and the scholastics on several key issues. I regret that I am not able to make more use of Payne's fine book, which arrived too late for the development of the present volume.

Bibliography

Primary Sources

Crisogono de Jesus, ed. *Vida y Obras de San Juan de la Cruz.* Madrid: Biblioteca de Autores Cristianos, 1955.

Biblioteca Autores Españoles. Vol. 1. Madrid: Editiones Atlas, 1948.

Silverio de Santa Teresa, ed. *Obras de San Juan de La Cruz. Doctor de la Iglesia,* 5 vols. Burgos, 1929–1931.

Kavanaugh, Kieran and Rodriguez, Otilio, trans. *The Collected Works of St. John of the Cross.* Washington, D.C.: Institute of Carmelite Studies, 1973.

Peers, E. Allison, trans. *The Complete Works of Saint John of the Cross.* 3 Vols. Westminster, Md.: Newman Press, 1949.

Lewis, David, trans. *The Ascent of Mount Carmel.* London: Thomas Baker, 1922.

Zimmerman, Benedict, trans. *The Dark Night of the Soul.* London: Thomas Baker, 1924.

Campbell, Roy, trans. *The Poems of St. John of the Cross.* New York: Pantheon, 1951.

Thompson, Colin, trans. "Spiritual Canticle." In *The Poet and the Mystic.* Oxford: Oxford University Press, 1977.

de Nicholas, Antonio, trans. *St. John of the Cross.* New York: Paragon House, 1989.

213

Secondary Sources

Aldrich, J. Ruth. "Teresa, A Self-Actualized Woman." *Carmelite Studies* 2 (1982).

Alonso, Damaso. *La Poesía de San Juan de la Cruz.* 4th ed. Madrid, 1942.

Ballestero, Manuel. *Juan de la Cruz.* Barcelona: Ediciones Peninsula, 1977.

Baralt, Luce Lopez. *San Juan de la Cruz y el Islam.* : Colegio de Mexico, 1985.

Barth, Karl. *Church Dogmatics.* Edinburgh: T. and T. Clark, 1939–1969.

Barthes, Roland. *Sade, Fourier, Loyola.* New York: Hill and Wang, 1976.

Baruzi, Jean. *Saint Jean de la Croix et le probleme de l'experience mystique.* Paris: 1924.

Bell, Rudolph. *Holy Anorexia.* Chicago: University of Chicago Press, 1985.

Bendick, Johannes. "God and World in John of the Cross." *Philosophy Today* 16 (1972): 281–294.

Bord, Andre. *Memoire et Esperance chez Jean de la Croix.* Paris: Beauchesne, 1971.

Braudel, Fernand. *The Mediterranean and the Mediterranean World in the Age of Philip II.* New York: Harper and Row, 1975.

Brenan, Gerald. *St. John of the Cross: His Life and Poetry.* Cambridge: Cambridge University Press, 1973.

Brice, F. *Journey in the Night.* New York: Pustet, 1945.

Brown, Peter. *Augustine of Hippo.* London: Faber, 1967.

Bruno de Jesus Marie. *Saint Jean de la Croix.* Paris: 1929.

Bynum, Caroline Walker. *Jesus As Mother.* Berkeley, University of California Press, 1982.

Bynum, Caroline Walker, ed. *Gender and Religion.* Boston: Beacon Press, 1986.

Campbell, Camille. "Creation-Centered Carmelites: Teresa and John." *Spiritual Life* 28 (1982):15–25.

Cawley, Martinus. "Vegetarianism, Abstinence, and Meatless Cuisine." *American Benedictine Review* 38 (September, 1987): 320–338.

Chevallier, Dom Philippe. *Saint Jean de la Croix.* Paris: Aubier, 1958.

Colville, Claudia. "The Wadi Es Siah: Contemplative Aspects." *OCDS Bulletin* IX (1989):2–3.

Crisogono de Jesus. *The Life of St. John of the Cross.* New York: Harper and Brothers, 1958.

Cristiani, M. *Saint Jean de la Croix.* Paris: Editions France Empire, 1960.

Daly, Mary. *Beyond God the Father.* Boston: Beacon Press, 1973.

Diaz, Emilio. *Poesía y Mistica de San Juan de la Cruz.* Madrid: 1959.

Dicken, Trueman. *The Crucible of Love.* New York: Sheed and Ward, 1963.

Dodds, E. R. *Pagan and Christian in an Age of Anxiety.* Cambridge: Cambridge University Press, 1965.

Dombrowski, Daniel. "Eating and Spiritual Exercises: Food for Thought from St. Ignatius and Nikos Kazantzakis." *Christianity and Literature* 34 (Summer, 1983):25–32.

———. "Gandhi, Sainthood, and Nuclear Weapons." *Philosophy East and West* 33 (October, 1983):401–406.

———. Review of John Ansbro, *Martin Luther King, Jr.: The Making of a Mind.* In *Idealistic Studies* XIV (September, 1984):279–280.

———. "Benne and Novak on Capitalism." *Theology Today* XLI (April, 1984): 61–65.

———. "Adam Smith's *The Theory of Moral Sentiments* and Christianity." *American Benedictine Review* 34 (December, 1984):422–438.

———. "The Virtue of Boldness." *Spirituality Today* 37 (Fall, 1985):213–220.

———. "Thoreau, Sainthood, and Vegetarianism." *American Transcendental Quarterly* 60 (June, 1986):25–36.

———. "Rorty and Mirror Images in St. Thomas." *Method* 4 (October, 1986):108–114.

———. *Hartshorne and the Metaphysics of Animal Rights* (Albany: State University of New York Press, 1988).

———. "Back to Sainthood." *Philosophy Today* 33 (Spring, 1989):56–62.

———. *Christian Pacifism* (Philadelphia: Temple University Press, 1991).

D'Souza, Camillus-Paul. "Poverty and Prayer in St. John of the Cross." *Carmelite Studies* 1 (1980):204–212.

Edward, Denis. "Experience of God and Explicit Faith: A Comparison of John of the Cross and Karl Rahner." *Thomist* 46 (1982):33–74.

Efrén de la Madre de Dios. *Tiempo y Vida de Santa Teresa.* Madrid: Biblioteca de Autores Cristianos, 1968.

Eslick, Leonard. "Plato as Dipolar Theist." *Process Studies* 12 (1982):243–251.

Farmer, David. *The Oxford Dictionary of Saints.* Oxford: Oxford University Press, 1982.

Fitzgerald, Constance. "Impasse and Dark Night." In *Living With Apocalypse,* ed. by Tilden Edwards. San Francisco: Harper and Row, 1984.

Florent, Lucien-Marie. "Spiritual Direction According to St. John of the Cross." *Carmelite Studies* 1 (1980):3–34.

Frost, Bede. *Saint John of the Cross.* New York: Harper and Brothers, 1937.

Furlong, Monica. *Therese of Lisieux.* New York: Pantheon, 1987.

Gageac, Pierre. *Saint Jean de la Croix.* Paris: Gabalda, 1958.

Garrigou-Lagrange, Reginald. *Christian Perfection and Contemplation According to St. Thomas Aquinas and St. John of the Cross,* trans. by Doyle. St. Louis: Herder, 1937.

Giles, Mary, ed. *The Feminist Mystic.* New York: Crossroad, 1982.

Gracia, Jorge. "Texts and Their Interpretation." *Review of Metaphysics* 43 (March, 1990):495–542.

Green, Deirdre. "St. John of the Cross and Mystical 'Unknowing.' " *Religious Studies* 22 (1986):29–40.

Gutierrez, Gustavo. *We Drink From Our Own Wells.* Maryknoll, New York: Orbis, 1984.

Haglof, Anthony. "Buddhism and the *Nada* of St. John of the Cross." *Carmelite Studies* 1 (1980):183–203.

Hartshorne, Charles. *Philosophers Speak of God.* Chicago: University of Chicago Press, 1953.

———. *The Logic of Perfection.* LaSalle, Ill.: Open Court, 1962.

———. *Creative Synthesis and Philosophic Method.* LaSalle, Ill.: Open Court, 1970.

———. "Mysticism and Rationalistic Metaphysics." *Monist* 59 (1976):463–469.

———. *Omnipotence and Other Theological Mistakes.* Albany: State University of New York Press, 1984.

———. *Wisdom as Moderation.* Albany: State University of New York Press, 1987.

Holmstrom, Nancy. "Do Women Have a Distinct Nature?." *The Philosophical Forum* XIV (Fall, 1982):25–42.

Irigaray, Luce. *Speculum of the Other Woman,* trans. by Gill. Ithaca: Cornell University Press, 1985.

James, William. *The Varieties of Religious Experience.* Cambridge: Harvard University Press, 1985.

Kazantzakis, Nikos. *Zorba the Greek.* New York: Simon and Schuster, 1962.

Knowles, David. *What Is Mysticism?.* London: Sheed and Ward, 1966.

Kohak, Erazim. *The Embers and the Stars: A Philosophical Inquiry into the Moral Status of Nature.* Chicago: University of Chicago Press, 1984.

Leech, Kenneth. "Dark Night and Revolution: St. John of the Cross and Karl Marx." *The Modern Churchman* XXIX (1987):1–10.

Lerner, Gerda. *The Creation of Patriarchy.* Oxford: Oxford University Press, 1986.

Levi, Albert William. *Philosophy as Social Expression.* Chicago: University of Chicago Press, 1974.

MacIntyre, Alasdair. *Marxism: An Interpretation.* London: SCM Press, 1953.

McFarland, Thomas. *Romanticism and the Forms of Ruin.* Princeton: Princeton University Press, 1981.

Maio, Eugene. *The Imagery of Eros: A Study of the Influence of Neoplatonism on the Mystical Writings of St. John of the Cross.* Master's thesis, UCLA, 1967.

Merton, Thomas. "Notes for a Philosophy of Solitude." In *Disputed Questions.* New York: New American Library, 1965.

———. "The Primitive Carmelite Ideal." In *Disputed Questions.* New York: New American Library, 1965.

———. *Zen and the Birds of Appetite.* New York: New Directions, 1968.

Moltmann, Jurgen. *God in Creation.* San Francisco: Harper and Row, 1985.

More, P. E. *Christian Mysticism.* London: Society for Promoting Christian Knowledge, 1932.

Nemeck, Francis. *Teilhard de Chardin et Jean de la Croix.* Montreal: Bellarmin, 1975.

Neville, Robert. *Soldier, Sage, Saint.* New York: Fordham University Press, 1978.

Nieto, Jose. *Mystic, Rebel, Saint: A Study of Saint John of the Cross.* Geneva: Droz, 1979.

Nygren, Anders. *Agape and Eros,* trans. by Watson. New York: Harper and Row, 1969.

Ong, Walter. *The Presence of the Word.* New Haven: Yale University Press, 1967.

Ortner, Sherry. "Is Female to Male as Nature Is to Culture?." In Rosaldo and Lamphere, editors, *Women, Culture, and Society.* Palo Alto: Stanford University Press, 1974.

Payne, Steven. *John of the Cross and the Cognitive Value of Mysticism.* Boston: Kluwer, 1990.

Peers, Allison. *Spanish Mysticism.* London: Methuen, 1924.

Plutarch's Morals, ed. by Goodwin. Vol. III. Boston: Little, Brown, and Co., 1870.

Porphyry. *De Abstinentia or Abstinence from Animal Food,* trans. by Taylor. London: Centaur Press, 1965.

Prado, Luis. *San Juan de la Cruz.* Madrid: Compania Bibliografica Española, 1963.

Quitslund, Sonya. "Elements of a Feminist Spirituality in St. Teresa." *Carmelite Studies* 3 (1984):19–52.

Scott, Charles. *The Language of Difference.* Atlantic Highlands, N.J.: Humanities Press, 1987.

Sontag, Susan. *Against Interpretation.* New York: Farrar, Straus, Giroux, 1961.

Stein, Edith. *The Science of the Cross: A Study of St. John of the Cross,* trans. by Graef. Chicago: Regnery, 1960.

Swietlicki, C. "Writing Femystic Space." *Journal of Hispanic Philology* 13 (1989):273–293.

Swinburne, Richard. *Faith and Reason.* Oxford: Clarendon Press, 1981.

Tavard, George. *Poetry and Contemplation in St. John of the Cross.* Athens: Ohio University Press, 1988.

Teilhard de Chardin, Pierre. *Activation of Energy,* trans. by Hague. New York: Harcourt, Brace, Jovanovich, 1971.

———. *Toward the Future,* trans. by Hague. New York: Harcourt, Brace, Jovanovich, 1975.

Thompson, Colin. *The Poet and the Mystic: A Study of the Cantico Espiritual of San Juan de la Cruz.* Oxford: Oxford University Press, 1977.

Thoreau, Henry David. *Walden.* New York: New American Library, 1960.

Tillich, Paul. *Systematic Theology.* 3 Vols. Chicago: University of Chicago Press, 1951–1963.

Tracy, David. *The Analogical Imagination.* New York: Crossroad, 1981.

Vilnet, Jean. *Bible et Mystique chez Saint Jean de la Croix.* Paris: Desclee De Brouwer, 1949.

Weber, Alison. *Teresa of Avila and the Rhetoric of Femininity.* Princeton: Princeton University Press, 1990.

Werblowski, R. J. Zwi, "On the Mystical Rejection of Mystical Illuminations." *Religious Studies* 1 (1965–1966): 177–184.

Wojtyla, Karol. *Faith According to Saint John of the Cross,* trans. by Aumann. San Francisco: Ignatius Press, 1981.

Index of Names